VENICE

How to use this book

The main text provides a survey of the city's cultural history, from the beginnings of civilization in the lagoon to the present time. It is illustrated with paintings, sculpture, architecture and general views.

The map (pp. 262-263) shows the principal monuments, museums and historic buildings, using symbols and colours for quick reference.

To find a museum or gallery turn to Appendix I, which lists them alphabetically, with their address, opening times and a note on their scope and contents. The larger collections are sub-divided into departments. Page numbers indicate where these are mentioned or illustrated in the text

To find a historic building or church turn to Appendix II, which gives a similar alphabetical list of important buildings, landmarks, monuments, fountains, squares, etc. References to vaporetto stations enable the most important places to be easily located on the map.

For information on artists—painters, sculptors, architects, goldsmiths, engravers, etc.—turn to Appendix III. Here are listed those who contributed to the cultural greatness of Venice and whose works are now to be seen there. Each entry consists of a biographical note, details of where the artist's works are located, and references to the main text where they are mentioned or illustrated.

World Cultural Guides

To. Margaret .

25-12-76,

R.....

VENICE

Terisio Pignatti

190 illustrations
in colour and black and white

special photography
by Mario Carrieri

Thames and Hudson · London

... Sometimes, when walking at evening on the Lido, whence
the great chain of the Alps, crested with silver clouds,
might be seen rising above the front of the Ducal Palace, I
used to feel as much awe in gazing on the building as on the
hills, and could believe that God had done a greater work
in breathing into the narrowness of dust the mighty
spirits by whom its haughty walls had been raised, and its
burning legends written, than in lifting the rocks of granite
higher than the clouds of heaven, and veiling them with
their various mantle of purple flower and shadowy pine.

John Ruskin, The Stones of Venice, ch. v

Translated from the Italian
by Judith Landry

The World Cultural Guides
have been devised and produced by
Park and Roche Establishment, Schaan

ISBN 0 500 64001 7
Printed and bound in Italy by Amilcare Pizzi S.p.A.

Contents

Aerial photographs pp. 22 (below), 84, 122, 158, 204, 206, 234, 238 by Borlui, Venice pp. 22 (above), 24, 110, 185, 188, 212 by Marzari, Schio

End-paper illustration: Detail from a fifteenth century coloured engraving of Venice. Biblioteca Marciana, Venice.

Significant dates
in the history of Venice

450   Destruction of Aquileia by Huns; refugees settle on islands of the Venetian lagoons.

489   Establishment of Ostrogothic kingdom at Ravenna; Venice governed by 'maritime tribunes'

553   Ostrogothic kingdom, including the Venetian islands, reconquered by Byzantines under Belisarius

c.570 Invasion by Lombards, but the islands remain under Byzantine protection

639   Bishop of Altino moves to Torcello and builds S. Maria Assunta

727   Venice assumes independence, centred on Cittanova. First Doge elected

774   Venice besieged by the Franks. Administrative centre moves to Malamocco, on the Lido

814   Treaty with Byzantium. Centre moves to Rivo Alto (modern Rialto). Agnello Partecipazio becomes Doge. Building of the first Doge's Palace and Basilica of San Marco. Body of St Mark transferred from Alexandria to Venice.

887   Venice unified under Doge Pietro Triburio

1000   Venice controls the coast of Dalmatia and Croatia. Democratic constitution established

1003   Present San Marco begun

1124   Doge Domenico Selvo present at the conquest of Tyre

1177   Meeting in Doge's Palace between Emperor Frederick Barbarossa and Pope Alexander III

1192   Beginning of Fourth Crusade. Venetians under Doge Enrico Dandolo take Zara

1204   Capture of Constantinople. Many classical works of art brought to Venice including Bronze Horses of San Marco

1234   Church of San Zanipolo

1270-95 Travels of Marco Polo

1310   Council of Ten established. Election of Doges confined to a restricted oligarchy

1312   Dante visits Venice

1330   Church of the Frari begun

1340   Present Doge's Palace begun. Paolo Veneziano initiates a Venetian style of painting. Venice begins new period of expansion on the mainland

1406	Venice controls the mainland as far as Verona
1420	Cà d'Oro begun
1425	Uccello in Venice
c.1400-70	Jacopo Bellini
1442	Andrea da Castagno in Venice
c.1430-1516	Giovanni Bellini
1453	Fall of Constantinople to the Turks
1454	Peace of Lodi; Venetian territory extends as far as Bergamo
c.1460	Beginning of Renaissance architecture in Venice; Pietro Lombardo
1490	Carpaccio begins the *Legend of St Ursula*
1508	League of Cambrai formed against Venice
c.1476-1510	Giorgione
c.1487-1576	Titian
1529	Jacopo Sansovino comes to Venice
1518-94	Tintoretto
c.1528-88	Paolo Veronese
1556-59	Sammicheli in Venice
1565-80	Palladio in Venice
1572	Turks defeated at Lepanto
1574-77	Fires damage Doge's Palace. Restored with paintings by Tintoretto and Veronese
1630	Santa Maria della Salute founded in memory of Venice's surviving the Plague
1697-1768	Canaletto
1696-1770	Tiepolo
1712-93	Francesco Guardi
1797	Abdication of the last Doge. Venice under Austrian rule
1805-14	Venice part of Napoleon's 'Regno Italico'
1814	Venice becomes part of Austro-Hungarian Empire
1841-46	Railway built between Venice and the mainland
1848	Revolt under Daniele Manin against Austrians
1866	Venice incorporated in the Kingdom of Italy under Victor Emmanuel

The Face of Venice

Venice is a fascinating but elusive city: demanding, difficult to love and understand, but always rewarding. Thinkers, poets and artists of all times and from widely differing backgrounds and cultures have tried to distil and portray her essence. Rarely, except in unqualified admiration for her extraordinary aesthetic appeal, have their judgments coincided. Which of the hundred faces of Venice, drawn throughout a literature exceptional in quality and quantity, emerges as valid for the man of our time — often a breathless visitor, hurried by the stresses of mass culture and no longer in touch with the broad view of history seen as a living adventure of the mind?

By the eleventh and twelfth centuries Giovanni Diacono and other very early chroniclers were describing the island of Rialto and the Basilica of San Marco as 'the wonder of the world': the face of Venice had already changed beyond recognition and the idea of a city was taking shape. For Philippe de Commynes, at the end of the fifteenth century, the Grand Canal was 'the most beautiful street I think that there be in the whole world'; and innumerable sixteenth-century writers, from Sannazaro to Aretino, from Calmo to Vasari, all exalted the glorious myth of Venice '*la Dominante*'.

In the writings of men of the seventeenth century, however, enthusiasm was mingled with regret, for they — Boschini, for instance, and Sarpi — were torn between admiration for the splendour of Venice's art and distress at her military defeats at the hands of the Turks, a presage of her imminent decline. In the eighteenth century, Casanova's *Memoirs* offer a cloudy and deceptive vista, while Goldoni in his comedies mocks customs in *calli* and palazzi; foreign travellers were particularly delighted with the easy life and near hysterical gaiety. Napoleon saw the Piazza as '*un salon auquel le ciel seul est digne de servir de voûte*' (a great hall for which the sky is the only worthy ceiling). But the Romantic era was in agreement with the tone of Goethe's gloomy epigram, which compared the gondola to something midway between the cradle and the bier, eternal symbols of love and death. A silent gondolier accompanied Lord Byron through a decaying Venice:

> *Her palaces are crumbling to the shore*
> *And Music meets not always now the ear:*
> *Those days are gone, but Beauty is still here.*

◁
Fondamenta di Santa Maria Maggiore.

Late nineteenth- and early twentieth-century Romantics had an infinite variety of things to say about the face of the city, now irreparably marked by time. The theme of death in the novels of Maurice Barrès and Thomas Mann was now more relevant than ever. For Mann, the face of Venice was deceptive and ambiguous, like certain characters in his works; the whole atmosphere of Venice was suffused with the breath of relentless decay. As Bettini pointed out (*Venezia,* Milan 1963), for the late Romantics Venice was fickle, treacherous, deeply decadent. The philosopher Georg Simmel actually used the city as a prototype of 'deceitful beauty', to be contrasted with the natural 'limpidity' of Florence. For Simmel the face of Venice, analysed as an artistic form, was all appearance: it offered no rational certainty, nor peace; on the contrary, it was deeply disturbing to anyone who tried to plumb its secret depths. Gabriele d'Annunzio, in *Il Fuoco,* gave an extreme interpretation of a mature and tragic Venice, mirrored in his own Foscarina, a Venice where love, like the city, was dying.

An interpretation that comes nearer to the modern mood is to be found in Marcel Proust. The image with which the protagonist of *Du côté de chez Swann* dreams of Venice (a spring sunshine tingeing the waves of the Grand Canal with so dusty an azure, with emeralds so splendid that they washed and were broken against the foot of one of Titian's paintings) is already a thoroughly modern vision, in its temporal mobility: that of a city whose formal elements are constantly moving and changing in time, whose endless colours and reflections vary with the passing of the seasons and the movement of the sun.

It is this mode of existence, rather than the sentimental myth-making of the romantics, that seems to characterize the face of Venice as it is to-day: a Venice closely linked to her original human genesis, within the limits of the mobile and changeable element of time. Here it might be as well to consider the very particular environment from which Venice emerged: a stretch of water, an infinite arch of sky. Unique among the world's cities, Venice is not linked to any elements of reality, to any natural relief, mountains or hills, rivers or trees. Everything we see is man-made, artificial. This is a unique, unmistakable feature, which binds the nature of Venice essentially and inescapably to the work of man, her maker.

'What Venice lacked, as she emerged, was limitation in space; any kind of feature which Riegl would have called *tactile.* As far as artistic morphology was concerned, the expanses of both sea and sky are almost absolute surfaces of colour: they cannot be determined by geometrical formulae or expressed by the syntax of perspective, and they elude the classic laws of composition. So it is not surprising that Venetian art, and Venice herself, had always been orientated towards an order that was anti-geometry and anti-perspective, or, more exactly, fostered a transient and specious geometry which multiplied, entwined, broke down and built up, and finally left the spectator with nothing but fields of blue and gold, marked only with the shifting, exultant notation of an endless song of colour.'

Here Bettini has pinpointed Venice's most striking formal characteristic: the element of light. This is also the key to the romantic misunderstanding which led many to accuse Venetian architecture of falsity, with its palazzi like temporary backdrops, its deceptive vistas measurable only in terms of their theatrical effect: they failed to see that the essence of the place lies not in deception but in eternal variety, with its endless watery echoes of the skies. Modern criticism has located the origin of this aesthetic vision firmly in the art of the late Roman period.

Palazzo Zorzi at the Ponte dei Greci, San Zaccaria. The urban structure of Venice is a complex web in which the houses of the poor are adjacent to the patrician palaces. The water, with its shifting reflections, is the element that binds them all.

Venice was in fact the daughter of Aquileia, Ravenna, Byzantium, late Roman cities par excellence, and through them she absorbed the basic element of the late Roman tradition: a changeable artistic form linked to the continuity of the narrative style, to life lived in time, to experience translated into the factors of light and colour. 'The mosaics on the walls, the *opus tessellatum* of the floors, have something of the sea about them in their washed brightness: as though the tide had only just gone down from those churches built on the seashore or on islands, leaving behind it layers of stranded shingle, speckled pebbles, chips of iridescent shell, their design still bearing the mark of the curved path of the waves'.

Anchored to this basic aesthetic element of light, the face of Venice developed with an extraordinary continuity and unity over the centuries; it emerged, from a mass of divergent detail, as a genuine, living work of art. 'Venice as a work of art', then, is the historically determined, aesthetically definable object of our analysis: as though this were a gradually formed structure that had moved towards an ideal perfection, predetermined by an inner conviction, by its own formal reality.

Venice is almost uniquely well suited to such a critical exercise, for a variety of reasons. Above all, Venice is not only a city. Venice is the capital of a state, or rather she is herself the State. Even to-day, deep in the real Venetian, there is an echo of the civic pride of a people whose world existed for them within the perimeter of the lagoon. For centuries Venetians weighed anchor from here with their merchant fleets or set out over the *terraferma,* the mainland, but always with the secret thought of their return to the island that was their whole spiritual domain; they were a people tied to their own traditions, alive to the memories and myths of their own history. Within these limits, during the thousand years of her independence, Venice developed politics, economic doctrines, financial practices, a whole culture that was autonomous in character and development. To talk of Venice is to talk of a completely self-sufficient world, of a city state, whose archives still contain miles of shelving holding the entire official documentation of its thousand years of activity. Literature, music and the figurative arts were equally independent; for long periods of time Venice was a world in itself.

Today's visitor to Venice is offered a unique and fascinating opportunity: to go back into the distant past. With a minimum of imagination we can eliminate violent lights and noises; walking along the *calli* and small canals before dawn, we can go back centuries, to the atmosphere of the old city, re-creating the space and time of a Venice that is alternately medieval, Renaissance or Baroque, depending on the visual angle from which we happen to be viewing it. Passers-by in modern dress do not need to jar — they might be actors in a gigantic modern-dress performance in the old historic setting. Certainly no other city in the world has a historic centre as totally preserved as that of Venice: a work of art completed in 1797 — if we take the date that officially marks the end — where later interpolations are luckily so few and insignificant that they do not shatter the feeling of completeness in space, nor the possibility of experiencing it in time.

The face of Venice has come down to us with the coherent uniqueness of a supreme work of art. I shall now attempt to analyze it as it grew, suggesting an itinerary that is historically valid and should ultimately enable anyone who loves and understands Venice to make the critical synthesis which leads to her real, but intriguingly enigmatic essence.

Byzantium and Ravenna

The first step in this reconstruction of Venice must inevitably be in the direction of the ancient, lonely lagoon. Here we find all the environmental conditions that preceded the founding of the city, though naturally there are no traces of the settlements of the earliest peoples.

The oldest documentary information goes back to the time of the Roman Empire, of which this district was part, already bearing the name Venetiae. It was included in the *X Regio,* a boundary march which had several flourishing cities, including the capital Padua, Aquileia, Oderzo, Concordia and Treviso. In the loop of the Adriatic a broad lagoon stretched from north to south for about twenty miles, with a width varying between three and seven, cut off from the sea by a long thin sand bar (*lido*), broken by natural gaps. A Roman city, Altino, was situated towards the extreme north-east of the lagoon, where three important roads met: the *Emilia Annia* which ran eastwards towards

Rio della Fornace, at the Salute. The canal, a thoroughfare both vital and ornamental, is the basis of the city's structure. The bridges unite the hundred islets that make up the city.

Aquileia, Illyria and Byzantium, the *Popilia* which ran southwards to Rome and the *Claudia Altinate Augusta* going northwards.

The inhabitants of the lagoon itself must have been relatively few: it was just a stretch of marsh, its salt water diluted by the rivers that flowed into it, stagnant and evil-smelling and mosquito-ridden. This is indeed how the Venetian lagoon appears in the letter that Cassiodorus, Praetorian Prefect of the Goths' king Vitigis, adressed in 337 to the 'maritime tribunes' who governed the earliest Venetians in the name of Ravenna: 'They live,' he writes vividly, 'like marsh birds, in nests of reeds raised on piles, to protect themselves against the waters.' Their life was poor and hard, devoted to maritime trade with nearby towns and Ravenna itself; they also extracted the salt from the sea water, in the great sandy expanses bounded by low walls of which there are still many traces, clearly visible in aerial photographs.

The lagoon's population increased greatly during the barbarian invasions. Attila's invasion in AD 450, which destroyed Aquileia, drove many families to seek refuge in the area protected by the waters and considered safe from the horrors of war. In the fifth century, after the collapse of the Roman Empire in Italy, the Veneti had their first constitutional organization, under the rule of the Goths established in Ravenna. The representatives of the central government were the maritime tribunes, who exercised their power through small assemblies, meeting where inhabitants were most concentrated. The first settlements were near Altinum: the documents actually talk of a capital of the lagoons, where the tribunes lived — Heraclea, also known as Cittanova.

In AD 535 the Roman Empire in the east sent its generals to reconquer Italy. Belisarius brought Ravenna and the Venetian lagoon under the rule of Justinian; the lagoon was an important element in Byzantine strategy because it offered possibilities for replenishing naval food and salt supplies, and indeed for the repair of ships. This was a very important turning-point in the history of the Veneti and the future Venice: the link with Byzantium, which for centuries was to be the dominant theme of the Republic's policy and the reason for her commercial and cultural leanings towards the east.

A new invasion, by the Lombards, was now under way, and the Veneti took precautionary measures: for instance, at Grado, a few miles away from Aquileia (now in the enemy's orbit), they set up a new patriarchate of all the Veneti and of Istria. Politically, the government of the lagoon was still dependent on the Byzantine emperor's representative in Ravenna, the Exarch; but the relationship with Byzantium was of little help to the Venetians in their struggle against the invading Lombards at the end of the sixth century. The worst was yet to come: about AD 640, Rothari destroyed Oderzo, then Concordia, near the sea, further east; then the inhabitants of Aquileia, still faithful to Byzantium, moved to Grado, barricading themselves on the island, linked with the Venetian lagoon and Ravenna only by sea. Finally the bishop of Altino left his small town on the edge of the mainland and moved, with the wealthier portion of the population, to one of the nearby islands, Torcello. There, in AD 639, a church was founded, and took on the name of Santa Maria Assunta. It is still there, and is the oldest evidence of the life of the Venetians in the lagoon, the first trace of the Venice of the future.

We must move on to the year 697 for a hint of any autonomous political organization of the lagoon's inhabitants: it was then that the leaders of the various small islands and main centres (the most important of which were Cittanova and Torcello) agreed to name a leader of the Venetians: 'Paulucius Dux': the first Doge of Venice. This is how the story is told in the oldest chronicles, but it is disbelieved by most modern historians (Cessi, *Un millennio di storia veneziana,* Venice 1964). Paulucius was more probably the Exarch of Ravenna who assumed dictatorship of the maritime Venetians during the crisis of the Iconoclasm. In fact, according to the most credible sources, the series of Venetian doges began only in 727, with Ursus Ypatus, elected after a military plot and assassinated soon afterwards; the Venetians were able to exploit the Byzantine government's temporary weakness to obtain from the Exarch a definite recognition of the new state, with its capital at Cittanova.

This first regime did not last long. Violent internal struggles shook Cittanova and caused its destruction. The centre of power moved to the lagoon. When Doge Deusdedit settled in Malamocco, on the Adriatic shore, many groups followed him and began to populate a hitherto little-known district nearby: Rivo Alto, 'deep channel' (hence the modern name Rialto). This was a group of relatively high-standing islands along the edge of an easily navigable channel. In the move from Cittanova

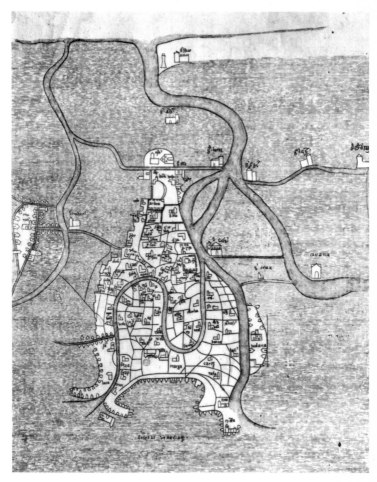

Ancient map of Venice. From a 12th-century manuscript in the Biblioteca Marciana. The shape of the city, bisected by the Grand Canal, had already been established.

to Malamocco, the second step in the direction of the future Venice had been taken.

Meanwhile struggles, assassinations and conspiracies continued among the chief families, made even more crucial by the complex political situation: the Byzantines of Ravenna found themselves faced with the Franks, who had recently made a bid for supremacy in northern Italy. The Venetian lagoon, with its shipyards and safe waters, was potentially a military base of enormous importance.

Unfortunately, nothing remains of the second Venetian capital, Malamocco, situated on the site of the small town that still bears its name. But the importance of this choice of site, on the Lido and near the opening of the Porto di Albiola, emerged when, in the year 809, a Byzantine fleet trying to re-establish full sovereignty over the Venetians was driven back into the sea; similarly, the year 810 saw the defeat, also in the Porto di Albiola, of the counter-expedition of the Franks, led by King Pepin and supported by a group of Venetian intriguers hoping to consolidate their own power. For the first time, the lagoon was threatened by enemy fleets and armies. This was one reason for a fateful decision in Venice's destiny: the transfer of the Doge's seat from Malamocco to Rialto.

In 814 the lagoon once more fell under the sway of Byzantium with the *Pax Nicephori* (Nicephorus was the reigning emperor), though it was granted a certain degree of independence under the rule of the Doges. Agnello Partecipazio built a Doge's Palace on the islands of Rialto: now all that was lacking to the formal constitution of the new state was its name.

The era of the Partecipazio family (Agnello, Giustiniano and Giovanni) marks the physical birth of the future city of Venice, with the foundation of the basilica of San Marco on one of the Rialto islands, next to the Doge's Palace.

This event was crucial in many ways; it was closely connected with the complex struggle waged by the Doges against the Byzantine Empire and the Papacy. On the one hand, the Venetians had hitherto in a sense admitted their dependence on Byzantium by choosing the Greek St Theodore as patron saint of the city and venerating him in a small church near the Doge's Palace (probably where the Piazzetta dei Leoncini now is). On the other hand, while Aquileia and Grado were competing for the title of cathedral city of the Patriarchate of the Venetians and Dalmatians, Rialto was electing its own bishop, with his seat on the island of Olivolo, near the Porto di San Nicolò (now Porto di Castello). Five suffragan sees depended upon this metropolitan bishop, those of Malamocco, Equilio (now Jesolo), Caorle, Cittanova and Torcello. Relations between these lagoon bishops and the Doges were always tense, and frequently exploded into violent conflicts over recognition of nominations.

Doge Agnello Partecipazio probably intended to put an end to all this with a popular gesture when he announced his intention of transferring the patronage of the city to another saint, one untarnished by imperial and ecclesiastical politics — St Mark. A legend, soon widespread in Rialto, claimed that the saint had preached in the lagoons and had seen an angel who said 'Peace be unto thee, Mark, my apostle'. This was taken as a prophecy that his mortal remains would find peace in Venice. *'Pax tibi, Marce, Evangelista meus.'* With this in mind the saint's remains, laid to rest in Alexandria in Egypt, were stolen by Venetian sailors and deposited in the Doge's Palace. And immediately, to underline the significance of the new choice, an anti-Byzantine and anti-papal gesture, Agnello Partecipazio ordered the building of a 'Doge's chapel' to house the bones of the new patron: the future basilica of San Marco.

So the image of the original city looms out of the mists of ancient chronicles and legends, with the Doges' fortified palace and the basilica of the patron saint looking out over the basin in the centre of the lagoon. Though nothing remains of these two architectural complexes, there are sufficient traces to enable us to define exactly their architectural make-up and their position within the town.

But the only sure sources for the identification of the remaining part of the original city are the relevant documents. They enable us to follow the movements of many churches and monasteries on the basis of their present-day positions. The Bishop had his residence at San Pietro in Castello, and nearby were the churches of Santa Giustina, San

▷

Rio della Verona, near San Marco. The grey-green waters move with the tide twice a day, and mirror the play of light on the ancient façades.

The Grand Canal, from the Rialto. The main axis of the city is lined with the city's most renowned palaces, which in the past were the private dwellings of Venetian merchants.

Giovanni in Bragora and Sant'Antonin. Nearer the centre, in the ninth century we can identify the churches of Santa Maria Formosa, San Teodoro, San Gemignano and San Salvador. Towards the centre of Rialto were Santi Apostoli, San Giacomo and Sant'Angelo; at the extreme west, Santa Croce and Santa Chiara, San Nicolò and the Angelo Raffaele. The original city had now spread broadly from the present-day site of the Porto del Lido to that of the railway station. There are no genuine maps before AD 1000, but we can still gain some idea of it from what seems to be the oldest topographical representation of the city, the so-called Temanza plan in the *Chronologia Magna* of the Biblioteca Marciana (a twelfth-century manuscript). Rialto stretches from the Lido towards the mainland, an elogated form a mile or so long, roughly corresponding in position to the present-day city. A deep

channel (the future Grand Canal) forms its axis of development, while the wider Canale della Giudecca marks its boundary to the south.

It is hard to say what the city looked like at the time of the Partecipazio doges, but obviously it did not vaunt the magnificent series of buildings and marbles that characterize Venice as she is today. The churches themselves were largely of wood. Some, like San Giacomo, were roofed with thatch. Most of the dwellings were even more simple and unassuming; only around San Marco, perhaps, did the buildings soon have a hint of grandeur, anticipating future developments.

But before considering San Marco, anyone wishing to understand the history of early Venice must go to Torcello, which in the ninth century was a thriving trading and ship-building centre, and the seat of a bishopric. That small island, now semi-deserted, had a population of many thousands of souls, the centre of whose life was the Piazza where, long ago in 639, the exiles from the mainland had founded Santa Maria Assunta, with an adjacent baptistery and mausoleum *(Martyrium),* as was the custom in the oldest examples of late Roman architecture, in Aquileia, Concordia and Ravenna.

Santa Maria Assunta in Torcello exemplifies the state of our knowledge of Venetian architecture before the eleventh century. There are no extant structures from this period; but the forms of earlier buildings are often apparent in those which succeeded them. Thus, in this case, despite successive rebuildings (records note the date 1008 for the

▷
Rio Menuo, near the Teatro della Fenice, San Marco.

P. 22/23, above
Aerial view of Venice, from the south. The ancient city is composed of a hundred islets. In the centre, San Marco with its campanile and the Doge's Palace. In the foreground, the glass works island, Murano, and on the horizon, the strip with the international Marco Polo airport.

P. 22/23, below
Aerial view of San Francesco del Deserto. From a deserted lagoon rises the monastery where, according to legend, St Francis preached to the birds.

broadening of the nave), the building still bears the mark of an original basilical ground plan in the 'Exarchal' tradition which grew from the meeting of late Roman and Byzantine influences in Ravenna. The broad nave and side-aisles, marked by a series of rather close-set columns, have a slow rhythm which emphasizes the even diffusion of the light as it falls from the numerous windows in the high central face; the main apse draws this movement of shapes into a wide arch, which diminishes and counteracts the effect of depth so created. The dense, slow light of the Ravenna basilicas, Sant'Apollinare in Classe and San Vittore (now destroyed), reappears in this Torcello basilica, built by

men whose eyes still held the image of the very similar churches of their birthplaces, Aquileia and Caorle, Oderzo and Altino.

On the exterior the use of brick, particularly on the apses, to form slight fillets, pilasters and geometrical friezes, has its origins in Ravenna. The brickwork has a soft surface, rich in chromatic possibilities and varying according to the way the light falls on it at different times of day and year. And here one of the unfailing rules of Venetian architecture was established: that of the use of light values, emphasized on the surfaces, irrespective of the plasticity of the geometrical volumes.

It is no coincidence, in this context, that pictorial decoration should also make its appearance in Torcello. There is scarcely a trace of the original decoration, dating back to the first seventh-century church; but the mosaic of the ceiling of the *diaconicon* (in the smaller apse on the left) which represents the Lamb of God, supported in a medallion by four angels in white tunics, is doubtless very close to it in mood. It is an absolutely unmistakable reference to the similar mosaic in the presbytery of San Vitale in Ravenna: evidence of a genuine stylistic and iconographic affinity. As in San Vitale, the colour spreads into great scrolls of greenery and flowers, with roundels showing symbolic animals, in a way that is delightfully natural, and suggests memories going right back to the late Roman period or the Milan of Theodosius, the sources of that Early Christian art which took on new life in Torcello. The mosaic also tends to remove all feeling of depth and all dynamism from the walls and ceilings; in fact, it tends to transform built architecture into painted architecture; it dissolves it, with a mysterious formal process that points a way soon to be followed even in the mighty San Marco.

Torcello is thus in many ways both the inspiration and the matrix of Venetian art. Its haunting remains suggest the shape of many of the churches that grew up on the lagoon and later disappeared. Looking down from the tall campanile of Torcello, one is bound to reflect on the passing of time. In old Venice, as in Torcello today, the waters and the lonely *barene*, the grass-covered shoals awash at high-tide, scarcely coloured by a fuzz of purplish flowers, once reflected great public buildings and crowded hovels; and there too the piercing cry of a white gull once echoed under the vast emptiness of the sky, against which the odd red brick tower marked the first trace of man's triumphant foothold.

Begun about two centuries after the Torcello basilica, San Marco is basically a very different matter. Five domes set out in a Greek cross define the internal space, giving it a centralized plan, whereas Torcello was elongated longitudinally according to the traditional design of the late Roman basilica. No church in Ravenna or anywhere else in the district of the Exarchate could be compared to this cluster of gigantic bubbles of air held down by the, elastic wave of the domes. But was the original San Marco, built by the doges Agnello and Giustiniano Partecipazio in the few years between 828 and 832, more or less the building that we see today? Specialists are locked in passionate disagreement over this. For the old school (represented by Cattaneo in 1876) San Marco was built at first as a close copy of the cathedral at Torcello, replacing the old San Teodoro. A part of the old walls, it was claimed, was incorporated into the present north side; while a trace of the foundations was said to be visible in the part of the crypt that runs under the centre nave. But more recent investigations (Forlati, 'Il primo San Marco', *Arte Veneta*, 1951) have confirmed that, in all probability, San Marco had a cruciform plan from the very beginning, with its domes inspired by Byzantine architecture. Original foundations have been discovered in the four great piers that support the main dome; and this could never have been conceived above a nave of the early Christian or Ravenna type. Basically, the very uniqueness of the plan of San Marco is a confirmation of the significance consciously conferred upon it by the Doge who gave it so important a part to play in the establishment of the new state. Even the very oldest chronicles attest this uniqueness, when they point out than the architect was ordered to build a chapel that was to be 'the finest that ever could be seen'.

It is no wonder, then, that the unknown builder should have sought his model in the capital of that cultural and political world in which Venice was still firmly rooted: in Constantinople itself. Here, examples of cruciform plans had abounded since the glories of the age of Justinian. The huge dome of Hagia Sophia, the masterpiece of Anthemius of Tralles and Isidore of Miletus, has been endlessly compared to the interior of San Marco. Furthermore, much of the sense of colour, the rarefied atmosphere, built up from optical rather than dynamic effects, was to be found in the buildings of Byzantium before reappearing in San Marco. In fact, the prototype of San Marco can be found, with its five domes arranged in a Greek cross, in a church that was very famous at the time, also built in the sixth century but altered in the eleventh: the Church of the Holy Apostles (Apostoleion) in Constantinople. Today this is no longer in existence, but written accounts and some illuminations make it possible to reconstruct its architectural form and to recognize it as the prototype of the first San Marco (Bettini, *L'Architettura di San Marco,* Padua 1946). The cultural link between the Doge's chapel of the proud young state and its distant historical and aesthetic origins was strengthened; and this explains the sense of colour, the architecture of enclosed space, solemn and imposing, a legacy of the late Roman era. This was no journey into uncharted territory: the art of the Exarchate itself largely derived from the same source, absorbed through Ravenna.

Here, with San Marco and the Doge's Palace about to take on their definitive shape, we may pause to take up the account of historical events. Briefly, after a period of internal struggle and violent upheavals, the city embarked upon a period of development and peace under the Doge Pietro Tribuno, elected in 887. It was to be he who first gave Venice her form and definitive name, girding most of the islands extending from Olivolo to Cannaregio with a defensive wall: it was no longer the island of Rialto, but *civitas Venetiarum:* Venice.

The whole of the tenth century saw Doge and people working to establish and consolidate their new achievement. Under the Candiano dynasty, Venice extended the power over the Adriatic which had been recognized in 840 by the Western Empire with the *Pactum Lotharii*. Istria was conquered; and on Ascension Day, AD 1000, Doge Pietro Orseolo II set out against the Narentines and other pirates who infested the Adriatic, defeated them finally and assumed the government of the whole coast as *Dux Dalmatiae et Chroatiae:* a sonorous title, accepted by the German Empire and Byzantium, and one which made Venice a mediator of great political and military value.

Well (11th century). Venice, Museo Correr. The influences of Ravenna and the Barbarians mingle in the stylized decoration of early Venetian sculpture.

In 1001, Emperor Otto III met Doge Orseolo in Venice; from that moment, the little city of Venice entered the ranks of the great European powers.

San Marco and the Rise of the Republic

From the very beginning attempts had been made to ensure that the election of the Doge should be really democratic: he was to be elected by popular vote. But for a long time violence and intrigue led to troubled governments and untimely deaths, and power tended to remain within the hands of a single family. After the Orseolos, the electoral system operated by the assembly ensured greater constitutional guarantees and permanently replaced the irregular methods followed hitherto. Venice became a democratic republic, with a Senate or Council of Elders which controlled and regulated her activities. Growth and social participation in public life encouraged well-being and stability, and by the eleventh century the community was flourishing and growing rapidly: Venice was now adult and independent in her civic life.

This growth was not even impeded by the wars and other difficulties in which Venice found herself involved, mainly in her capacity as

dominant power in the Adriatic, and as a maritime trading power. With the help of Byzantium, and of good fortune, Venice also freed herself from the danger of the Norman kingdom which threatened, with the conquest of Apulia and Albania, to lock her up in her own sea. Having emerged from this crisis, Venice resumed her mercantile expansion eastwards, came to terms with the Moslems, became a trading centre for merchandise imported from the east, and distributed it to the whole of continental Europe.

This position as a go-between was the secret of all Venice's wealth and the keystone of her own art and culture. The city was growing rapidly, so that between the eleventh and thirteenth centuries we see her spreading, in all her architectural magnificence, along the banks of the canals, glorying in her Arsenal, which Dante describes in the *Divine Comedy,* and in the breathtaking beauty of her churches and palazzi.

In 976 a serious fire destroyed part of the basilica of San Marco and more than three hundred houses, as far afield as Santa Maria Zobenigo. But in the chronicles for the year 1000 many churches and palazzi are mentioned as having been rebuilt. San Marco itself, at the command of Doge Contarini, was restored and modernized from 1063 onwards. In 1093 Doge Falier reopened it for worship.

◁
Relief of two lions (11th-12th centuries).

◁
Two lions fighting (11th-12th centuries). Campanile of San Paolo.

Finestrella *with winged lions (11th-12th centuries). Rialto, Riva del Carbon.*

It is quite clear that, two centuries after its founding, San Marco had become the real and symbolic centre of public life, the focus of patriotic feeling for the Venetians. The patron saint had taken hold of their imagination; his symbol, the winged lion with claws gripping a book bearing the famous inscription *Pax tibi Marce . . . ,* appears everywhere, in sculpture, painting and manuscript illumination, the very symbol of the Republic, *la Dominante.* Meanwhile, the actual pattern of the city's development could be said to justify and explain so much interest on the part of the magistracy. In fact, San Marco stood at the focal point of what one could call the administrative and political centre of Venice; even as early as 1000 the economic centre could be said to be around Rialto. By San Marco stood the Doge's residence, the Palazzo della Giustizia and the Palazzo Pubblico, which soon came together to form the complex of the Doge's Palace. At the sides of the square, in the very earliest times, there had been hotels for pilgrims (founded by the Orseolos, who gave their name to them) and the offices of state, the so-called Procuratie (on the north side, where the Procuratie Vecchie stands today). The Rio Batario, the canal which ran through the centre of the present square from north to south, completed the scene, with the gardens of San Gemignano on its far bank. The basilica (according to the interpretation given by

Bettini, *L'Architettura di San Marco,* 1946) thus dominated an enclosed space, comparable in many ways to the 'ceremonial courtyards' of late Roman imperial palaces — for instance, the palace of Diocletian still preserved at Split. Napoleon called it a magnificent hall with the sky for a ceiling; and, historically, the Piazza was thought of precisely as a ceremonial hall set in front of the church: a church, it should be remembered, conceived not exclusively as a place of worship but also as a state chapel, a patriotic shrine.

Miraculously enough, the Contarini basilica of San Marco has come down to us practically intact. Inside, nothing of the original scheme seems changed. The system of the five cupolas is supported by piers and vaults of gigantic proportions which, at the crossing, give a particular impression of concentration and fusion of space. Looking at the central nave, we realize that light has become a basic element in this space: spreading blandly, seeping between the columns into the dim shadows of the gynaecea and side aisles, it seems, magically, almost to dispel the intervening structures and recast the space into a single whole again. Originally, this light effect must have been even more striking. As Bettini has noted, the small windows in the south face, through which the light enters, were probably filled with translucent slabs of alabaster, so that the lighting would have been even more diffused; it would have been undirectional, static rather than dynamic. Also, the small windows which run under the impost of the domes were set in a wall much less substantial than the present one, which was almost doubled in thickness in the fifteenth century, to support the outer covering of lead. The result of this was that the direction of the light changed: originally it had fallen more or less vertically and was diffused everywhere, reflected by the mosaic floor; but now, with the thickening of the walls, it was concentrated half-way up the nave, creating a contrasting pool of shadow below. To counter this unforeseen darkness, the great arch of the Apocalypse was opened on the façade (it was originally filled by an openwork screen), and the Gothicizing rose-window on the south arm of the transept was added later. The result was the crossing of violent bands of light in two directions, with disastrous results: 'almost', says Bettini, 'like two Gothic cathedral naves'.

This tampering with the sources of light may have been ill-considered, but the fascination of the interior was ensured by the mosaics which entirely cover its surface. They date from various periods, but here we can reasonably consider all the thirteenth-century examples together, because they have a complete unity whose very divergencies point to the complex cultural situation of early Venetian painting.

Beneath the marble facing of the masonry, there are a few traces of the original mosaics, commissioned by Doge Domenico Selvo (1071-85) according to the chronicles, but they are hard to identify. However, it does seem that the faintest echo can still be seen, through the alterations and restorations, in the series of small mosaic-covered niches above the main door, inside the porch. They represent the Virgin and the Apostles, in a simple pictorial style, with long stylized streaks of light, and are clearly related, as in the fixed gaze of the Virgin, to the Ravenna mosaics (for instance the panels of Justinian and Theodora in San Vitale). The monumental saints, too, in the lower part of the apse, probably reveal something of the original character, exemplifying the two basic strands of Venetian painting at the beginning of the twelfth century: the Early Christian tradition, which the first artists brought from Ravenna, and the fascination of the

Byzantine, as seen in the monumental style of mosaics like those of San Luca in Focide. From the very beginning these essential elements in the formation of the Venetian figurative language worked upon a 'vernacular' substratum, which implied the presence of local artists. They were probably fresco-painters who (judging by the extremely faint traces in the monastery of San Nicolò di Lido) seem to have worked within the ambit of Greek provincial forms, possibly even producing a 'popular' version with a western flavour. Their work must have been a major factor in the formation of Venetian painting.

The domes, too, appear in the first plan of the basilica. They were destroyed in the fire of 1106 and rebuilt probably after 1156, according to an old inscription preserved in the church, which commemorates the resumption of work on the marble decoration. The mosaics undoubtedly had an organic design, probably deriving .from that of the Apostoleion in Constantinople, which had served as a model for the architecture. The Emmanuel and Pentecost cupolas are thus part of the second cycle of activity, which continued until about 1200 with

Archway in Marco Polo's house (11th-12th centuries). Campiello del Milion.

the *Life of Christ* in the great southern arch of the Ascension cupola. An examination of one of the mosaics in this group, the *Palm Sunday,* makes it plain that Venetian painting had acquired considerable expressive independence: references to Byzantium are purely external by now, and the dynamic emphasis reveals the influence of Ottonian painting. Towards the end of the twelfth century Venetian artists already had a style of their own, similar in many ways to the vernacular 'Benedictine' style so widespread in southern Italy. The outline of the figures is extremely emphatic: this is the so-called *stile frecciato,* the 'arrowed style' which is evident for instance in the Archangel in the Pentecost cupola.

The actual pictorial design is sharply detached from the golden background, which loses its typically Byzantine abstractness — as a sort of musical comment — and takes on a dialectical value: the intense, dramatic colours stand out against it, creating an unmistakably Romanesque effect.

The great mosaic of the Last Judgment in Torcello belongs to this period; it has an expressionistic strength that is often almost grotesque, though it has a Byzantine background in the linear style of Daphni. Datable after the middle of the twelfth century (in 1153 certain mosaicists with Greek names made their appearance in Torcello) it shows Christ sitting in judgment amid the figures of the Apocalypse and of Heaven and Hell. In the last scene, particularly in the realistic representation of the nude, the unknown artist takes the first steps towards that 'naturalistic' style which was often to constitute one of the most striking features of independent Venetian painting, especially in the field of colour. The relationship between the Torcello mosaics and those of San Marco remains obscure; but it is not improbable that, when the decoration of the latter was resumed after 1156, all the masters previously employed at Torcello would have been employed there, leaving the decoration of Santa Maria Assunta half-finished and initiating the irreversible process of decline for the little island, which since then has always been a suburban outpost of the Venetian metropolis.

The development of the style of Venetian painting is more evident in the third period of the decoration of San Marco, which may be dated between 1200 and 1250: this was the period of the Agony in the Garden (*c.* 1200-20) and the Arch of the Passion. These are the masterpieces of San Marco and are among the finest creations of Italian Romanesque painting. The Agony in the Garden depicts a complex and dramatic scene: the figure of Christ, shown on the hillock beside the Apostles, is part of a plastic system which has the tension of a bas-relief. The great luminous patches of colour emphasize the feeling of the various planes, resolving the complex tangle of figures into a spacious composition. The gold background is forced to retreat, while the plastic vitality of nature comes to the fore, authoritatively expressed and bristling with energy. The colour here is particularly sophisticated, woven together from a very fine web of deep blues and golds, greens and subdued yellows. This is the work of a

▷

Levantine merchant (13th century) in Campo dei Mori, Cannaregio. Popular tradition attributes the name of 'Moors' to the three figures of the turbaned Oriental merchants. The square (campo) near the Fondaco degli Arabi was called after them.

craftsman of some individuality, who already clearly belonged to an original and vital culture.

The scenes of the Arch of the Passion (*c.* 1250) are part of the same dramatic dialogue, which is born of exclusively formal elements. Christ stretches out his arms to embrace almost the whole composition in an agonized framework, contrasting with the contained grief of the Marys and the violent invective of the soldiers. Even the angels break ranks to form a disjointed, quivering line; while the browns, reds and dark blues have an extraordinary brilliance and novelty. Here we have elements of line and colour typical of the most definite Romanesque expressionism, possibly even influenced by the Salzburg school of illumination.

This was the most novel strand in Venetian painting in the mid-thirteenth century. But other forms coexisted with it, for instance in the almost archaic Lives of the Virgin and of Christ in the north transept, or that of St Mark in the organ loft. These are traditionally regarded as the oldest mosaics in the Basilica, but they were probably restored at the beginning of the thirteenth century, which would mean that only the iconography is original.

The style of the Master of the Passion was dominant in the decoration of San Marco until half-way through the century, as can also be seen in the mosaics in the atrium on the side nearest the Piazza, which were probably completed about 1258. Of the *Genesis, Life of Abraham* and the first series of the *Life of Joseph,* the oldest are those of Genesis in the first dome and adjacent arch. These show a narrative variant of the expressionism of the mosaics of the Passion; it has been postulated that they were inspired by lost mural paintings and perhaps by the flowing realistic style of the so-called Cotton Bible, in the British Museum, a sixth-century Alexandrian manuscript.

The figures of Adam and Eve, the Flood sequence, the Earthly Paradise and the animals offer opportunities for work of great natural freshness, executed in colours rich in atmospheric vibrations, far removed from the conventional Byzantine depiction and use of light. This can be seen, for instance, in the way the white doves and peacocks emerge from the Ark beneath the glittering curve of the rainbow, while the tawny spotted coats of the wild animals, vividly and skilfully represented, stand out against a craggy landscape dotted with tender green.

The fourth period of the decoration of San Marco began, after a ten-year pause, about 1258 and probably ended about 1275, with the last *Lives of Joseph and Moses* in the atrium and the mosaics of the *Finding of the Relics* in the transept. Of the lunettes on the façade, representing the *Life of St Mark,* only the one on the extreme left has been preserved, with the view of the old church. The sophistication of the colour and the subtle vibrancy of the line already clearly anticipate the forms of Gothic painting. But the iconography shows an unexpected return to Byzantium in the stylized composition, almost a sort of neoclassicism. This is the first hint of a tendency which was to become more pronounced in the last quarter of the century and may have been related to the political rapprochement with Byzantium, at the time of the Palaeologue emperors, after the peace of 1268.

A whole century is therefore spanned by the mosaics of San Marco, from the primitive forms influenced by Ravenna to the dawning of the Gothic age. Venice, a latecomer in the field of Romanesque art, rapidly forged herself a powerfully expressive style: she inherited a taste for colour from Byzantium, but also retained something of the

Relief of monsters (13th century). Palazzo del Camello, Misericordia.

Relief of camel (13th century). Palazzo del Camello (Palazzo dei Mastelli),
Misericordia. The insignia of the Mastelli, the three
Levantine merchants shown in the statue of the 'Moors' in the adjacent
square. Symbol of the enterprise and vitality of the Venetian merchants.

dry strength of northern art, extracting from it that incisive line and plastic tension which suggest movement.

Sculpture played an important part in defining the face of Venice between the eleventh and thirteenth centuries. The earliest examples show it used purely decoratively, as a superimposition on the façades of churches and palazzi. Interestingly, it reflects the particular character of the city, and the acquisitive nature of its inhabitants: a city trading with distant lands, a city of merchants avid to bring home mementoes of their experiences overseas. During these two centuries, so crucial for the formation of the Republic, the city was gradually

Torcello Cathedral and Church of Santa Fosca. Of this city of thousands of inhabitants, to which the first refugees from the mainland came in the 7th century, before they founded Venice, only a few ruins and this wonderful complex of buildings remain: the older Cathedral (7th-11th centuries) and Santa Fosca, its elegant central plan showing Macedonian influence.

bedecked with all manner of trophies, usually sculptural, coming mainly from the eastern seaboard: Byzantine reliefs, *paterae* and *tondi*, friezes and cornices and door and window panels. Naturally, there were also local imitations, and the Venetian *tagiapiera* (stone-cutters) carved Byzantine Madonnas, or 'Langobard' doorways, like the famous door in the Corte del Milione in the house of Marco Polo, the traveller who carried the name of Venice to the fabled countries of India and China, and described them in his book *Il Milione*, perhaps the most famous of medieval travel books (1298). The sculptures of the so-called *Mori*, too, at the Madonna dell'Orto, and the

famous *Camel,* incorporated into the bas-relief in the palazzo of the same name, in Cannaregio, are examples of the spirit of exoticism which dictated the choices of the Venetians in the field of sculptural decoration.

Venice's participation in the Crusades was a basic element in the cath-olicity of taste which was so noticeable in the growth of the city between the eleventh and thirteenth centuries. Here, the Venetians always acted as astute merchants and calculating politicians, extract-ing the maximum profit from an ostensibly religious enterprise. From the First Crusade onwards, Venetians settled in many eastern Mediter-

ranean ports, including Rhodes, Jaffa, Modon, Ascalon and Chios. In 1124 Doge Domenico Selvo took part in the conquest of Tyre; in 1192 Doge Enrico Dandolo, a key figure in the Fourth Crusade, reconquered Zara. In 1204 Dandolo took part in the capture of Constantinople and the foundation of the Eastern Latin Empire, of which Venice obtained a large part; there was even talk of making the Doge Emperor and moving the capital there, but luckily the prudence of the Venetians prevailed. During this period Venice's merciless plundering of the eastern provinces reached its peak. As early as 1172 Doge Ziani had erected two columns from Syria in the Piazzetta of

Cathedral apse, Torcello. Early Venetian architecture was inspired by Ravenna, as the red brick walls of Torcello indicate. The surfaces are enlivened with small arches and pilasters.

39

San Marco, with the symbols of Venice, the lion of Mark and the old patron St Theodore (*Marco e Todaro,* as the Venetians now say); in 1204 the four famous *Horses* of gilded bronze, probably late Roman, torn by Dandolo from the Hippodrome in Constantinople, were placed triumphantly on the façade of the golden basilica, amid the innumerable columns, reliefs, *plutei* and screens which adorned the walls of San Marco. At the same time, Venice extended her trading and political bases throughout the eastern Mediterranean, conquered Crete, and dotted the Greek and Syrian coasts, the Sea of Marmara, the Black Sea and Egypt with her *fondachi* (trading settlements). In this way she carried out her function of intermediary between east and west: a historic function which was the basis not only of the city's prosperity, but also of her culture.

A complex of varying, sometimes contradictory influences formed the basis of Venetian taste in the field of sculpture, in many ways repeating the process that applied in the field of mosaics. But, as far as sculpture was concerned, Venice began to look intently in the direction of the mainland. There was a primitive background inspired by Ravenna or Byzantium, as can be seen in reliefs like those of the *gynaecea* in San Marco or *plutei* like those in Torcello; but at the beginning of the thirteenth century the influence of mainland Romanesque sculpture was decisively superimposed upon it. There are many examples of this, for instance the *Adoration of the Magi* in the Seminario Patriarcale, or the *Joseph's Dream* on the main door at San Marco, works of artists who were adopting a style that was already mature and somewhat severe, though veined with psychological subtleties and tense linear forms.

The masterpiece of thirteenth-century Venetian sculpture is the main porch of San Marco, whose three great arches are decorated with bands of sculpture. On the bottom are representations of the *Earth, Sea,* and *Human Life;* on the central one, the *Months, Seasons* and, on the face, the *Virtues;* and on the third arch the *Crafts,* on the soffit, and on the face, the *Prophets.* The complex decoration is certainly not the work of a single master, indeed it was worked on throughout the whole of the thirteenth century, and the dates generally given — c. 1240 until 1275, the year the mosaic of the left-hand lunette with the view of the church was completed — are probably too restricted. This revision of the dating offers further evidence for the turn that Venetian art took in the thirteenth century, towards the Romanesque manner of the mainland. This can be seen on the first arch (certainly earlier than 1240), which shows Lombard influence, and in the series of *Months* and *Seasons* of the second arch, reminiscent of the Antelami carvings of the months in Ferrara, particularly in their haunting realism.

On the face of the second arch, the *Virtues* indicate the return of Byzantine modes complicated by Gothicizing French forms, which are a sort of prelude to the picturesque, incisive vision of the third arch, with the *Crafts;* these last sculptures may perhaps be dated from the last quarter of the thirteenth century, and it is not impossible that they indicate a Gothic way of working, possibly even with a certain Pisan influence. Their genesis was complex; the result was an exceptionally lovely work of art. After the tense complexities of the first arch, and the sophisticated interplay of the forms within the

▷
Campanile, Torcello.

decorative backgrounds of the second, we come, in the third arch, upon a representation of astounding vitality: a popular poem, given a quite extraordinary picturesque intensity by the play of light.

Even alongside the ultimately Gothic tendencies of the Masters of San Marco, after the middle of the thirteenth century we note the appearance of rhythmically decorative forms which are related to Byzantine art (particularly the backgrounds of the *Months* and some aspects of the *Virtues*). The same phenomenon, as we have seen, occurs in the late mosaics of the atrium, corresponding to the resumption of relations with Greece in the last quarter of the thirteenth

century. This tendency seems fundamental to the development of other sculptors, working on the north side and minor porches of the basilica, at the time when the decoration of the façade was being started. Among these sculptors, it does seem possible to pinpoint one personality whom we can call the 'Master of the Evangelists', after his most significant works, on the north side of the church. This sculptor moves between the Byzantine-inspired subtleties of the 'painterly' bas-relief and a tense style, involving strong contrasts of light and shade, which has its precedents in the 'arrowed' style of the Roman-esque mosaics in San Marco, with their typical linear inflexion.

The Ship of St Mark
(11th century). Treasury of San
Marco. Enamel.

P. 42/43 and left
Basilica of San Donato, Murano.
Contemporary with San Marco, this
red brick basilica still looks very
much as San Marco must have
looked in the 11th century, with
reminiscences of Padua and Ravenna.

P. 46/47
The horses of San Marco
(4th century)

Certain reliefs incorporated into the north façade, and the Portale dei Fiori with its exquisitely decorative *Nativity,* are reminiscent of the *Evangelist,* as are some *Reliefs* on the doors opening on to the Piazzetta; the Angels beneath the main crossing are probably works of the same period, with their brilliant sense of movement and feeling for depth emphasized by the play of light. The bundle of folds follows the movement of the angel playing the trumpet, then falls to drape itself in the background together with the elegant lines of the great elongated wing. For all its echoes of Byzantium, this is one of the most lively works of Venetian sculpture.

The Master of the Evangelists is the last great thirteenth-century figure.

Towards the end of the century, when the force and liveliness typical of the best works had vanished, Venetian sculptors sank back into a flaccid imitation of Byzantium, which reduced plastic forms to modest reliefs over which light spread lifelessly. Examples of this are the many bas-relief icons scattered throughout Venetian churches, for instance the *Madonna dello Schioppo* in San Marco, or the one in Santa Maria Materdomini, where the light falls delicately but unincisively.

Venetian art of the thirteenth century thus ended, in painting as in sculpture, with a homage to Byzantium, anticipating what was to be its dominant mood for at least the first half of the fourteenth century.

The visitor to Venice at this stage in time would already have found her beginning to look like a modern city, bursting with strange riches, scattered with the exotic curiosities which bore witness to the Venetians' habit of travel, and the scene of numerous cultural encounters. Martino da Canale, one of the old chroniclers, wrote that at that time 'merchandise was pouring from everywhere into that noble city, like water from fountains': an image which gives a vivid idea of the fantastic speed of change, and of the Venetians' insatiability.

An obvious example of this mood would be the unquenchable explorer Marco Polo; or Enrico Dandolo the conquering Doge, the Loredan, the Farsetti, the Barozzi, the Businello or Da Mosto families, the innumerable successful merchants who perpetuated themselves in their splendid palazzi, still in existence. The thirteenth century was one of the golden ages of the Republic. This new city of politicians and merchants had managed to establish a stable and well-ordered system of government, with her Doges, Senate, lesser councils and Maggior Consiglio (Great Council); the famous gold ducat, struck in 1284, was to remain stable until the Napoleonic era.

By now, Venice had about 100,000 inhabitants and was divided into thirty *contrade,* themselves grouped within larger divisions called *sestieri.* Their names are still in use today. Starting from the harbour mouth, we find Castello, with the Arsenal, the district of sailors and fishermen; San Marco, with the seat of the government and main commercial activities, extending up the Grand Canal as far as Rialto; Cannaregio, occupying the whole of the northern area facing the

◁

Column of ciborium. San Marco (12th century). Sometimes the Venetians searched for masterpieces to adorn their basilica in the most distant of their conquered countries; the horses (p. 46/47) came from Constantinople (1204). Sometimes they preferred to imitate, with superb mastery, the most ancient works; the columns of the ciborium were sculptured in the 12th-13th centuries, on late Roman models.

mainland; Dorsoduro, with the Giudecca, facing south; and San Polo, with Santa Croce, facing south-west.

The urban intermingling of the various classes has been characteristic of Venice from the earliest times to the present day. Practically speaking, there are neither 'smart' districts nor dreary suburbs. The merchant-patrician was to build his palazzo where he judged best for his trade in ships and goods: that is why, in every *sestiere,* sometimes on a small side-canal or *rio,* there are magnificent palazzi side by side with the modest dwellings of the ordinary people. The only exception to this feature of the pattern of Venice is the Grand Canal, destined to become the Republic's ceremonial way.

There are still many traces of this thirteenth-century townscape, so that we can reconstruct the city as it was at its most impressive. There are numerous examples along the Grand Canal.

The Fondaco dei Turchi (formerly the Palazzo Pesaro) at San Stae, is a typical example, though it was clumsily restored in the nineteenth century; the original division into storeys was respected but much of the marble facing was replaced. The plan develops longitudinally, so that the façade is much narrower than the sides; this was clearly also partly a consequence of the high cost of building land along the canal. The façade looks out over the water and is typical of the early Venetian pattern: an arcade on the ground floor, loggia on the first floor and cresting hiding the pitch of the roof. At the sides, the two small towers indicate its derivation from late Roman villas, of the kind that were to be found not only along the African and Adriatic coasts, but as close as Altino, on the north shore of the Venetian lagoon (indeed. the poet Martial wrote: *Aemula Bajanis Altini litora villis;* 'the shores of Altino rival the villas of Baiae'). It is interesting that this architecture — completely open, with its porticos and loggias, because it evolved in a time of peace, with no concern for wars or invasions — should have found the ideal place for rebirth, centuries later, in the Venetian Republic, equally protected by its well-defended lagoon. The Venice of the thirteenth century, in short, was already well on the way to becoming that splendid assemblage of highly coloured backdrops and burnished balconies that looked out on to the most beautiful street in the world, the Grand Canal.

The history of the palazzo now know as the Fondaco dei Turchi is long and complex. It was built in the thirteenth century by a merchant from Pesaro, Giacomo Palmieri. In 1381 it was given by the Republic to the Marchese di Ferrara, who turned it into so splendid a residence that sovereigns and princes passing through Venice would stay there. It then became the property of the Aldobrandini, Priuli and Pesaro families, and finally (in 1621) of the Turks, who made it into their headquarters and warehouse; hence its present name. At present, converted into a museum of natural history, its interior still has the airy, luminous feeling of early Venetian architecture, of which it is undoubtedly the masterpiece.

Many other similar palazzi were built along the Grand Canal, most of them concentrated aroud the Rialto. There is the evocative Cà da Mosto, with its lovely ground-floor portico (partly filled in by restorations) and its delicate, graceful little loggia on the first floor (originally the top, but other floors were added later). As at the Fondaco, its brick walls are covered with a thin layer of delicately coloured marble. This was a typical late Roman habit (the marble slabs were called *crustae*), and several examples from the Early Christian period are still preserved in Ravenna, where the Venetians plainly found

Cupolas. Basilica of San Marco. In the original plan San Marco probably had five cupolas, but they were much lower, in the Byzantine style. In the 14th century they were topped with the present lead outer domes, which give them a picturesque élan.

their inspiration. The navigator Alvise da Cà da Mosto, who explored the coasts of Africa in 1445, set out from this palazzo; in the sixteenth century it became the Albergo del Leon Bianco, the favourite haunt of many famous travellers including, in the eighteenth century, the Russian archdukes whose visit in 1782 was immortalized in the paintings of Francesco Guardi (Pinakothek, Munich).

Then, beyond the Ponte di Rialto towards San Marco, on the left, are the Palazzi Loredan and Farsetti and on the right the two Donà palazzi and Palazzo Barzizza. All are characterized by the elegant first-floor loggias, with their many arches, set above ground-floor colonnades. We can imagine the merchants' vessels moored outside these buildings which served both as store-rooms and patrician residences. Dotted with these exquisite houses, Venice was now a splendid and mature medieval city.

What was going on at the Doge's Palace, amid such energetic building activity? The thirteenth-century documents tell us of three different elements that made up the whole. Probably the oldest was the Palatium Ducis, a private house for the chief magistrate of the Republic. It was situated along the Rio di Palazzo (behind the present-day Bridge of Sighs). On that side, on the Molo, stood a *torresella* (small tower); it probably served some military purpose, because that part of the palace held the armed men and weapons for the use of the Signoria.

Along the Molo, looking south, another building had taken on definitive form by the time of Doge Sebastiano Ziani (1172-78): the Palazzo Pubblico, which many documents call *palatium comune*. This housed the larger government bodies, such as the Maggior Consiglio, as well as the officers of the magistrature (Signori di Notte) and the tax officials. Most space was probably given to the Maggior Consiglio, the supreme magistracy of the Republic, whose task it was to elect the Doge and advise in event of war. A curious document of 1255 talks of it in connection with a ruling prohibiting anyone from remaining in the adjacent courtyard to disturb the work of the magistrates with games of dice and shouts, on pain of being thrown into the water! It would therefore seem that the councillors may have gathered on the ground floor; it does not seem that this section of the Palace was very big.

The third part of the Doge's Palace was the Palazzo di Giustizia (*ad jus reddendum*) situated on the west side, looking on to the present Piazzetta. On that side, on the ground floor, were the Doge's stables, opening on to inner courtyards as well as on to the Piazzetta.

Pietro Ziani, Doge from 1205 to 1229, must have felt the need to bring some order into this chaotic mass of buildings; furthermore, with the rapid growth of the Republic, they were fast proving inadequate and requiring costly restorations and improvements. Ziani has been credited with the idea of transferring the capital to Constantinople; luckily for Venice, this never took place. Also at the time of this revolutionary Doge we hear of a small church dedicated to San Nicolò; this too was within the Palace precincts. Its demolition in the sixteenth century leaves us uncertain of its position, which must have been somewhere at the side of the Palace, possibly facing on to the Rio del Palazzo, not far from the *torresella*.

Meanwhile, the Doge's Palace had been the silent witness of great historical events: in 1177, there was the meeting between Pope Alexander III and Frederick Barbarossa, under the auspices of Doge Sebastiano Ziani, and in 1204, the setting up — on the ruins of the old Byzantium — of the Latin empire of Constantinople, with Venice as co-ruler of 'a quarter and a half a quarter'; the victory over the Genoese at Saint-Jean d'Acre in 1257 meant that Venice dominated trade with the Orient.

In 1297, Doge Pietro Gradenigo brought about the *serrata* or 'locking' of the Maggior Consiglio, concentrating power into the hands of a restricted oligarchy of families, through the election of the Doge. With this reform of the Maggior Consiglio, the Venetian constitution was definitively established. The Senate *(Pregadi),* consisting of about three hundred members and elected annually, was set up, with legislative and advisory functions. The executive power was subdivided among various groups of *Savi* (wise men): one group concerned with the navy, another for mainland affairs, one for finance, one for internal affairs, and one for war. All these together formed the Collegio (led by the Doge), which had begun virtually to embody the government of the Republic (a sort of 'presidential republic' as one would say today). An offshoot of this was the Signoria, a cabinet consisting of the Doge, six counsellors and three judges. Judicial power was exercised by the three supreme courts of the Quarantie, the criminal and old and new civil courts, with a total of forty judges.

It is obvious that the growth of the numerous magistracies, and their increasingly broad fields of operation, made more accommodation necessary; the Signoria's consideration of alterations and additions to the Doge's Palace thus became more pressing than ever.

As early as the end of the thirteenth century, at the time of Doge Gradenigo's *serrata*, there was talk of enlarging the Sala del Maggior

▷
Bronze central door (12th century). Basilica of San Marco.

Consiglio on the Rio di Palazzo and of decorating it with frescoes. Authoritative evidence comes to us from Dante Alighieri, present in Venice in 1312 and received, on that occasion, in the hall on the east side of the Palazzo. Numerous other documents of the beginning of the fourteenth century tell us of this problem, which had now become chronic.

One can only guess at the exact architectural situation of the Palazzo Pubblico on the Molo. It is probable that by then the building destined to hold the Sala del Maggiore Consiglio (consisting of over a thousand persons) occupied a considerable portion of the frontage on to the Molo and extended as far as the eastern end of it, possibly taking in the *torresella*. Recent excavations have uncovered remains of what must have been the thirteenth-century building, so that it is not too far-fetched to imagine that at the end of the thirteenth century a real Palazzo looked out over the basin, with colonnaded façades and loggias just like those of the same period which have been preserved, from the Cà da Mosto to the Fondaco dei Turchi, including the Palazzi Loredan and Farsetti and the Palazzo Barozzi at San Moisè. The latter, no longer in existence but recorded in the De Barbari plan of 1500, is probably a guide to the layout of the Palazzo Pubblico begun by Doge Ziani, which was in existence at least until the beginning of the fourteenth century. This, too, seems to have had a *rio* running along its east side, and was built as an almost square block, with crenellated walls and towers. The south façade of the Palazzo Barozzi corresponds to what the façade of the Doge's Palace might have looked like: a broad ground-floor portico topped by a loggia, running the whole length of the building. Above it, a smooth wall broken only by small windows, and, on top, the typical *falconatura* (cresting) of which we find distant examples in Ravenna, the artistic ancestor of Venice.

So, through the Palazzo Barozzi, it is possible to reconstruct the most probable forms of thirteenth-century Venetian architecture, which provided the model for the Doge's Palazzo Pubblico: forms which recent studies have identified as part of the late Roman heritage of the Adriatic, with geographically nearby examples like the villas of Altino or Diocletian's palace in Split.

Even in the absence of contemporary graphic documents, we may perhaps attribute some value to the later illustration of the Palazzo Pubblico in the illumination of the 'Book of the Great Khan' in Oxford (fourteenth century). Despite undoubted inaccuracies and flights of fancy, there is no denying that the porticoed Palazzo Pubblico looking out over the Molo is clearly identifiable; there are other buildings inside the inner courtyards, probably the Doge's apartments and the small church of San Nicolò.

But in 1340 we come to a turning-point in the growth of the Palace. Weary of conflicting proposals and inadequate restorations, the Signoria decided to give the problem of the headquarters of the Maggior Consiglio a radical solution: and thus they laid the foundations for the final elaboration of the whole architectural complex. The drafting of the plan was promptly entrusted to three senators, the so-called *Tre Savi:* Marco Erizzo, Nicolò Superanzio and Tommaso Gradenigo; in that same year of 1340 they presented their conclusions, which were immediately accepted and put into execution. The new hall was to occupy the whole area looking on to the Molo, from the *torresella* to the side of the Palazzo di Giustizia on the Piazzetta. The Palazzo Pubblico must thenceforth have had broadly the same frontage

Angel of the Apocalypse (13th century). Basilica of San Marco.

on the Molo as it has today; it has been rightly noted in this context that the great balcony completed in 1404 is already indicated in the documents as 'central'. It is certain that, in the Palazzo designed by the *Tre Savi,* the *torresella* disappeared, being incorporated into the façade; but, perhaps because it had different floor levels, the curious asymmetry of the two first windows on the right remained, and they are still a little lower than the other four, which correspond to the Sala del Maggior Consiglio. Further evidence of this incorporation of the tower can be found in the earliest engraving to show the new façade when it was completed: this is the woodcut by Reeuwich, made in 1486 in Mainz. On the right corner of the palace one can clearly see the upper part of the *torresella;* it was finally demolished in the sixteenth century.

The 'palace of the *Tre Savi'* was built between 1340 and 1419, the year of the Council's first meeting in its new quarters, to an overall plan which was strictly architectural in nature and not just a craftsman's rehandling of the earlier structures, and which must have seemed novel, even revolutionary, at the time. In addition, decorative styles had changed in the meantime, from the early Venetian style of the thirteenth-century palazzi to the fully-fledged Venetian Gothic. The new forms of Gothic architecture had first appeared in Venice from 1330 onwards, at the Frari and San Zanipolo, in the Palazzo Ariani near the Angelo Raffaele and the abbey of San Gregorio at San Vio.

Who was the unknown architect of the palace of the *Tre Savi?* From their own report we know that they consulted numerous *magistri e protomagistri,* taking advice and designs from them before drawing up their plans. The chronicles mention the name of Filippo Calendario (executed after the Bajamonte Tiepolo plot of 1355) as the main creator of the Palace, together with a Pietro Baseggio, *'magister protus'* (which means architect of the building) and another *protus* or foreman called Enrico.

It is certainly hard to believe that the idea of the fourteenth-century Palace, built like a fabulous backdrop to the ship-filled harbour, beside the golden basilica, was not the fruit of a single independent creative imagination. This building had so much that was traditional and at the same time so much that was extraordinarily new; in its luminosity and resonance, it is unique in the world.

Over the portico and the loggia, clearly of Venetian (and ultimately late Roman) descent, developing the idea of the Palazzo Barozzi, the body of the building rises in its marble covering, worked with a design of rhomboids in pink and white marble, of infinite shades of colour. At the edges, these walls look as if they have been sewn together with a highly original marble stitching reminiscent of rope, and this makes them extraordinarily light, almost weightless, as though one could feel the limits of their physical thickness. This airy effect — typical of later Venetian architecture — is accentuated in the large openings of the windows, which create a contrast of shadows on the dazzling wall, while above, the traditional cresting mediates between the mass of the building and the transparent clarity of the sky.

With the building of the Doge's Palace, under the direction of the *Tre Savi,* we enter the fourteenth century, when, as we have seen, the face of Venice changed greatly as her architects began adopting the stylistic forms of transalpine Gothic into the special Venetian or 'florid' Gothic. For about a century and a half the city was to make use of these forms until, in the middle of the fifteenth century, it reached a stage in its growth analogous to that of today, and attained an unparalleled beauty praised by contemporaries from every country.

The Gothic Flowering

If we leave the Doge's Palace, looking out from the Molo in the mid-fourteenth century, light and airy in its majesty, a tracery of light and shade like a precious piece of Venetian *merletto* lace, and enter the concealed Rio di San Sebastiano, we find ourselves facing the arcade of the Palazzo Ariani, with its six small Gothic windows topped by a stupendous screen of double quatrefoils, set within a branching pattern of slender marble theads, white in the dry light of the sun, or silver-grey — almost filigree — in the half-shadows of a rainy day. This is a new face of Venice: that of the Gothic city.

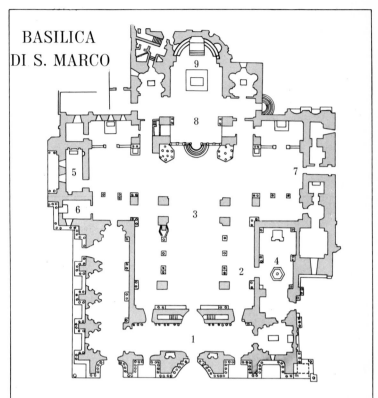

BASILICA DI S. MARCO

1 Atrio
2 Mosaico della Preghiera nell'Orto
3 Mosaici della Passione
4 Battistero
5 Cappella di S. Isidoro
6 Cappella dei Mascoli
7 Stanze del Tesoro
8 Coro
9 Pala d'Oro

The special interpretation of Gothic, as it developed in Venice from the first decades of the fourteenth century until half-way through the fifteenth, has come to be known as *Gotico fiorito:* florid, blossoming Gothic. It was probably imported by wandering monks who were responsible for the first religious buildings, including the great cathedrals of the Frari and Santi Giovanni e Paolo, the churches of Santo Stefano and the Madonna dell'Orto.

The process of the adaptation and transformation of the architectural elements, from the Veneto-Byzantine to the Venetian Gothic, was slow and gradual. Furthermore, the change was actually more apparent than real. Basically it concerned the decorative elements but did not affect the actual concept of space, and even less so the general plan of the city; most important of all, the new style maintained the traditional Venetian concern with effects of colour. Secular architecture retained its typical character, with the elongated ground plan, the façade overlooking the canal or an open space *(campo),* the ground-floor portico and upper gallery, the great central room (known as the *portego*) and the self-contained rooms on either side. The staircase was still usually external, in a broad courtyard to the side of the building, or else was set in a recess. Similarly, religious architecture kept its basilical layout, with very broad naves, and roofs supported by tall columns linked by wooden tie-beams. At most, we find a reflection of the Gothic concept of the interior in an increase in the vertical emphasis: the ceilings of the churches became higher, and the palazzi had two upper stories, with two superimposed windowed loggias.

In the strictly decorative field, sculpture became omnipresent: on the capitals, which took on bizarre shapes, with their mouldings of diamonds, cubes, pyramids, dogtooth and Venetian dentil; on the pinnacles of the cresting, which became tall and slender, sprouting out into fantastic buds; on the balustrades and on the windows, with their filigree quatrefoils or overlapping circles; lastly, on the arches, which took on the characteristic ogival shape rather than the round or semi-elliptical shape of the Byzantine period. In short, it was a composite style which adopted much of the decorative taste of transalpine Gothic, while setting it against a gentler background, particularly rich in colour, broader in movement and more relaxed in its surface rhythms; the frequent use of filigree tracery tended to reinforce the Islamic character of Venetian architecture, derived from models seen by Venetian merchants on their travels and often brought back in fragments for decorative purposes. The minor doors of San Marco are an obvious example of this; their decoration is Venetian in execution but inspired by Oriental examples.

This interest in the most disparate artistic cultures — in those of France and Germany, which came together in the Gothic, and in those of the Orient, linked with Islamic forms — was closely related to the political and economic situation of the city. In fact, from the middle of the fourteenth century. Venice began to build up her own empire on the mainland, conquiring the Marca Trevigiana (1339) and successively overcoming the surrounding *Signorie* from Padua to Vicenza and Verona (1404-06). At the same time her power at sea was strengthened, with the naval war against Genoa, which, after a number of initial defeats, was ultimately resolved in a succession of victories at remote naval bases, from Gallipoli to Salonica.

In 1423, the new Doge Francesco Foscari embarked on an expansionist policy. In his time, famous *condottieri* such as Carmagnola, Francesco Sforza, Niccolò Piccinino, Gattamelata and Bartolomeo Colleoni commanded forces for and against the Republic. Ultimately, too, Venice triumphed over the Milanese and the French (who had entered the fray with their claims on Lombardy), and set the seal on her conquests with the peace of Lodi (1454) which extended her western borders as far as Bergamo, and put her among the great European powers. In 1453, meanwhile, the Turks poured out of Asia Minor and conquerer Constantinople, the old capital of the eastern Roman Empire and the beacon of European civilization. Soon the consequences of this crucial event were to be felt throughout Christian Europe, and on Venice first of all.

It might seem logical that, at such a complex cultural crossroads, and particularly in relation to her mainland policy, Venice might have felt a decisive impulse to 'westernize' the character of her art. On the contrary, although the Gothic was an import from France and Germany by way of Lombardy, Venetian artists continued to be absolutely faithful to their traditional late Roman concern for colour, preferring if anything, particularly at first, to cling to contemporary forms of Byzantine art, both the aulic (i.e. of Constantinople) and the provincial (i.e. Macedonian, Serbian or Dalmatian). This is confirmed by an examination of the few remaining frescoes from the end of the thirteenth century, such as the ones in the little church of San Zan Degolà, one of the most fascinating monuments of early Venice. Both in the *Annunciation* and in the *St Helen,* with her great eyes staring out with the fixity of a Coptic icon, we find unmistakable references to the Byzantine provincial style of Macedonia (as in the frescoes of Mileševa, 1235). But here too the regal and solemn structure of the figures is built up on patches of luminous colour in the fashion that was by now typically Venetian.

In fact it is probable that various currents coexisted about the turn of the century: the Byzantine (particularly in its provincial forms, more appealing to western taste because of their stress on depth) and the indigenous, more sensitive to certain influences from the field of illumination and Gothic and Romanesque sculpture.

Mosaic pavement (15th century). Basilica of San Marco. The oldest pavements in San Marco are ones with figures, in the Christian tradition. Later, at the dawn of the Renaissance, Tuscan influence stimulated the use of geometric designs.

At this moment in time, the sophisticated literary culture and human-istic inclinations of certain important figures, such as Doge Andrea Dandolo, Petrarch's friend, determined the particular climate in which important complexes of mosaics could be created. And indeed San Marco was to inspire the last example of the great pictorial civiliza-tion of Venetian Gothic. About 1345 Dandolo turned the space to the south of the façade into a baptistery and began the mosaic de-coration with the scenes from the Childhood of Christ in the Ante-baptistery, then the lunettes and domes of the Baptistery itself, illus-trating the Life of St John and the Crucifixion.

Even within the evident unity of Venetian figurative culture, we find stylistic nuances, depending on which of the two tendencies had in-fluenced the master who drew the cartoons. An unexpected Gothic verve, chivalric and northern in flavour, breathes life into the forms of the *Adoration of the Magi* and the greatly restored *Massacre of the Innocents;* while the *Christ's Baptism* seems to look in the direction of the rather awkward, but always nobly restrained, Byzantinism of the Chora church in Constantinople.

The main scene in the Baptistery is the *Crucifixion,* in which the Doge appears as donor, and in it one can trace a long series of antecedents. The most immediate reference, in connection with the sense of space, is still the recently completed mosaics in the Chora. For the iconog-raphical motif of Mary and John at the feet of a Christ contorted in supreme human suffering, one can go back as far as Daphni, or the frescoes at Göreme in Cappadocia, and find successive stages of de-velopment in the small Crucifixions of the portable Byzantine mosaics. The portraits of the donors (the Doge, Dogess and Chancellor) are completely 'western', related, if at all — in their sharpness and vita-lity — to fourteenth-century painting in the towns along the Po valley.

The culture of the mosaicist of the Baptistery of San Marco is charac-terized by considerable stylistic novelty, creating remarkable contra-dictions in terms, with a strictly Byzantine iconography dotted with lively Gothic interpolations (for instance the portraits in the Cruci-fixion) and culminating in the extraordinary *Salome dancing,* where the influence of the Bolognese painting of the *stilo volgare* seems undoubted. Salome, dressed in ruby red, moves to a rhythm marked by the long tails of ermine which hang down from her wrists and along her thigh, daringly arched in a dancing step, completely free of any limiting stylization. It is as if the character had become a woman for the first time, treacherously lithe and beautiful even where, beneath the courtly trappings, one can still sense the harsh linear modelling of the previous century.

Thus, at the beginning of the fourteenth century, Venetian Gothic painting, still anchored in tradition, began to develop the themes which were gradually to launch it into the wider stream of Italian artistic culture. Despite trade and exchanges of all kinds with the towns of the Po valley and Venetian hinterland, the city had really been very isolated; nor did the new century lay Venice entirely open to the impact of Italian figurative culture, now fully mature. For in-stance, Venice not only long continued to be unacquainted with Tuscan painting, with its great protagonists Cimabue and Duccio, but contin-ued to ignore even Giotto, who was actually in Padua in 1304, work-ing on the Scrovegni frescoes. At least during the first part of the fourteenth century, Venice seems to have been susceptible only intermittently to influences of a 'western' type; these in turn were

Porta di San Clemente. Basilica of San Marco. Silver, orichalc and enamel: the loveliest of the doors of the atrium, probably a 13th-century Venetian imitation of a Byzantine model.

northern rather than connected with the Po valley, because northern forms were closer to the stylizations to which Byzantinism had accustomed her. Venetian artists seem always to have been haunted by a tendency to go back to some obscurely felt starting-point, whose paradigm was still constituted by the thirteenth-century mosaics, the major episode in primitive Venetian art.

A similar fact is found again in the later mosaics commissioned by Doge Dandolo, completed about 1355 in the chapel of Sant'Isidoro in San Marco. It seems probable that here the artist had in mind some source in the *stile cavalleresco,* the 'chivalric style' which appears in many illuminations and contemporary frescoes in the Venetian area.

The Virgin and the Apostles (1394). Basilica of San Marco. Masterpiece of Venetian Gothic sculpture, signed and dated by Jacobello and Pierpaolo dalle Masegne. From the iconostasis (rood screen).

It would be hard to find any other explanation for the extremely vivid and fluent detail of the horse dragging the martyred saint, or of soldiers visible here and there between the towered castles. But every time more typically Venetian episodes are dealt with, for instance ships approaching Chios or Doge Michiel emerging armed from the galleon decked out with the lions of St Mark, a sort of archaic feeling for tradition reasserts itself, and the blue skeined waves of the *Flood* and palmate fig leaves of *Genesis* reappear.

Venice, in short, did not veer from the path she had chosen; nor can the rare examples of North Italian influence in Venetian mural painting, such as the frescoes of the *Virtues* in the Museo Correr (taken from a house in San Zulian, where they had been painted in the early fourteenth century), really be said to attest any innovating tendency. In these frescoes, beneath series of tabernacles and pinnacles in the Venetian Gothic style, we see Charity holding out a piece of bread to a boy, Constancy gazing at a picture, Hope appealing to the heavens.

Temperance is very human and realistic, with her pots and her long scroll with beautiful courtly letters. Rather than the work of a Venetian artist, this was probably by some northerner who had travelled along the Adige, where many castles had paintings similar at least in taste and subject matter.

Further proof of the basic conformism of the Venetian painting of the first decades of the fourteenth century is offered by manuscript illumination, in both aristocratic and popular styles. It is worth examining some of the most important of these.

In a first group, we go back to the spirit of the Paduan school of the thirteenth century, with the Antiphonaries of Doge Zorzi (1311-12) in the Museo Correr, similar in many ways to the Evangeliary no. 110 and Missal no. 111 in the Biblioteca Marciana; while the great pages of the *Mariegola (matricula) di San Teodoro,* also of the beginning of the fourteenth century, take us right back to Constantinople, with their cramped space, as though the characters were moving in an airless void, weighed down by the archaic golden background.

Wherever Venetian illumination attempts popular subjects, with the liveliness typical of the Gothic movement, we are once again forced to postulate the presence of artists with foreign backgrounds. Probably it was an artist from Emilia, in the case of the *Mariegola del Pelizzeri* in the Correr (1334); or a Paduan from the circle of Cristoforo Cortese in the case of the *Registro di San Matteo di Murano* (1391) in the Seminario. In the first, one may note the nimbly realistic movements of the little figures within the limited space of the shop where the furs are; and, in the second, the avid grasp of the cashier taking the bag of money, piquant as a detail from a story by Boccaccio.

But these episodes remained peripheral to the development of Venetian culture, which was intent, on the one hand, on completing the historical mosaic masterpiece of San Marco; and on the other, with the first panel painters, on absorbing the influence of the *Madonneri* (the name given in Venice to painters of icons, particularly those of Greek origin), who put the traditional Byzantine goods back on the market again with a fresher local touch.

This basic confusion of styles is exemplified in the history of the Pala d'Oro, the golden altarpiece of San Marco, which was enlarged for the third time by Doge Andrea Dandolo in 1345, by mounting all the old enamels on a Gothic frame made by the goldsmith Paolo Boninsegna, amid countless precious stones which colour the whole work with a thousand reflections. According to the most recent studies, his altarpiece was bult up in successive stages. The earliest goes back to the time of Doge Pietro Orseolo I (976), and must have been mainly of metal; it is possible that the existing altarpiece still retains some of the original enamel medallions made by Byzantine craftsmen. The

Façade. Basilica of San Marco. The flamboyant crowning with foliage, angels and saints, above the terrace with the four horses, is the work of the Venetian artists J. and P. dalle Masegne and the Tuscan Lamberti, and was created at the end of the 14th and the beginning of the 15th century.

(below) Reliquary of the Blood of Christ (12th century). Treasury of San Marco. Byzantine coffer of embossed silver, originally meant to hold consecrated wafers.

P. 66/67
Piazza San Macro.

Mosaic of Translation of the Relics of St Mark (12th century). Basilica of San Marco. One of the oldest mosaics, in the vault near the organ, right transept; of a startling realism.

(below) Mosaic of Noah after the Flood (c. 1240). Basilica of San Marco. Mosaic from the atrium, the work of a master of chromatic tonalities.

second version was commissioned in 1105 by Doge Ordelaffo Falieri: it must have been more or less the size of the present lower tier, with most of the enamels done by artists from Constantinople. In 1209 Doge Pietro Ziani added the upper part, with the enamels of the Feasts of the Church, booty from the sack of Constantinople

▷

The Tetrarchs. Basilica of San Marco. Set on an outside angle of the tower of the Treasury, the figures are probably Syrian work of the 4th century. Because of the deep red colour of the porphyry of which they are made, they are popularly called 'The Moors'.

P. 70/71
Interior, showing the Pentecostal cupola. Basilica of San Marco.

after the Fourth Crusade; the panels of the outer border, with the Life of St Mark, are probably Venetian imitations of the others. The Pala d'Oro is therefore a composite work, and extremely eloquent because of it, an expression of the eclectic taste of the mid-fourteenth century and of the supreme distinction of the Gothic artists.

It was now that the first real personality emerged in the field of Venetian painting, Maestro Paolo Veneziano (*c.* 1290-*c.* 1362). His works, often Madonnas or Coronations of the Virgin on panels with gold backgrounds, traced with the patient finesse of the Byzantine masters, have long perplexed critics. 'Where exactly did Paolo part company with the Greek iconographers?' asks Bettini. 'He was the great Venetian interpreter of Byzantine art. He was able to assimilate Greek painting so completely that he became one of its greatest exponents, comparable only, discounting differences in character, to Andrei Rublev, another outsider, another interpreter. Paolo was the greatest of the Mediterranean Byzantine painters, the last non-Greek and the first of the Venetians.'

This moment in time, then, saw the emergence of a dialectical antithesis to the local tradition of mosaic (as seen in San Marco), which had lasted until the fourteenth century with increasing western sympathies. On the one hand, fidelity to Byzantium revived in the form of a sort of neo-Hellenism, drawing to a gradual halt with the swarthy Madonnas of the Veneto-Cretans; on the other, the artists of the Venetian school itself were feeling the somewhat inconclusive stirrings of independence and were preparing to align themselves with the Gothic forms of the mainland.

There is not much by Paolo Veneziano to be seen in Venice, but a brief discussion of at least one of his works is important to an understanding of the character of the city in the middle and late fourteenth century. For a long time it was believed that the first work by Paolo was the altarpiece of San Donato in the lovely basilica of that name in Murano. The attribution is now (rightly) contested; but it is certainly worth looking at this fascinating panel, dated 1310, when Paolo would have been very young. The saint is shown as carved in wood, set in a symbolic niche, and he is not very different from the typical bas-relief figures of the late thirteenth century. The novelty lies in the lively little figures of the two donors, Memmo, the Mayor of Murano, and his wife, detached in sharp outline from the golden background and built up with a touch that has little to do with the black and gold linear cobwebs of the icons of the *Madonneri*. Yet the combination of such elements with a use of the traditional Byzantine manner is an indication of an eclectic and partly contradictory attitude. Just as he is resigning himself to decorating the most conventional of icons, the artist reveals the presence of new forms, as they were developing on the mainland rather than in Venice.

It is also doubtful whether another similar work, the *Coronation of the Virgin* (1324) in the National Gallery in Washington, was actually by Paolo. Here we see mainland motifs (from Emilia or Rimini in this case) being incorporated into the Byzantine tradition, and it is they that explain the particular liveliness of the colour. The panel, until recently in the Dal Zotto collection in Venice, is a blaze of colour, set in a niche formed by the red cloth and green cushions against

◁
Nicopeian Madonna (12th century). Basilica of San Marco.

The Lion of St Mark. Piazza San Marco. Traditionally the symbol of the Evangelist St Mark, the winged lion quickly became the symbol of Venice, which had chosen the saint as its protector. This lion, on a column near the Molo, is an ancient chimaera, probably of Oriental make (4th century?), to which wings were added.

(below) Relief of winged griffins. Basilica of San Marco. One of the many ancient reliefs, brought from distant countries, that were set into the façade of San Marco.

which the blue and yellow of the clothes of Christ and Mary stand out sharply. The choir of angels, too, is arrayed in various very bright shades; this is the first appearance of a motif which was later to be typical of Paolo's painting. We find it, many years later (*c.* 1350), in his *Coronation* in the Accademia, confirming his love of decorative effects, and here his style, mid-way between the Venetian Gothic and the Byzantine, suggests that he might have been further influenced by

Façade, towards the Piazzetta dei Leoncini. Basilica of San Marco. In the upper right, the very beautiful Byzantine relief (10th century) showing Elijah ascending to Heaven.

an actual journey to Constantinople. A typical example of the confusion of styles which characterized the Gothic Venice of the mid-fourteenth century, Paolo's work always seemed to move uncertainly in a number of directions, so that the great panel in the Accademia is in many ways particularly significant. There is certainly a marked difference between the small scenes of the *Lives of Christ and St Francis,* at the sides of the composition, and the great *Coronation* in the middle. In the small scenes, Paolo's fondness for the Byzantine is able to express itself in graphic refinements in the incisive, gem-like colour: and it is typical that in many places a subtle patterning appears in the gold parts of the design, as if this were not so much a painting as an inlaid enamel. The gold background crushes the figures into two dimensions, removing all depth. This is the most 'Byzantine' of fourteenth-century Venetian paintings.

Certainly the sumptuous arabesques of the *Coronation* are quite a different matter: here the exultant rhythm of the composition laps the figures of Christ and Mary in restrained swirls and then breaks up into the wonderful garland of angels in blue and pink, green, red and orange, absorbed in the concert of their various instruments. A possible clue to the source of such an amazing novelty is to be found in certain equally penetrating and delicate details in the Gothic paintings of Rimini, particularly those by Baronzio, which continue the language of Vitale di Bologna and Giotto, in a more courtly tone.

It is undeniable that Paolo ultimately turned away from the influence of North Italian painting in general, although he did continue to utilize certain elements of it in his own stock of gilded preciosities. This is one of the constants of Venetian art: its exponents absorbed the best outside influences with ease and flexibility, while losing none of their own essential characteristics.

After Paolo, Venetian painting shows both an accentuation and a limiting of the traditional theme of the silent exchange between western and Byzantine art. Lorenzo Veneziano (fl. 1356-72, no relation to Paolo) refined Paolo's colours and softened them into delicate, bright shades against a gilded background. His figures become less other-worldly, milder and more human, probably because he was acquainted with the art of his neighbour Tommaso da Modena, who worked in Treviso. Among the greatest of his works in Venice is the great polyptych in the Accademia, with the donor Domenico Lion, dated 1359.

Paolo was not long dead; but the gulf between the works of the two painters is as great as though one had been from Byzantium and the other from Bologna. Lorenzo's Gothic verve is astounding: the forms have plastic relief; the design leaps out at the spectator and is on contrasting planes; the volumes are built up according to a diagonal perspective; the colour becomes pale and iridescent because of the light that saturates it. Here the light is no longer coloured in the Greek fashion, with a threadwork of gold on greenish or brown fields. The background, still empty of references to the reality of nature, fades away behind the spatial solidity of the forms. Some of the figures of the Lion Polyptych, including the Magdalene standing in one of the niches, have a relaxed sweetness of rhythmic line and colour that no other artist in Venice achieved at the time, apart perhaps from some of the sculptors of the capitals of the Doge's Palace, who drew their inspiration from France and whom we shall discuss later. Wrapped in her long pink cloak, revealing its green facing, and her damask gown, Magdalene is already touched with the quiver of that linear sensitivity which characterized the Venetian Gothic architecture of the end of the fourteenth century. The range of colour, too, is

▷

Relief of the Month of December (c. 1240). Basilica of San Marco. A relief in the second great arch of the principal door; work of a follower of Antelami, of remarkable realistic power.

completely original, with its delicate pinks heightened with touches of gold, a particular soft bloom about the colouring of the flesh, certain blues patterned with gold arabesques and edged with pearl grey: in the 1350s and 1360s only Lorenzo was producing colours like these, and they bear witness to a particularly refined way of life, suggesting images of delicate and gentle girls along the *fondamente* (quays) and on the bridges of Venice, now firmly established as the most beautiful, noble city in Europe.

Another important painting in the Accademia is the *Mystic Marriage of St Katherine*. Here, in 1360, Lorenzo adds movement to the traditional scene with the gesture of the Child who leans right over to put the ring on the Saint's finger. The sumptuous tunic and the soft blurring of the modelling are marvellously evocative, so that even this remote figure is drawn towards Venetian reality.

Some of Lorenzo's last works, like the *Annunciation* of 1371 in the Accademia, show that he was clearly influenced by the style of the Emilian school towards the end of his life: there is a physical sense of human solidity, decked out in splendid clothes. This was the sign of new interests in Venetian painting, although we cannot yet talk of a positive reawakening. On the whole, in fact, Lorenzo seems to have remained less aware of the very lively Emilian realism than of the cosmopolitan International Gothic style which brought the artistic activities of all Europe together, from Burgundy to Bohemia, from Lombardy to the 'paradise gardens' of Rhineland painting and to Tournai tapestry.

For Venice, his work was another invitation to indulge in that 'florid' version of the Gothic that was to maintain its hold on the city's vocabulary for another three-quarters of a century.

Rather than the last late follower of the Byzantine traditionalism of

◁

Mosaic of the Damned
(13th century). Torcello, Cathedral.
Detail with the Gluttons and the
Misers, from the Last Judgment
mosaic.

◁

Mosaics of the Crucifixion and the
Kiss of Judas (c. 1220). *Basilica*
of San Marco. In the early
13th century the masters of mosaic
stopped work on the decoration of
Torcello Cathedral and transferred
operations to San Marco, where they
created masterpieces like these in
the great central arch of the Basilica.

▷

Pilaster of San Giovanni d'Acri
(6th century). Piazzetta San Marco.
Syrian carving, so called because
of its provenance from the port of
Acre, conquered by the Venetians in
1256.

(below) Mosaic of the Pentecost.
Basilica of San Marco.

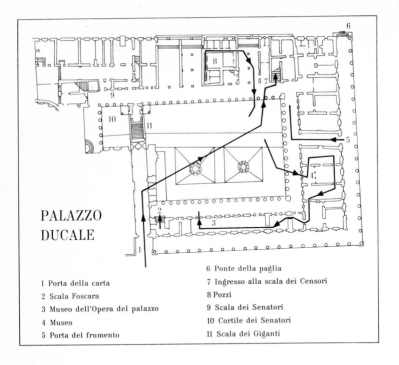

PALAZZO
DUCALE

1 Porta della carta
2 Scala Foscara
3 Museo dell'Opera del palazzo
4 Museo
5 Porta del frumento

6 Ponte della paglia
7 Ingresso alla scala dei Censori
8 Pozzi
9 Scala dei Senatori
10 Cortile dei Senatori
11 Scala dei Giganti

Paolo, Lorenzo Veneziano was the newest voice of the fourteenth century in Venice: the painter who helped to divert the path of Venetian painting in the direction of the international developments which were already under way in Lombardy and elsewhere.

There are many gaps in the picture of Venetian Gothic. After Lorenzo, there was a modest painter named Nicolò di Pietro, who painted a *Madonna* in the Accademia, but his works are of little interest; and it has not been possible precisely to identify the artist — through he probably belonged to the same circle — of the marvellous series of tapestries with the Life of Christ in the Museo Marciano. With their grotesque, un-Italian faces they are reminiscent of the Bohemian paintings of the early fifteenth century, and indeed this could well have been their source, because numerous travelling painters then present in Venice, including possibly Tommaso da Modena, could easily have acted as intermediaries.

The most important fruits of International Gothic painting in Venice were produced during the first decades of the fifteenth century, but unfortunately most of the material itself has been destroyed. In the late sixteenth century a disastrous fire destroyed the Sala del Maggior Consiglio in the Doge's Palace, where the best artists of that particular movement, Gentile da Fabriano (1408-19) and Pisanello (*c.* 1417), had left their frescoes. Anyone wishing to gain an impression of what they might have produced here should look at Gentile's *Adoration of the Magi* in the Uffizi, or the odd fresco in Santa Caterina in Treviso (for instance Saint Eligius tempted by the Devil), or the later

▷

Palazzo Ducale (Doge's Palace), towards the Piazzetta. This is the oldest part of the palace, reconstructed after 1340 to allow for the inclusion of the great hall of the Maggior Consiglio.

frescoes by Pisanello in Sant'Anastasia in Verona, with the *Life of St George*. As in a courtly poem, the characters in Gentile's works play their parts as though oblivious of surrounding reality, immersed in a gilded dream; while the protagonists in the chivalric story of St George are lit up with sinister metallic gleams, enveloped in enigmatic silence, filled with terror at the fearful monsters to be slain, and alarmed by the ominous flicker of fires along the horizon.

Certainly, the personality of the few Venetian artists of the late Gothic period is far less incisive, though they did elaborate their own particular versions of Gentile and Pisanello. Jacobello del Fiore (*c.* 1370-1439) dresses his *Justice,* painted in 1421 for the Doge's Palace — and now in the Accademia — in showy and extremely sophisticated drapery: an unbroken whirl of lines like an initial letter in a lavish Book of Hours; Michele Giambono (fl. 1420-1462) adorned his *St Chrysogonus on horseback,* in the church of San Trovaso, with a gem-like intensity and delicacy of colour. Antonio Vivarini (c. 1415-84) from Murano, the head of a family of artists active throughout the whole fifteenth century, was the last of the painters of the 'florid' Venetian Gothic, and was also in a sense a man of the Renaissance. However, he was an exponent of the late Gothic at least in the fascinating chapel of San Tarasio in the church of San Zaccaria. This is the old apse of a pre-existing church, and it still retains the mystery and beauty of Venetian Gothic in the three polyptychs that decorate it: two, of St Sabina and the Body of Christ, by Vivarini, and the one for the main altar, a composite work, by Maestro Stefano da Sant'Agnese (1385) and retouched by Vivarini. The ensemble is datable by the cornices, grandly carved and gilded by Ludovico da Forlì in 1443. We are now at the beginning of the fifteenth century and, with the work of these two artists, we can consider the Gothic phase of Venetian painting closed.

Sculpture took a very similar course and made an important contribution to the definition of the face of Venice in the second half of the fourteenth century. Its triumph was the decoration of the Doge's Palace, to which we must return once again.

When the building of the new palace (which was to combine the three pre-existing buildings) had been assigned to the *Tre Savi* in 1340, we may imagine the whole city absorbed in its progress. The architect is unknown, but those responsible for its external decoration are more easily identifiable, because of their stylistic peculiarities: the hordes of stone-masons, sculptors and master-builders who took part in the great work, which was to epitomize the grandeur of the government of the Republic.

The sculptural decoration proceeds, on the capitals of the portico and loggia, from the eastern corner on the Ponte della Paglia towards the Piazzetta, for the length of six arches, and ends, nowadays, with the relief of Justice in the centre of the loggia. During the period between 1340 — when work was begun — and 1419, when it was completed, there were at least two generations of sculptors. We believe that the portico and loggia, with their respective capitals, were not worked on immediately (as a document of 1342 would imply, deliberating the extension of the building *usque ad plateam,* as far as the square) but during the course of the work begun on the interior above the masonry structure of the thirteenth-century palazzo. The oldest capitals of the loggia therefore reflect the Venetian taste of the late fourteenth century, hesitating between the manner of the De Santis and the more advanced forms of the Dalle Masegne brothers: they are heads

Capital of the Human Race (14th century). Doge's Palace.

of warriors and animals, bizarre representations of plants, with a linear exuberance that implies the influence of the typically Gothic forms that were gaining favour at that time. The great window of the Sala del Maggior Consiglio should also be seen in this context; an old inscription says that it was completed by Pier Paolo and Jacobello Dalle Masegne in 1404, when Michele Steno was Doge: a great altar-like structure, with pillars and traceried pinnacles, and a small central tabernacle whose statues were mostly replaced after the great fire in the sixteenth century.

The first generation of Venetian sculptors elaborated a highly sophisticated and ornate stylization of the Gothic, anticipating the characteristic Venetian Gothic style; but the second generation came from quite different artistic territory and used means typical of western Gothic as it was developing in Milan.

Recent studies have conclusively proved the presence in Venice in 1410 of a famous Lombard draughtsman and painter, Michelino da Besozzo, who had provided designs for the Duomo in Milan, together with Giovannino de' Grassi. Also, we know that another sculptor from Milan was working in Venice during the same period; this was Matteo Raverti, already famous as the sculptor of the Giants in the Milan Duomo; the similar gargoyles on the façade of San Marco are attributed to him. Leaving Milan in 1404, Raverti appears in

The Doge's Palace, from the air. The façade on the Molo, going round on the Piazza to the seventh arch, was completed in the 14th century. The façade on the Piazza was completed between 1424 and 1440.

Venetian documents only in 1421 as the architect of the Cà d'Oro: but he had certainly spent these two decades in Venice, working on San Marco and the Doge's Palace.

The two tendencies evident in the capitals of the porch of the Doge's Palace have rightly been traced to these two Milanese artists, or rather to their hard-working workshops. Michelino was responsible for those in a 'courtly' manner, delicate, pictorial, narrative in inspiration, dealing minutely with the *Months,* the *Zodiac, Human Life,* the *Crafts, Vices and Virtues;* while Raverti's workshop was responsible for the sculptures with the more plastic line and more marked realism on the capitals of the *Crusades, Women, Races of Mankind* and *Nations.*

Some of the most impressive sculptures in the Palace were executed within the sphere of Raverti's influence. These are carvings level with the upper part of the arches of the portico, on the south-east corner, near the Piazzetta; they show episodes in the life of man and seem to be devoted to illustrating a very specific programme: the *Drunkenness of Noah* pardoned by his sons (the indulgence of good government) and *Adam and Eve* (the severity of good government). There can be no doubt that these sculptures, certainly made during the second decade of the fifteenth century, aroused admiration and astonishment in Venetian circles, culturally blinkered by the more modest Gothicizing local production. Animated by a completely new sense of spatial realism, the figures of Adam and Eve seem to start out of their niche as if they wanted to play their part in the luminous vitality of the marble façade, trimmed along its fairy-tale tiers of arches with lacy friezes of rosettes and dentils.

▷

The Drunkenness of Noah (early 15th century). Doge's Palace. Set on the angle towards the Ponte della Paglia, it is attributed to the Lombard Matteo Raverti.

Old Noah is bending outwards, going beyond the limits of the plane of the walls, in an anticipation of the full relief which later, in the figures of Adam and Eve, was partly to detach the forms from their background and to thrust them out into the surrounding atmosphere. The human faces, the psychology of the characters in their animated movements, the bold treatment of the bare bodies, which have elusive echoes of the late Roman tradition found in reliefs in Aquileia and Altino, are all elements which lead to a realistic bias. Raverti's influence, as it emerges from the representations of Noah and Adam and Eve on the Doge's Palace, was undoubtedly to be of great importance in the development of sculpture in Venice, for it was soon to constitute the main bastion in the face of the Tuscan invasion, and the fundamental element in a dawning local style.

In 1419, the seventh capital of the portico facing the Piazzetta concluded the façade of the Palazzo Pubblico of the *Tre Savi*. Meanwhile, we know that the interior of the Sala del Maggior Consiglio had been decorated with frescoes by some of the most famous artists of the time. The order, given in 1366, to delete the portrait of Marin Faliero proves that the frieze of Doges' portraits which runs just below the ceiling, and which was restored in the sixteenth century, was already in existence. In 1368 the Paduan, Guariento, had completed the fresco of the *Crowning of the Virgin* which occupied the whole of the end wall on the side facing east (as can be seen in an engraving by Furlano, of 1566), showing that even at that date the hall had exactly the same dimensions as it has to-day (the fire of 1577 was later to damage the fresco irreparably, causing it to be replaced by Tintoretto's famous *Paradise*.) At the beginning of the fifteenth century the walls of the Sala del Maggior Consiglio were decorated with other paintings and frescoes, some of which were the work — as we have already said — of Gentile da Fabriano and Pisanello; these too were destroyed in the sixteenth-century fire.

The Signoria had sustained enormous expense over the completion of the Palazzo Pubblico, and it seems that it was therefore agreed that no one should propose any further alterations to the Doge's Palace on pain of heavy penalties. But in 1422 Doge Tommaso Mocenigo is said to have paid this fine and proposed a resumption of work. Naturally none of the *Tre Savi* of the fourteenth-century palace, nor the shadowy 'foremen' Filippo Calendario and Baseggio and Enrico, were any longer alive; but Mocenigo's decision, implemented by his successor Doge Francesco Foscari, to extend the Palace along the Piazzetta as the Palazzo Pubblico had been extended along the Molo, simply completed the work they had so brilliantly begun.

In 1424 work on the Palace was resumed, from the seventh column, and continued, with twelve more arches, almost as far as the basilica, where the new main entrance was: the Porta della Carta (possibly so-called — Paper or Letter Gate — because the public letter-writers sat nearby). About 1443 the gate, resplendent with its sculptures and decorations, its expanses of ultramarine and gold stars, was completed, and Doge Foscari began the porch which lies behind it, further towards the inner courtyard of the Palace, and which is called the Arco

▷

Apse (15th century). Church of San Gregorio. During the intensive work on the Doge's Palace 'florid' Gothic architecture developed in Venice, and influenced most of the new churches and palaces built in the 14th and 15th centuries.

Foscari, although it was completed by his successors, Cristoforo Moro and Giovanni Mocenigo, by 1485.

In this way the ambitious work of Doge Foscari gave a new face to the Doge's Palace, now unified along the whole outer perimeter of the Molo and Piazzetta. Inside, however, the legacy of the previous state of affairs was more obvious, and probably there were different court-yards leading to the original separate buildings of the Palazzo Pub-blico and the Palazzo di Giustizia. Furthermore, to the north-west stood the buildings containing the Doge's apartments, still completely isolated, together with the little church of San Nicolò: looking at the engraving by Reeuwich one can see that, along the canal, the building of the Doge's Palace was succeeded by two or three lower buildings with typical brick façades, long pointed windows and even the remains of medieval battlements.

The sculptural decoration was worked on while the new wing on the Piazzetta was actually being built; it was popularly called the 'Loggia Foscara', after its courageous champion. The capitals of the new portico and loggia were largely imitations of the fourteenth-century ones, and in some cases identical copies. But the workmen were no longer the Lombards, who had proceeded meanwhile to work on the Cà d'Oro in the wake of Raverti; Tuscan stoneworkers had arrived in Venice, and the reliefs of the Palazzo, like those of the top of San Marco, bear witness to it.

We know in fact that in 1415 Niccolò Lamberti arrived in Venice from Florence; he had worked on the cathedral in Florence, Santa Maria del Fiore, with a large number of assistants including his son Pietro, who was to succeed him. Admittedly, in the age of Donatello and Ghiberti, Lamberti was hardly of the greatest importance in the context of Tuscan art. Indeed, one may reasonably suspect that Lam-berti was chosen for his somewhat mediocre, non-revolutionary qua-lities, which enabled him to fit without difficulty into the basically conservative atmosphere of the Venetian Republic. Apart from the uppermost parts of San Marco, Lamberti's work can be identified in part of the capitals of the Foscari wing portico, completed after the Lombard masters had left. A completely Tuscan elegance character-izes these small carvings, whose subject matter was inspired by the previous ones but whose plastic treatment is far more fluent and animated. Another Tuscan masterpiece is the capital on the corner nearest the church, with the symbols of Justice below, and signed, apparently, according to a vanished inscription, by *due sotii florentini,* two Florentine companions: Pietro Lamberti and Giovanni di Mar-tino da Fiesole. In continuation of the series of statues level with the arches, started at the beginning of the century with Noah and Adam and Eve, we find, above the capital, the *Judgment of Solomon,* possibly the work of the Florentine Nanni di Bartolo, and so majestic that Jacopo della Quercia has been suggested as its inspiration.

The Tuscans also played a part in the adjacent Porta della Carta, with the sculptures of the lower order, *Fortitude* and *Temperance* attributed to Pietro Lamberti; but by now this gate was a sort of testing ground for the new generation of Venetians, leading up to

▷

Mosaic of Salome dancing. Baptistery of San Marco. This is part of a cycle of mosaics in the Baptistery, masterpieces of the Venetian Gothic period. They were commissioned by Doge Dandolo (1345), who employed the youngest, most sophisticated and realistic artists of the day.

Paolo Veneziano:
Madonna (c. 1339).
Accademia.
Paolo was the first
major figure in
Venetian painting.
The style of his
Madonna is
balanced between
Western and
Byzantine.

(below)
Lorenzo Veneziano:
Annunciation
(1371)
Accademia. A
masterpiece by
Lorenzo Veneziano,
whose work was
more realistic than
Paolo's, and whose
use of colour was
more decorative.

▷
Jacobello dalle
Masegne. Doge
Venier (end of
14th century). The
artist achieves a
synthesis of incisive
realism and Gothic
stylization.

Giovanni and Bartolomeo Bon. It was Bartolomeo who signed the work on the architrave in 1443. The sculpture of these Venetians differed considerably from Raverti's group or from the Tuscans: it had a more outward sophistication and was supremely decorative, all linear flutter and flurry. This was the last fling of the fifteenth-century Venetian Gothic manner; in Tuscany and even in Padua, the arrival of Renaissance forms had meanwhile already revolutionized the figurative vocabulary.

Monster Head. Campanile. Santa Margherita. Venetian gargoyles represent a remarkable encounter between Venetian and northern taste. The influence of 14th-century French artists is also documented.

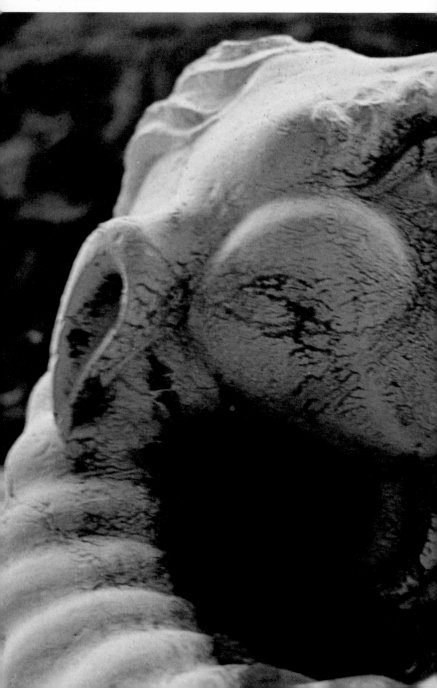

The works of another workshop, mid-way between Lombard and Tuscan and headed by a master from Como, Antonio da Rigesio, known as Bregno, should also be considered as part of this last Gothic phase. After 1450, he played an important part in the decoration of the Palace, of which he probably became *proto* or foreman, being responsible for most of the Arco Foscari. He carved the statues above the Porta della Carta and also the *Archangels* set at the three corners of the Palace, level with the loggias: complex, rhetorically decorative, with

Paolo Veneziano and assistants: Polyptych of the Coronation (1354-58). Accademia.

their too ample draperies, but rich in unexpected light effects, fresh and delicately elegant. Many of the statues on the pinnacles on the side of the Foscari nearest the Doge's apartment are by Bregno; two

▷

Ludovico Da Forlì: Incised and gilded polyptych (1444?). San Zaccaria.
The polyptych, in the 'florid' Gothic decorative style, was characteristic
of the 14th and 15th centuries. The pictorial part of the polyptych of
San Zaccaria was reworked, for the most part, by Antonio Vivarini
and Giovanni d'Alemagna, except for the Madonna and the two saints at
the sides, which are signed by Stefano da Sant'Agnese (1585).

or three of them stand out as being more stylized, and recent criticism has attributed these to his pupil and successor Antonio Rizzo. But since Rizzo was now working with the elements of a new style that was completely different from that of his predecessor, we must once again take up the general discussion where we had left it and complete the historical panorama of Gothic Venice.

We shall therefore go back to the Grand Canal, just where it takes one of its biggest bends, between the Accademia and Rialto. On the west side we see a series of Gothic palaces which seem to sum up all the characteristics of late Gothic: half-way through the fifteenth century the Giustiniani and Foscari, two of the most important Venetian patrician families, lived in them. Cà Foscari, in fact, was begun in 1452 by Doge Foscari himself, shortly after the completion of his work on the Doge's Palace. The high, luminous façade of the Giustiniani and Foscari palaces, extending along a frontage of several hundred feet, give us an idea of how Venice's ceremonial route must have looked in those days. Majestic but airy with their tracery of double windows, looming impressively but refined and lightened by the Venetian Gothic tracery, warm with the intense colour of the brick but clear-cut, their graphically slender structures like the strokes of an etching against the peerless sky, these buildings were the quintessence of fifteenth-century Venice. More or less within the first half of the fifteenth century, hundreds of other palazzi similar to these were dotted throughout the city. A survey of Gothic palazzi would reveal that, even today, beneath the evident violence done to them, about half the old buildings in Venice date back to that period of extraordinary economic prosperity.

In 1457 the magnificent chambers of Cà Foscari (now the headquarters of Venice University) witnessed the death of Doge Francesco Foscari, who had been driven out of office by the intrigues of his political adversaries. In 1574 Henry III of France stayed there during his visit to Venice; and even today, with its impressive courtyard and open staircase, it still retains traces of its former majesty.

The district around Cà Foscari has largely retained its original character, and many other Gothic palazzi still look on to the Grand Canal; there is the Palazzo Pisani Moretta facing Sant'Angelo, with its beautiful double six-light windows, once the home of a famous art collection including Paolo Veronese's *The Family of Darius* (now in the National Gallery, London), Piazzetta's *Death of Darius* (now at Cà Rezzonico) and Canova's *Daedalus and Icarus* (now in the Museo Correr). The best-preserved example of Venetian Gothic secular architecture is probably the nearby Palazzo Bernardo, built in 1442, with its three Gothic stories and two ground-floor doorways in their original state. It also has characteristic sloping panels round the windows, with casings of coloured marble, which give the surface greater splendour and richness, preserving the picturesque character that the use of brick might otherwise have ironed out.

There are various other examples of similar architecture on the Grand Canal, so that one can imagine the effect of the original whole. We need only think of Cà Giustinian (1474), now the centre of the Biennale d'Arte; and the nearby Palazzetto Contarini Fasan, right opposite the

◁
Madonna with the Foscari and Mocenigo coats of arms. Ponte del Paradiso. Typical Venetian Gothic decorative piece, probably set up in 1407 as boundary stone for the Paradiso district, near Campo Santa Maria Formosa.

Salute, with its two balconies whose tracery is quite extraordinarily complex. Legend has it that this was where gentle Desdemona lived, victim of the jealous Moor of Venice, Othello, captain of the eastern fleet.

Of the many Gothic palazzi that are not on the Grand Canal, we shall mention in particular Palazzo Soranzo-Van Axel, near San Zanipolo. Looking on to the *fondamenta,* and with a narrow canal running by its side, it still has its wonderful decorated doorway in the courtyard wall. The inner courtyard still has its beautiful open staircase; in the centre is a Gothic well-head. Here one feels a lingering atmosphere

of the Gothic city, as it appears in certain paintings, of a slightly later date, by Gentile Bellini or Carpaccio (we shall see them in the Accademia).

One palazzo in particular seems fitted to conclude this panorama of the Gothic city: the Cà d'Oro, near Rialto. It was built between 1420 and 1440 by Marino Contarini, a merchant rich enough to employ the architects and sculptors who were just finishing work on the Doge's Palace. That illustrious model did in fact inspire the marble decorations of the double multi-lighted windows and the portico, just as the upper cresting is reminiscent of that on the Doge's

Scuola Vecchia della Misericordia (c. 1450)

S. MARIA GLORIOSA DEI FRARI

1 Monumento a Tiziano
2 Coro dei Frati
3 P. LOMBARDO - Monumento a Jacopo Marcello
4 NANNI di BARTOLO - Tomba al Beato Pacifico
5 J. DELLA QUERCIA - Monumento a Paolo Savelli
6 G. BELLINI - Madonna e Santi (Sacrestia)
7 DONATELLO - S. Giovanni Battista
8 TIZIANO - L'Assunta
9 A. RIZZO - Monumento al Doge Niccolò Tron
10 Cappella Corner
11 TIZIANO - Pala Pesaro
12 Monumento a Canova

Interior plan of Santa Maria Gloriosa dei Frari.

Palace. But two typical anomalies distinguish Cà d'Oro: firstly, the asymmetry of the façade, which has an extra wing on the right, to include a broad courtyard and open staircase; secondly, the gilding of many decorative elements (for instance the window surrounds, the various panels and the cresting), from which it takes its name (House of Gold). This extraordinary decorative effect is heightened by the freedom of the ground plan, conceived with a truly organic vision of the structure and adhering closely to its functions as a whole. It is still particularly interesting to visit because it houses an art collection, the gift of the Barone Giorgio Franchetti, who decided to re-create the atmosphere of the splendid Contarini residence with works of art and fifteenth-century furnishings.

▷
Façade (1340-1443). Santa Maria Gloriosa dei Frari.

Thus secular architecture was changing the face of Venice, but naturally the Church, too, continued to make numerous and important contributions to its development. The grandiose basilicas of the Frari (Franciscan) and of San Zanipolo (Dominican) belong to the early fourteenth century, while the churches of Sant'Alvise and the Madonna dell'Orto, Sant'Elena, the Carità, San Gregorio and Santo Stefano were completed at the beginning of the fifteenth.

The oldest Venetian Gothic church is that of Santi Giovanni e Paolo, known as San Zanipolo. It was begun after 1234, the year in which Doge Jacopo Tiepolo gave the land to the Dominicans, but was completed only at the beginning of the fifteenth century. It is not certain that its original plans were the work of a Fra Benvenuto da Bologna or, as tradition has it, of Fra Niccolò da Imola; but from the very beginning it certainly followed the layout typical of the great basilicas of the conventual orders: a broad central nave with two lesser side aisles, flanked by chapels and numerous small apses. The striking thing about San Zanipolo is the great height of the nave, whose pointed arches are supported by enormous piers. If one looks closely, however, one finds that in comparison with other masterpieces of Italian Gothic architecture (for instance, San Francesco or San Petronio in Bologna) it lacks that dynamic feeling, that typical sense of soaring upwards, which characterizes genuine Gothic architecture. On the contrary, the typically Venetian interpretation more or less consciously drew the architect of San Zanipolo towards a more relaxed use of space in the wide expanses between the piers, causing him rather to stress an awareness of colour, to strive for an effect that was optical rather than plastically dynamic. Long wooden tie-beams support the heavy thrust of the vaulting, which is unusually broad, constituting a characteristic Venetian use of space. The light floods the nave fairly evenly, coming from the rose window and apse windows as well as from the transepts and, above, from windows set over the arches. It thus falls calmly and harmoniously, so that the dramatic feeling of the genuine transalpine Gothic interpretation is lost.

Basically, the Venetians instinctively sought to give these great basilicas of theirs a popular, communal atmosphere, to make them into meeting-places and shrines of civic glory. They are structured to favour contact between men rather than to isolate them in the ascetic shadows, typical of the medieval mainland taste but which had never been adopted in Venice. And indeed, San Zanipolo was used as a civic shrine; its walls house the monuments of Doges and *condottieri*. Some of these go back to the original Gothicizing forms (like the monument to Doge Tommaso Mocenigo, by Tuscan masters), but the others are usually mostly in the Renaissance style, of which we shall see more later.

The second Venetian Gothic basilica, Santa Maria Gloriosa dei Frari, was the work of the Franciscan Friars Minor, and was begun, on the site of an earlier church, in 1330. However, as late as 1415 the original thirteenth-century church is mentioned as still being in existence; it follows that most of the presence building dates from the fifteenth century. By 1443 its façades had been built; it was soon to be named Cà Granda because of its impressive size and because of the adjacent monastery. Here too the architect is unknown, though some scholars identify him as the Fra Pacifico to whom a tomb was put up inside the church. Meanwhile, between 1361 and 1396 — as one reads on the stone at the base — the beautiful campanile had been completed, second in height only to that of San Marco. Much more elaborate and rich in its interior decoration than San Zanipolo, the Frari puts the emphasis on the space of the main nave, reducing the aisles to a minimum and further encumbering them with altars, since there are no side chapels. In the nave one can still see the monks' original choir, separated from the rest of the nave by a marble screen. This choir is particularly noteworthy for the juxtaposition of Gothicizing forms (possibly still from the Bon workshop) with motifs that are already Tuscan and Renaissance in form.

Apse. Santa Maria Gloriosa dei Frari.

Well-head, now in the Scuola Vivaldi, at Santa Giustina
near San Zanipolo.

The most striking element in the Frari is the magnificent transept, on to which opens the chancel with its six terminal chapels and also to the right and left, two chapels added in Renaissance times (Corner and Sacristia). See from the outside, the apses of the Frari spread like a great screen, set with tall stained glass windows; through them the light falls evenly on to the most important part of the church, lighting the great works that are kept there: altars by Vivarini and Donatello, and Titian's monumental *Assumption*, the greatest single work of Venetian painting and the youthful masterpiece of the greatest artist of sixteenth-century Venice (1518). The Frari, too, is a magnificent shrine of the Republic, with its numerous tombs of Doges and members of the great aristocratic families. Apart from that of Fra Pacifico, attributed to Nanni di Bartolo and Michele da Firenze (1437), and the tomb of the *condottiero* Paolo Savelli, referred to the style of Jacopo della Quercia (after 1405), the most important monuments are by Renaissance sculptors such as Rizzo, and I shall say more about them in due course.

Traces of the original interior decoration of these fourteenth-century Gothic churches are visible both in San Zanipolo and the Frari: and

▷

Façade. Madonna dell'Orto. Like the sumptuous Morosini well-head,
the doorway of Madonna dell'Orto illustrates the Venetian Gothic
decorative style. The sculptures at the sides of the Annunciation
are youthful works of Antonio Rizzo (c. 1450).

perhaps the most typical example of the same style is in the lovely church of Santo Stefano, with long flowery strips, frescoed in red, pale green and grey on the pale plaster: a sort of poetic branching accompanying the dark cornices, as they run along the beams, worked with 'rope-moulding', of the typical wooden keel-like roof.

In one of the remotest parts of the *sestiere* of Cannaregio there are two more Gothic churches, completed between the mid-fourteenth and early fifteenth centuries: Sant'Alvise, of which only the interior is original, apart from the façade with the prothyrum or lobby, very rare in Venice, and the Madonna dell'Orto. This is one of the most

important and best preserved buildings of its period, particularly appealing because of its position by a quiet out-of-the-way canal, and because of the size of the really impressive ground plan. Begun half way through the fourteenth century by Fra Tiberio da Parma, the Madonna dell'Orto was completed, with its façade, by the beginning of the fifteenth. An unusual feature of the façade is the small loggia at the sides, almost too reminiscent of the Lombard Romanesque, with which the architect does not seem to have been very familiar. The beautiful statues of the Apostles, in the niches, by the Dalle Masegne — the greatest Venetian sculptors of the beginning of the fifteenth century —

Antonio Bregno: Doge Foscari (c. 1440). Doge's Palace, Museum. Taken from the Porta della Carta, its original site, this powerful portrait immortalizes the lineaments of the Doge who was involved in the completion of the Doge's Palace towards the middle of the 15th century (p. 110/11).
The Venetian Gothic palaces of the Foscari on the Grand Canal were also built in this period (p. 108/09).

like the little pinnacles and charming brick decorations at the edge of the roof, complete the most thoroughly Venetian Gothic or 'florid' façade to be seen anywhere in Venice today. As in the case of the Frari, here too the main porch is Gothic, and the white of its gleaming marble helps magically to lighten the monumental brick covering of the façade.

There are many other Gothic churches to add to the vista of Gothic Venice at the beginning of the fifteenth century; I shall mention only the most interesting of them, formally or historically. The small island of Sant'Elena, between Castello and the Lido, has a lovely church,

with the original beautiful dimensions of the nave and chapels and the brick decorations of the façade. In the church of the Carità (now the Gallerie dell'Accademia) there are polygonal apses, with high, slender windows and a beautiful façade (which appears in many of Canaletto's paintings, such as the one now in the Royal Collection at Windsor). The church of San Gregorio (now a regional laboratory for restoration) has a beautiful façade and highly elaborate apses looking on to the Campo della Salute; while the nearby abbey still has a small, intimate fourteenth-century cloister, once the monastery of the monks of the very ancient Sant'Ilario.

The Renaissance

The phenomenon of the Renaissance, pivot of the spiritual and stylistic development of modern Europe, did not easily find a place in Venice, where it often takes on surprising and idiosyncratic colours. Firstly, the actual contact with the new humanist philosophies, the renewed interest in the literature and art of antiquity, the resultant surge of creativity, all come very late in Venice. In comparison with Florence, the cradle of the new movement, Venice was half a century behind. While Brunelleschi in Florence was erecting the dome of Santa Maria del Fiore, in Venice the coping of San Marco was being garlanded with a picturesque cornice of gilded foliage; and there was certainly no comparison between the powerful Apostles gathered in a circle around Masaccio's Christ in the Carmine, Florence, and Vivarini's tenuous filigree in the chapel of San Tarasio in San Zaccaria.

However, despite difficulties and delay, the Renaissance vocabulary did come to Venice gradually, from the second half of the fifteenth century onwards; and, if at first it was more a superficial than a basic variation, ultimately it took root and developed a character of its own, resuming the old colouristic tradition, to triumph in the field of painting with personalities of the stature of Bellini, Carpaccio and Giorgione.

There is another observation that anyone wanting to identify the face of Renaissance Venice should bear in mind: this is that the new forms penetrated into the architecture and general fabric of the city not so much through monuments or sculptural decorations, as through the apparently more fragile channels of painting. The reason for this is to be found in the very origin of the Renaissance in northern Italy as a whole, which took its impetus from Padua, a famous university city and cultural centre of prime importance. Tuscan painting had taken root in Padua as early as 1430, with the presence there of Filippo Lippi; soon afterwards the Paduan, Squarcione, formed an unique workshop of decorators, painters, sculptors and fabric designers who took their models from the antique and the Tuscan school, ranging from a drawing by Pollaiolo to a cast of Donatello; and in 1443 Donatello himself moved to Padua where he worked for ten years producing, among other things, the bronze altar of the basilica of Sant'Antonio and the equestrian statue of Gattamelata.

From this inspired and productive forge of new forms, an indigenous pictorial genius emerged in Padua. Andrea Mantegna created his masterpiece in the frescoes of the Eremitani, painted between 1448 and 1455, grandly 'classical' compositions inspired by Donatello's feeling for depth but enriched with a tension, in the sharp, incisive design and strongly expressive use of colour, which was entirely Venetian.

Not completely unaware of the Tuscan Renaissance, even Venice, about the middle of the fifteenth century, girded herself for a thorough change. The first timid forms, with a greater sense of depth and human expressiveness, appeared in the sculptures of the highest part of San Marco, partly the work of Lamberti, and in the capital depicting Justice on the corner of the Doge's Palace nearest the Porta della

◁

Cà d'Oro (c. 1440). Completed by Raverti, in the style of the Doge's Palace, it is the masterpiece of the Venetian Gothic style. It takes its name from the frieze of gold leaf decoration on the façade.

The Porta della Carta (c. 1441). Doge's Palace, While Raverti was finishing Cà d'Oro, Giovanni and Bartolomeo Bon decorated the main entrance to the Doge's Palace with an abundance of elegant Gothic ornament. The figures of Doge Foscari and the Lion are modern copies; the original head is on p. 106.

Carta. In 1425 Paolo Uccello, one of Florence's new men, was brought to Venice by the Procuratorie to restore the basilica's mosaics; and in 1442 Andrea del Castagno painted several frescoes on the ceiling of the Gothic chapel of San Tarasio in San Zaccaria. But these brief visits left no immediate trace. Traditionally, Venice absorbed novelty gradually, through lines that lay within her own history: so the Renaissance made headway through the work of the local painters, who had had brief contacts with the main centres where the new forms were being elaborated. These were artists whose activity went little beyond the middle of the fifteenth century, and who thus bridged the gap between Gothic and Renaissance Venice. The first of these was Jacopo Bellini (1396-1470?), the founder of a great family of painters. A typical figure of a moment of transition, the father of

Doorway (c. 1440). Cà d'Oro. The crowning of the exterior door of the entry to the splendid courtyard in the style of the Doge's Palace.

Gentile and Giovanni was already active in Venice about 1430, but most of his work for public places has unfortunately been lost. However, his portrait of the city can still be seen in the books of drawings in the Louvre and the British Museum: these show the vision of a new Venice, with arcades of round-headed arches, broad, measured vistas, spacious squares paved with regular stones and solemn campanili, majestic stairways leading to airy loggias. If these drawings are to be dated no later than 1450, as now seems to be the case, we already have a foretaste, in the painter's brilliant vision, of the new Venice that was emerging, inspired by Tuscany and Padua.

From 1450 on, Giovanni Bellini, son of Jacopo, was painting his first works which, being panels and not frescoes, have luckily been preserved. His Madonnas, delightfully tender towards offspring

◁

Palazzo Nani, San Trovaso. On the lonely campo of San Trovaso, near the ancient squero (gondola boatyard stands the enormous Palazzo Barberigo, later Palazzo Nani, a typical example of Venetian Gothic of the mid-15th century. The well-head is of the same period.

P. 118, above

Jacopo de' Barbari: Ponte di Rialto (1500). Detail of wood engraving of plan of Venice. At that time the bridge was made of wood, and could be opened to allow ships to pass under it.

P. 118, below right

Bartolomeo Vivarini: Madonna and Child (c. 1460). Museo Correr. With its sculptural form, Tuscan-inspired via Mantegna's work in Padua, this Madonna is characteristic of the early Renaissance.

P. 118, below left

Jacopo Bellini: Madonna and Child (c. 1450). Accademia. By 1450 Venetian Gothic had completed its historical cycle. Artists like Jacopo Bellini, father of Gentile and Giovanni, had already presaged the transition to the Renaissance.

P. 119

Palazzo Contarini-Fasan, Grand Canal. Commonly known as 'Desdemona's House', notable above all for its magnificent balconies, whose fretwork has the delicacy of lace.

117

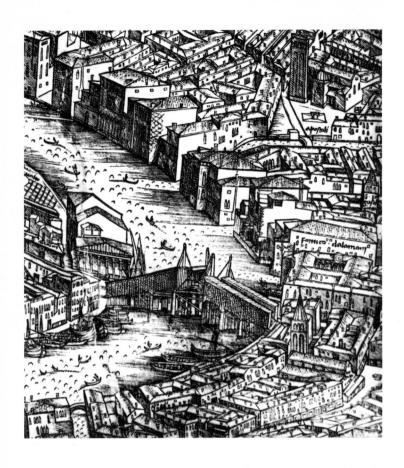

who are as sturdy and graceful as Donatello's *putti* (Venice, Accademia), his *Pietàs,* softly melancholic, in atmospheres of mild, haunting colour (Milan, Brera), his landscapes at sunset beneath the even, mellow light of the Venetian countryside (*Transfiguration* in the Museo Correr, Venice) already reveal a new attitude, both formally (because it was inspired by Tuscan techniques) and in spirit, since

*Entrance to the Arsenal (1460).
The work of Antonio Gambello,
inspired by Roman triumphal arches.
It heralded the appearance of
Renaissance architecture in Venice.*

▷

*An Arsenal Lion. Before the
entrance, numerous lions, some of
them spoils of war, symbolize the
naval power of Venice.*

they were touched by feelings of a hitherto unknown humanity. Anyone
looking at the four Carità polyptychs in the Accademia cannot fail
to notice, in the one with St Sebastian — the only one by Bellini —
the architectonic unity of space which, uniquely, draws the three
panels with their gold backgrounds into a harmonious whole, by
means of a tenuous line of hills; and the language of the mighty,
heroic figures of the saints in the altar of San Zanipolo is clearly that
of the resurgent humanistic vision to which Bellini lent such decisive
strength.

These are the voices heard in Venice during the decisive decade, from
1450, and they constitute the ideal basis of the figurative culture that
was soon to change the face of the city. The changing taste in painting was soon to lead to radical changes in architectural forms.

The first monument to fit into the new Renaissance vision was built
in 1460: the Porta dell'Arsenale, the gateway of the Arsenal. In the
old circle of the walls, next to crenellated towers still medieval in
style, Antonio Gambello erected a gateway with a broad round arch,
framed by double columns which support an entablature and tabernacle housing the lion of St Mark. Clearly, the lure of antiquity, here
inspired by some Roman triumphal arch, has made its appearance on
the lagoon. With its massive power, which positively jolts the delicate
balance of the surrounding space (still Gothic, with its brickwork and
crenellated walls), and the rarer and more precious quality of the
marble from which it is made, Gambello's triumphal gateway assumes
in retrospect a historical significance which may perhaps go beyond
the builder's original intentions.

From this point on, the introduction of the new Renaissance style to
Venice took place by degrees, gradually changing the face of the
Gothic city. The process took place in various stages: a new façade
would replace an old one, an old building would be restructured, a
whole complex would take on a new aspect. But the basic continuity
of the architectural vision was still there; so that, whereas the Porta
dell'Arsenale constituted an act of violence, other changes took on an
aura of tradition and fitted more easily into the existing urban fabric.
Thus, suitable dimensions were almost always respected in the new
buildings; more important still was the perpetuation of the traditional
concern with colour, which had made the whole city into a fragile-
looking stage-set, embellishing its details with touches reminiscent
of embroidery or filigree. Now it was the loveliness of the design of
the architectural details, the elegant outline of the small semi-circu-
lar arches, the delicate moulding of antae and capitals, of slender

pilasters and fillets and fascias, that ensured that the Venetian architecture of the early Renaissance kept its fresh, traditional character. This was how the miracle of adding the charmed Venetian touch to a Tuscan or Roman language was achieved.

The district where the Renaissance impact was immediately felt was in the centre of the *sestiere* of San Marco, with the houses of the great families and main public buildings. Here two currents met and clashed — both Tuscan in origin but developed in very different forms by their respective promoters, Pietro Lombardo and Mauro Codussi. For greater clarity, we shall consider their activities separately.

Pietro Lombardo (1435-1515) came to Venice in 1467, after spending four years in Padua, in an enviroment permeated with Donatello's

Scuola Grande di San Marco and Church of San Zanipolo. The rebuilding of the Campo San Zanipolo was one of the most important projects of the early Renaissance in Venice. The Scuola's picturesque façade contrasts with the equestrian Colleoni monument, the work of Verrocchio.

influence, and worked on the rebuilding of San Giobbe to look at the very elegant line of the porch, with a lunette and three statues of saints carved by Lombardo himself (like many artists of his time, he was both architect and sculptor). The best feature of the church is the chance, where a light dome with pendentives set on exquisite cornices recalls the spirit of Brunelleschi and Michelozzo, evidently used as models by Lombardo. This choice of models was probably influenced by the donors, the Martini, who were wealthy silk weavers from Lucca; they left very definite traces of their tastes in the adjoining chapel. Here, in the Tuscan-influenced pattern of the vaulting, there are echoes of Rossellino, while the terracotta is in the manner of Della Robbia: a corner of Tuscany in the hearth of Venice.

Façade (1480-1500). San Zaccaria. Designed by Mauro Codussi, it is one of the most impressive Renaissance monuments in Venice.

The character of this Tuscan-oriented architecture of Lombardo is not hard to define. A sculptor by vocation, the artist adapted his architectural space to the effects of light, obtaining very striking chromatic surfaces with a delicate and subtly suggestive touch. Essentially, he thus emerges as a superbly skilled and engaging decorator, characterized by a particular plastic virtuosity and awareness of colour. In this context two of his other masterpieces in Venice at the beginning of the Renaissance are extremely characteristic: the church of the Miracoli (1481-89) and the Palazzetto Dario on the Grand Canal near the Salute (1487). The artist's whole interest is focused on the external wrappings which cover the structures without any real relation to the internal space; he thus negates the very essence of Tuscan architecture (though he does draw upon the Tuscan tradition for the separate elements of the composition). Linear cornices on the façade, carved fascias, multi-coloured discs of rare marble, embellish these exteriors of Lombardo's with a lavishness that would make

▷

Andrea Verrocchio: Colleoni Monument (1496).

Portal (c. 1471). San Giobbe. Pietro Lombardo, like Codussi, was one of the greatest architectural craftsmen in Renaissance Venice. San Giobbe was one of his first works.

(right) Pietro Lombardo: Monument to the Doge Pietro Mocenigo (c. 1485). San Zanipolo. Typical Venetian Renaissance sepulchral monument. As a sculptor, Lombardo was Tuscan-influenced.

them worthy of a place in the exuberant — and contemporary — paintings of Bellini and Carpaccio.

The second tendency of the new architecture was represented by Mauro Codussi (c. 1440-1504). In many ways his works were the antithesis of the pictorial and decorative modes of Pietro Lombardo, for he affirmed the values of the Tuscan plastic-spatial vision and produced buildings all of whose structures and spaces were organic and vital.

Not much is known about Codussi's artistic education, but his first Venetian work, the little church of San Michele in Isola, already presents us with a singularly concrete and valid spatial vision. From the orderly façade, which reflects the internal division into three small naves, to the rhythmic clarity of the arches and square chancel where a cupola is set above a beautiful cornice, it is as though Codussi were thinking back to that simplified taste, inspired by Brunelleschi, such as Michelozzo had adopted in Florence (and possibly also in Venice too, in the monastery of San Giorgio, where it seems he designed a library, subsequently destroyed). This interest in Michelozzo made Codussi, unlike Lombardo, a real constructor of spaces, within a light-filled masonry framework.

This is exemplified in Santa Maria Formosa, completely rebuilt by Codussi from 1492 onwards, and certainly his masterpiece. An interior so passionately organized as a whole, with the rhythmic undulation of the waves of light as they flow along the bare walls, just barely marked by two-coloured fascias, had never before been seen in Venice. Supported by slight pillars, the whole complex roof of the church (with cross vaulting over the main naves, small domes in the

Apse (1489). Church of Santa Maria dei Miracoli. An imposing marble structure, the Miracoli shows the evolution from classical origins of the style of Pietro Lombardo and his sons.

(right) Santa Maria dei Miracoli (1489). The architectural concept of the church, by Pietro Lombardo, is simple; it has a single nave, and is gracefully adapted to the curve of the canal.

side ones and barrel vaulting in the chapels) seems almost to rise and hang suspended in the air, so much so that people on the ground feel as if they were standing in boundless space, concentrated and unified in the quiet vibration of the light.

Codussi's work was certainly decisive in transforming the face of the city. Combining his vigorous ideas of spatial structure with exquisite subtlety of design, he built the church of San Giovanni Crisostomo (1497-1504) based on an ingenious Greek cross plan which stresses the altars to great effect, with their well-placed masterpieces, including Bellini's altarpiece and Tullio Lombardo's bas-relief. He then concerned himself with buildings left unfinished by the Lombardo family, for instance the Scuola Grande di San Giovanni Evangelista (near the Frari) and the Scuola di San Marco (near San Zanipolo), creating the monumental staircases which further confirm his remarkable plastic feeling for the spacing of interiors.

But Codussi's last masterpieces are in the field of secular architecture, where he undoubtedly produced plans that were followed throughout the centuries to come. Palazzo Corner-Spinelli (c. 1500) looks on to the Grand Canal, near Sant'Angelo, its façade bordered by corner pilasters and an entablature, with a rigour of design which, miraculously, does not inhibit the wild inventiveness of the rows of windows and balconies. Codussi here combined an absolutely Tuscan moderation with Venetian elegance, and he more than any other architect seemed to understand the demands of the city's watery setting. The Palazzo Corner-Spinelli did not go beyond the usual dimensions of Venetian Gothic, but in his last palace, the Palazzo Vendramin-Calergi, the architect launched into monumentality. The two-lighted windows are flanked by columns, and long balconies give unity to the whole façade. This solution was to be a turning-point, providing the model for numerous Venetian façades to come, rising from the water in a picturesque play of light and shadow, with a majestically classical effect.

Codussi's work on Piazza San Marco ends his activity, and indeed actually goes beyond the span of the artist's own life. Until 1496, the year in which Gentile Bellini painted his great canvas *Procession in Piazza San Marco* (now in the Accademia), the whole of the north side was occupied by the thirteenth-century Procuratie, a long building with a portico and loggias very reminiscent of other architecture of the time, such as the Fondaco dei Turchi. Towards the basilica, the Procuratie were almost joined to various Veneto-Byzantine buildings, leaving the entrance to the important Strada delle Mercerie, which leads directly to Rialto, almost invisible.

Codussi's brilliant feeling for town-planning attracted his attention to the importance of this focal point of the city's traffic, and inspired him to provide it with monumental dignity in the form of a clock tower, the Torre dell'Orologio, which must have been built between 1496 and 1500, since it appears on Jacopo de Barbari's panoramic plan. As one still feels today, he thus created a landmark figuring in the prospect of anyone looking at San Marco from the Basin: between the two columns of Marco and Todaro, the Torre dell'Orologio, built like a triumphal arch (soon extended to include two side wings and terraces), completed a second magnificent vista on the axis of the Piazzetta, which crossed the axis of the Piazza in front of the basilica; as a result, the whole complex had an unparalleled majesty.

Codussi then decided to rebuild the Procuratie themselves, which were to constitute the necessary continuation of the Tower; he recast the original Veneto-Byzantine building in the purest Renaissance forms. Thus, under the spur of Codussi's genius, the Piaozza San Marco received the first touch of the Renaissance, which was to be of great importance for its future development.

Meanwhile, in another part of the city, a complete and equally exemplary work of renovation was taking place: this was the Campo di San Zanipolo. Half-way through the fifteenth century, the great Dominican basilica had been completed, and began to assume its function as the Venetian Pantheon, the shrine of the state. In front of the church, a smallish square stretched to the canal, while to the north the buildings of the monastery adjoined the Scuola Grande di San Marco. In 1485 a fire largely destroyed the Scuola, and Pietro Lombardo was commissioned to rebuild it.

Complex problems were posed by the existing buildings and the spaces contained between them, particularly since Lombardo knew of the plan to site the equestrian statue of Bartolommeo Colleoni, which had been commissioned from Verrocchio, level with the façade of the church. One of the landmarks of Renaissance Venice, the statue by the great Tuscan sculptor thus came to exercise a certain influence on Lombardo's solutions. With its concentrated energy, the broad firm movement of horse and rider, and its monumental base (later completed by Leopardi and placed on its site in 1496), the

▷

Antonio Rizzo: Eve (c. 1480). Doge's Palace. Rizzo's sculptural masterpiece was created for the Arco Foscari (where it is now replaced by a bronze copy).

128

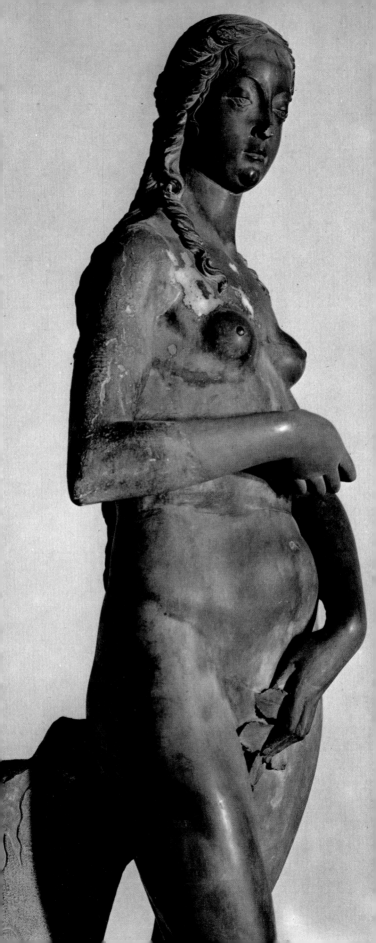

equestrian statue was an absolute novelty for the Venetians and deeply impressed them. Pietro Lombardo realized this and was inspired to set the façade of his Scuole back 'optically', through the device of the curious perspective panels on the lower part of the church, with their arcades and lions. The result is very strange indeed, perhaps an unsuccessful attempt to repeat the miracle of the Doge's Palace, where the solid upper part seems to be supported by the shadow of the porticoed lower part. Here Lombardo obtained at best a piece of elegant scenery, to act as backdrop to the massive statue.

But though this is a qualified success architecturally, the façade of

Barovier Cup (2nd half of 15th century). Museo di Murano. Typical 'nuptial cup', made by the Renaissance glassblower Barovier. Portraits of the bride and groom, and allegory of youth.

the Scuola Grande di San Marco is a mine of marvellous elements of Renaissance vocabulary: cornices carved like engraved work, columns and capitals picturesquely elaborated, highly elegant arches and windows, pale-hued marble. The building is topped by a series of rhythmically bounding lunettes, added by Codussi when, in 1495, he was asked to complete the work to end a disagreement between Lombardo and his employers.

It was often Codussi's lot to have to complete a work begun by someone else, and his impact on the face of Renaissance Venice was all the more considerable because of it. Under just such circumstances

◁
*Tullio Lombardo: The Lion of
St Mark (c. 1490). Scuola Grande
di San Marco. This, together with
the three other perspective reliefs,
the work of Pietro Lombardo and
his sons Antonio and Tullio,
decorates the base of the façade
of the Scuola.*

P. 134/35
*Scuola Grande di San Marco.
(c. 1495). Lombardo's work on the
façade was interrupted midway, and
Codussi, an artist of the most mature
Venetian Renaissance style, replaced
him. His picturesque and vivacious
building is an imposing backdrop to
the splendid Campo San Zanipolo.*

we find him at work on the stupendous façade of San Zaccaria, where the famous monastery protected by the Doges of Venice once stood. When Gambello's work was interrupted in 1465 at the level of the entrance, Codussi continued the exterior vertically, so as to cover the high Gothic naves of the interior, and drew the various levels together with half-lunettes, which are faintly reminiscent of the flying buttresses of the Gothic era. The Renaissance façade, in short, seems to interpret the Gothic interior with amazing critical subtlety, thus constituting an absolutely exceptional example in Venice.

One last worthwhile document of the early Renaissance is the curious Scala del Bovolo (spiral staircase) next to the Palazzo Contarini at San Luca. This is a cylindrical tower, inspired by campanili of that style, which were once common in the Veneto (there are still examples at Tessera and Caorle), adjoining a building with five superimposed galleries corresponding to the floors of the palazzo. As the galleries

become lower towards the top, so the spiral staircase, in its tower, regulates its progress so as to give access to the various floors, a brilliant feat of engineering. The design of the architectural details is very elegant, apparently by a certain Giovanni Candi (*c.* 1499) who seems to have been one of Codussi's many followers.

There are various other palazzi along the Grand Canal and lesser canals inspired by Lombardo and Codussi. It should be noted that, between the end of the fifteenth century and the first decades of the sixteenth, at least a quarter of the houses in Venice were more or less basically altered, adapting themselves to the new fashion.

The Gothic phase in Venetian sculpture had reached its peak, as we have said, in the Porta della Carta, completed about 1450 by the Bon and Bregno workshops. Soon afterwards, Doge Foscari commanded work to begin on the Arco Foscari which linked the square to the courtyard of the Doge's Palace.

Palazzo Dario (c. 1487). By Pietro Lombardo. With its fanciful use of marble, and the inlaid discs, rosettes and plaques around its elegant windows, this is the liveliest and most picturesque façade on the Grand Canal.

Antonio Bregno (1426-85), another typical transitional figure, was the foreman of most of the works. Born in Rigesio, near Como, he had brought the characteristics of the Lombard tradition to Venice, with a markedly foursquare, plastic sculpture, still late Gothic in many of its decorative aspects. These characteristics can be seen clearly in the structure of the tomb of Doge Foscari in the Frari (*c.* 1457). In the northern manner, we find a hanging sarcophagus topped by a big conical awning. The figures of the two warriors who hold the hangings on the two sides are very reminiscent, in their solid poses, of the giants in Milan cathedral, where Bregno is believed to have worked. But a new spirit is felt in the *Virtues* which appear between the pillars of the sarcophagus, and their forms have nothing of Bregno's plastic structure. Here it is possible to identify the first steps of a new personality in the field of Venetian sculpture, Antonio Rizzo (*c.* 1430 - *c.* 1498). A pupil of Bregno's, he was traditionally said to have been born in Verona, but according to Giovio he came from Como, like his master. Apparently he was the person who (in 1464-65) provided columns and capitals for the Certosa in Pavia. The first of his authenticated works was probably the tomb of Orsato Giustinian, once in the Certosa di Sant'Andrea, now known only through the old drawings in the Museo Correr in Venice and a few remains. This tomb too, significantly, recalled Lombard models, consisting as it did of a ground level sarcophagus surrounded by six statues of the Virtues and decorated with medallions in the Tuscan style. On it is the recumbent figure of Giustinian. The model, which is neither Florentine nor Paduan, must have come from Milanese circles or the Certosa in Pavia, known to Rizzo in his youth, yet another link between himself and the great matrix of the North Italian Renaissance. About 1467, after having completed the decoration for the porch of the Madonna dell'Orto, with a delicate but still very Gothic Annunciation, Rizzo reappears in the porch of Sant'Elena of about 1467. Beneath an arch, with a lunette, subtended by a classical entablature supported by medallions, the *condottiero* Vittorio Cappello kneels before the saint.

No other sculpture of the time presents the viewer with such harsh and significant stylistic contrasts. While in fact the architectural setting is clearly inspired by Tuscan models realized in Padua by Donatello and Pietro Lombardo (in the Rosselli monument at Sant'Antonio, also of 1467) the figure of the *condottiero* might have come down from some northern cathedral. Tall and gangling, the warrior has had to kneel so as not to touch the roof with his great head, seen in profile, while the saint puts forward a bent knee and inclines her head, in an intense and convincing movement. Surprisingly realistic, the human portrait jars with its classical setting, as if revealing the effort the sculptor had had to make to adapt to a not entirely congenial culture. Certainly, this is a work of great liveliness, and in many ways it was to act as an example for the still dozing Venice, soon to be visited by Pietro Lombardo, still in Padua, and, in 1469, by Mauro Codussi the great regenerator of Venetian architecture.

After 1473, the year of the Doge's death, Antonio Rizzo began his monument to Niccolò Tron in the Frari, which was to be of fundamental importance in the development of Renaissance sculpture in Venice. The architectural setting is certainly somewhat confused, and reveals the imitation of early works by Codussi, particularly of San Michele and the façade of San Zaccaria. The scheme is that of a triumphal arch of Tuscan inspiration, supported by two niched pillars linked to an upper gallery complicated — and this is Rizzo's distinctive northern hallmark — by a protruding porch, in which the figure of the Doge advances familiarly. By him are *Prudence* and *Charity,* smiling mournfully. The sarcophagus, almost identical to the earlier one for Giustinian, is once again in the Lombard style, with the body lying stretched out upon it, uncovered.

A variety of elements come together in this impressive composition, which must have cost Rizzo many years of labour and is thought to have been finished about 1480. Deeply realistic in the portrait of the Doge, whose physiognomy is carved with a patient concern for reality, Rizzo then created the models of the Virtues with a limpidly clear, painterly softness reminiscent of his contemporary Antonello, represented in Venice by the altarpiece of San Cassiano. But one must not overlook the extremely subtle modelling, smooth as ivory and highly sensitive to light in the drapery and faces; inevitably it reminds us of the Lombard elements found in the Certosa of Pavia by the Mantegazza brothers and Amadeo, and clearly known to the sculptor who appears in documents as having been their companion a few years earlier.

This irrepressible Lombard background reappears as completely as ever in Rizzo's two masterpieces, the *Adam* and *Eve* of the Doge's Palace, carved in marble for the Arco Foscari about 1480. These two impressive statues (they are over six foot in height) have a northern touch about them once again, and are reminiscent of the Giants of Milan cathedral, or Amadeo's *Virtues* in the Colleoni chapel. As for Eve, the slender shoulders above the broad pelvis and the nervous outline of her hands and feet actually seem to anticipate, inexplicably, the physical types which were to be introduced into Venetian art from Nuremberg at least ten years later, in the prints of Jacopo de' Barbari

▷

Torre dell'Orologio (1500), Piazza San Marco. Mauro Codussi built this tower, and also designed the Procuratie Vecchie, built after his death.

Arcade in courtyard (c. 1500). Palazzo Zorzi, Piazza San Severo. This Renaissance work by Codussi is supremely elegant even in its present neglected state.

and Albrecht Dürer. The authenticity and vivid life of the figures of Adam and Eve can be better understood, in northern rather than Venetian terms, if one bears in mind that Antonello and Giovanni Bellini were creating their masterpieces at that time. The exquisitely graphic character of the structure, too, with its striking relief, is reminiscent of northern models, rather than of the melodious colour-orientated local Venetian strain.

Rizzo was an artist of absolutely first-class importance, all the more so because, together with Codussi — another complete outsider — he acted as mediator for a very vital culture, and grafted it on to the tired, conservative fabric of Venetian artistic life. But Rizzo stayed in Venice for a remarkably short time, leaving in 1498 after accusations of sharp practice while he was working on the modernization of the courtyard and apartments of the Doge's Palace. Beginning in 1483, assisted by Lombard stonecarvers he had designed the monumental new stairway (later known as Scala dei Giganti, stairway of the Giants), daringly bringing the focus of ducal ceremonies into line with the axis of the façade of the Arco Foscari. Even the internal façade, in this theatrical vision, was to appear as an enormous decorative back-cloth, and act as a chromatic contrast to the bare walls of the surround-

Detail of capital, (right) balcony (c.1500). Palazzo Zorzi, Piazza San Severo.
The detail exemplifies the graphic poetry of the work of Mauro Codussi,
the supreme master of the early Renaissance in Venice.

ing buildings. As well as designing this impressive complex, Rizzo
was probably also responsible for the sculptural decoration of the
stairway, with its carved heads of a delicacy and naturalism utterly
typical of the Lombard style. The façade, over-burdened with carving
and other irrelevant ornament, was completed by the other great
sculptor present in Venice at the time, Pietro Lombardo, and his
numerous assistants.

We have already discussed Lombardo in connection with architecture,
but we must now consider him, and his sons, as creators of Renaissance
sculpture, particularly in relation to the monuments of the Doges in
San Zanipolo. Lombard by origin, he probably visited Florence in his
youth. This can be deduced from his first known work, the monument to the jurist Antonio Rosselli in the Basilica del Santo in Padua, between 1464 and 1467, where there are evident borrowings from
the Bruni and Marsuppini monuments, by Rossellino and Desiderio
respectively, in Santa Croce in Florence. Naturally, the Tuscan idiom
of Pietro Lombardo was also fed, in Padua, by the legacy of Donatello, still very marked in those years. But an examination of his
plastic style confirms the impression of a 'northern' culture which
definitely prevails, as for instance in the clear, incisive delineation of

the marble carving of the Madonna in the lunette of the Rosselli tomb, or the rigid, realistic hardness of the face of the dead man, which clearly recall the style of the Mantegazza brothers and Amadeo.

It is interesting to speculate on the reaction produced by Pietro Lombardo when he arrived in Venice, perhaps soon after 1467 and certainly before 1474, the year in which there is documentary evidence for his being there. At that time, the personalities of Codussi and Rizzo were prominent in architecture and sculpture and there is no doubt that, despite his 'Paduan' beginnigs, Lombardo must have been particularly influenced by Rizzo, who came from the same northern background and was at that time hesitating between the late-Gothic tradition of Bregno and the liberated Lombard Renaissance style as seen in the work of Amadeo.

There are evident signs of this in the naturalistic features of his first Venetian work, the monument to Doge Pasquale Malipiero in San Zanipolo, dating from shortly after the death of the Doge in 1462. Here too one can see the homage to a local tradition, for instance that of Bregno's Foscari monument: the presence, for instance, of the broad awning over the sarcophagus. The architectural framework is simpler and more linear than that of the Rosselli monument: a small Donatellian tabernacle, with pillars and architraving supporting a lunette, in which there is a relief of a Pietà in distinctly Paduan taste. But three Virtues on scrolls at the sides and top of the lunette give the ensemble an odd 'local' flavour, a distant echo of the Gothic, with its spires and pinnacles against the red background of the brick walls of the church; while the harsh linear modelling of the figures seems rather to point to Mantegna or to the early Gentile Bellini, whose great polyptych of San Vincenzo Ferrer, completed about 1464, stands opposite.

Pietro Lombardo really became established as official sculptor in the service of the Republic with the monument to Pietro Mocenigo, also in San Zanipolo, which he worked on between 1476 and 1481. This time Lombardo's design was clearly based upon a really inspired architectural idea, which contrasts strikingly with the confused agglomeration of themes in the contemporary Tron tomb, by Rizzo. The architecture of the Mocenigo monument is based on Codussi, and for the first time it rejects the characteristic Donatellian tabernacle to base itself on a more functional architectural structure. The sarcophagus, supported by giants and topped by the standing figure of the Doge, completely fills the void beneath a positive triumphal arch, flanked by a triple series of niches, with figures of Virtues and Warriors. Below, a broad base bears the elegant funerary inscription, while on the top there is a limpid and flawless relief of the Marys at the Sepulchre. The mask of the Doge is impressive in its incisive realism, with the light emphasizing the strong muscular structure of the face; the pictorial reliefs on the lower step are particularly remarkable, reminiscent yet again of contemporary examples by Bellini, and possibly already implying the collaboration of Antonio, Pietro's son, of whom we shall say more later.

This masterpiece by Lombardo may be considered as a parallel, perhaps even a rival, to Rizzo's Tron monument. It is nobly decorative, lacking the inspired sallies of Rizzo's incisive fantasy but all the more harmonious for it, a measured and simple example to the following generation of Venetian sculptors, among whom were Tullio and Antonio Lombardo, who became his faithful collaborators.

The next monument in San Zanipolo, to Doge Niccolò Marcello, was

Palazzo Corner-Spinelli, Sant'Angelo. Built by Mauro Codussi at the end of the 15th century, it has clear Tuscan references in its mullioned windows and rusticated base.

probably completed after 1485, and marks a further move in the direction of classicizing abstraction, which seems to have seized Pietro Lombardo with the passing of time. Ingeniously placed in a Codussian setting, the sculptural complex has the usual sarcophagus under the triumphal arch, flanked by four great figures of Virtues. Moving away from the original Lombard naturalism, Pietro makes expressions and movements increasingly perfect, balanced, almost glacial, obtaining a precious, literary result, a sort of imperial prose of noble if rhetorical anonymity. As has been noted, Pietro was here revealing a cultural attitude that was by no means uncommon, and we shall find it again in the consciously classical ornaments of certain paintings, from Cima to Mantegna, and in the world of illustrated books printed by Jenson and Aldus Manutius, including the famous *Hypnerotomachia Poliphili.* In this way, Pietro Lombardo's development played a crucial part in the growth of classically inspired Venetian culture at the end of the century.

At this point the figures of his son Tullio and Antonio emerge beside him. In the church of the Miracoli, a work known to be by the three artists, every inch of surface seems to have been carved with patient

Palazzo Vendramin Calergi (1504), San Marcuola. One of the last and most complete works of Mauro Codussi. The great cornice tops a façade in which Tuscan monumentality and Venetian elegance are perfectly balanced.

precision, with an effect of superlative delicacy. Here too, polychromy brightens the façade, and it is irresistible to compare it with contemporary representations by Carpaccio, so close in time and spirit to these picturesque creations. In the strictly sculptural field, the *stile antico* predominates at the Miracoli, and now emerges as characteristic of the older son, Tullio, sculptor of the *Annunciation* on the façade of the presbytery.

From now on Tullio Lombardo (*c.* 1455-1532) adopted a more independent position. In 1493, in fact, he was working on his masterpiece, the monument to Doge Andrea Vendramin at the Servi, later altered and removed to San Zanipolo. This is undoubtedly the most impressive tomb, in size and number of statues, ever made in Venice. Combining elements of the Mocenigo and Marcello tombs in San Zanipolo, Tullio enlarged the structure of the triumphal arch monumentally, deepening its projection in foreshortened perspective and giving the whole a carefully calculated static credibility. The sarcophagus appears on a porticoed structure, surrounded by Angels and Virtues; in the side niches were Adam and Eve (only the former still survives, but in the Metropolitan Museum, New York) while two warriors were placed outside the pilasters (they are now in the niches). Above, between two architraved niches of Tuscan purity, there is a classically lucid Annunciation.

▷

Torre dell'Orologio, Piazza San Marco (c. 1500). By Mauro Codussi.

P. 146/47
Savin: Moor (1497). One of the quarterjacks on the Torre dell'Orologio.

With the Vendramin monument, Tullio's sculpture achieves its full plasticity. The warriors, locked in their ponderous armour, have a metallic solidity, within which the living parts of the body — the hands, the feet, the faces with their steadfast, almost angry gaze — seem to tremble with life and power. In the figure of Adam the surfaces, polished with consummate technical skill, have a flawless quality; his pose, a sort of erudite transposition of the antique, now falls within the ideal category of an authentic neoclassicism.

These effects are also found in the numerous portraits, or double portraits, in classical dress, in the Cà d'Oro. The reference to Roman funerary iconography is clear, although in Tullio the tendency to soften

Vittore Carpaccio: St Augustine's Study, Scuola degli Schiavoni. This was one of a series of canvases painted for the School by Carpaccio between 1502 and 1507. The scene is an early Renaissance Venetian interior.

and blur surfaces chromatically never disappears; this is reminiscent rather of contemporary pictorial production, for instance of Giovanni Bellini's nude in Vienna. But even while tending in this neoclassical direction, Lombardo does not lose the extremely naturalistic touch he had found in the Vendramin monument and whose finest expression is to be found in the smile, frozen by death, of Guidarello Guidarelli, sculpted in Ravenna in 1525.

As early as 1505 the youngest and most mysterious member of the Lombardo family, Antonio (1485-1516) had produced the *Miracle of the New-born Child* in the Santo in Padua. His figures go beyond the neoclassical orbit of his brother; they have an animated sense of

(above) Giovanni Bellini: Madonna degli Alberetti (1487). Accademia.
(below) Giovanni Bellini: Pietà (c. 1450). Museo Correr.

(right) Gentile Bellini: Doge Giovanni Mocenigo (1478). Museo Correr. ▷

human involvement, and a richer pictorial quality, also noticeable in some reliefs of the bases of the Mocenigo and Vendramin tombs in San Zanipolo which have recently been attributed to his sphere of influence. In 1506, before leaving for Ferrara, he made the *Madonna* in the Zen chapel in San Marco: a bronze structure of solemn proportions, yet touched with a delicate pictorial softness reminiscent of Giorgione.

The works of Tullio and Antonio took the Lombardo dynasty right into the sixteenth century. The family's innumerable contacts with sculptural, architectural and pictorial circles are a further proof of the basic importance assumed by Venice in the last classicizing phase of the Renaissance in northern Italy.

To conclude this survey of early Renaissance Venice, we must now turn to painting. As we have noted, it was painting itself, rather than the other arts, that had been most important in the introduction of the first Renaissance forms. In the first period undisputed supremacy belonged to the Bellini family, with Giovanni pre-eminent from the middle of the fifteenth century. We have also observed how his very personal stylistic tone immediately set him apart from the traditional school, represented by the masters of Murano, more faithful to the forms of the late Gothic, even where they seemed to have been affected by the plastic transformation of the Tuscans.

A significant example of the art of this hesitant phase, which characterized Venetian figurative culture during the 1450s, is to be found in the four polyptychs of the Carità, still in their original church, now part of the Accademia. The four polyptychs — in the church's lovely apse — speak two different languages; it can definitely be stated that Giovanni Bellini (*c.* 1426-1516) was entirely responsible for the *St Sebastian,* while the other three confirm the continued influence exerted by more backward-looking styles, with their more brilliant, glassy colour and absence of a three-dimensional vision of space (annulled by the gold background) and of genuine plasticity in the design. If one had to hazard a guess at their authorship, it would not be unreasonable to suggest the most important master of the school of Murano, Bartolomeo Vivarini (*c.* 1430-99), who was capable of modelling a pictorial substance that was brilliant but clearly rigidified by a lingering Gothic linearity derived from stained glass. One fine contemporary window is still in San Zanipolo, in the south transept. There is no doubt that Bartolomeo Vivarini, too, was familiar with the novelty brought by the Tuscans to Padua: indeed, we very soon find him collaborating with Mantegna in the church of the Eremitani. But it is also certain that his formative years in Murano made him irredeemably 'conservative', whereas Giovanni Bellini emerges as the only really innovating spirit. Bellini's first 'Paduan' phase is admirably represented in Venice in a small room in the Museo Correr, looking on to the Piazza near the campanile: here there is a *Transfiguration of Christ,* originally designed with an ogival top, in which the figures of the apostles and Saviour have the plastic marble incisiveness of the figures of early Mantegna. But Bellini's distinctive timbre, deeply realistic and human, is already identifiable in the diffuse, melancholy luminosity: the light, which seems to emanate from the countryside just before nightfall, contains and caresses the crystalline angularities

◁
Scala del Bovolo (end of 15th century). Palazzo Contarini, San Luca.
Remarkable spiral staircase, in the Codussi style.

Antonio Rizzo: Monument to Doge Niccolò Tron (c. 1473). Santa Maria Gloriosa dei Frari. This work by the greatest Venetian Renaissance sculptor is a complex monument on a Lombard model, enriched with niches containing figures of the Virtues, and with a full-length statue of Tron (not shown).

of the hillock from which Christ rises, diaphanous in his gleaming robe. Mantegna's contribution was immediately re-elaborated and subjected to the growing lyricism of a colour which was soon to become the precise and confident voice of the new Renaissance painting in Venice.

In the same room in the Correr, however, the *Pietà* demonstrates Bellini's direct relationship with the leader of the new Tuscan school in Padua, Donatello. Bellini, in fact, was not satisfied with having adopted Mantegna's erudite vocabulary, basically poles apart from his own impassioned and lyrical sensitivity; and he was to find in Donatello that dramatic, richly human breadth which best suited him. In the Correr *Pietà,* the reference to Donatello is very clear in the two cherubim supporting Christ, positive copies of the bronze ones on the altar of the Santo; once again the dominant aspect is the harmony of colour, which moves gradually from the grey-violet of the backgrounds to the ivories and mellow brown of the figures.

Savelli Monument (1st half of 15th century). Santa Maria Gloriosa dei Frari. Of a somewhat earlier date than the monument to Doge Tron, this is in the tradition of the wall-mounted tombs of the late Gothic and the early Renaissance. The equestrian statue, the delicate figure of Virtue and the Madonna, are attributed to a Tuscan hand.

To follow the development of this Renaissance genius of colour would mean going back to San Zanipolo, where we have already seen his polyptych of 1464; but it may perhaps be simpler to go to the Gallerie dell'Accademia, because here, too, his successive phases are documented. Here, in the intimate light of the beautiful little rooms (recently laid out by a brilliant Venetian architect, Carlo Scarpa), we can move from the sharper brilliance of the youthful Madonnas to the sumptuous splendour of the *Madonna of the Little Trees (Alberetti)* of 1487, remarkable for the easy serenity of its colour relationships, softened into a shadowy mellowness of tone. The great altarpiece of San Giobbe also dates from these years: it presents the typical scheme of the late fifteenth-century Venetian altar, with the *Sacra Conversazione* of the Madonna and Child with six saints, accompanied by the music of three angels, in a chapel seen in foreshortened perspective: an architectural setting worthy of Codussi or Pietro Lombardo at his finest.

The decade 1480-90 was one of the most successful for Bellini, who was now in the absolute forefront of Venetian art. His works are found in the most important buildings: in the sacristy of the Frari, the triptych of the *Madonna and Child with Saints,* still in its original frame, with its stupendous atmospheric fragmentation of light, dates from 1488; the votive altarpiece of Doge Barbarigo in San Pietro Martire in Murano is of the same year, with a broad landscape that sets the protagonists in the real atmosphere of nature; while the church of San Zaccaria in Venice houses one of his last masterpieces, an altarpiece of the *Madonna and Child with Saints* dating from 1505, and comparable, with its *sfumatura,* its harmonious softening and blending of tonal values, to the paintings of Giorgione.

Few artists are as valuable as Giovanni Bellini — though his large canvases *(teleri)* of public ceremonies, painted for the Doge's Palace from 1480 onwards, have been destroyed — in portraying the mood of the Renaissance city and in suggesting the cultural and stylistic elements that enable us to reconstruct its lost face. His clarity of style and deeply human sensitivity help us to understand the Venetians' keen desire for grandeur, in their period of greatest expansion. But we shall be introduced to late fifteenth-century Venice even more directly in the works of the other great painters of ceremonies and episodes in everyday life: Gentile Bellini and Vittore Carpaccio.

Luckily, despite the irreparable loss of their *teleri* in the Doge's Palace, we still have ample documentation of their activities as unparalleled recorders of the face of the city.

Gentile Bellini (1429-1507) succeeded his father Giovanni as portraitist and painter of ceremonies and enjoyed such widespread fame that he was actually sent by the Doge to the court of Sultan Mahomet II in Turkey to paint his portrait. His rather timid approaches in the direction of Renaissance style can be seen in the Museo di San Marco, where the panels of the old organ (before 1465) are kept. Within the slender limits of a graphic style that is almost that of a medallist, the influences of Jacopo and Mantegna mingle with the persistent inspiration of Pisanello. Gentile's forms are flat, painted in very veiled tempera and with a palette of pale pinks and greys, softly reflected blues and whites. The artist is naturally drawn towards the portrait, whether he is outlining the chiselled profiles of the Doges (for instance that of Giovanni Mocenigo in the Museo Correr) or executing the most various and crowded portraits of Venice, with her bridges and palazzi, upper-floor loggias, chimneys, canals and quays, described with as much exhaustive minuteness as if they were human beings. This was the time when the Scuole of fraternities were modernizing their buildings, and a series of great mural decorations (on canvas, because fresco never lasts in Venice) now began. Gentile was the main artist involved with the Scuola di San Marco and the Scuola di San Giovanni Evangelista, making *teleri* a speciality of his (sometimes not of a very high quality either, particularly when they were completed by collaborators such as Bastiani or Mansueti). If we examine Gentile's contribution to one of these great pictorial undertakings — the *Legend of the True Cross* painted for San Giovanni Evangelista, now in the Accademia — we find an absolutely descriptive vision of Venice, a lucid literary prose with each phrase in its right place and beautifully expressed. From *fondamenta* to *fondamenta* on the Rio San Lorenzo, where the miracle takes place of the Cross falling into the water and being rescued (1496), from façade to façade of the red-

Alvise Vivarini: St Antony (c. 1485). Museo Correr. Among the masters of the end of the early Renaissance in Venice, Alvise Vivarini, a follower of Antonello da Messina, is outstanding for his crystalline limpidity.

(right) Lorenzo Lotto: Madonna (c. 1524). Museo Correr. Lorenzo Lotto, like Alvise Vivarini, was at first influenced by Antonello. Then as in this Madonna in the Correr, his work became sweeter and more painterly, and characteristically melancholy.

plastered Gothic palazzi, the space is static and lifeless; light is not really described, everything is subordinated to Bellini's insatiable desire to depict the rows of palazzi along the canals, the crowd of Caterina Cornaro's attendants, the portraits of the fraternities. Here we see a style of the highest graphic quality, which marks both the grandeur and the limitations of the last survivor of a world ordered according to vanished formal hierarchies.

In fact one need only compare Gentile's faded images with those which is young colleague Vittore Carpaccio (*c.* 1465-1526?) was painting at the same time and place. Carpaccio's *Miracle of the Cross,* in which a possessed man is being cured opposite the Rialto bridge, was painted when he was about thirty (*c.* 1495), and working alongside Bellini on the same series of paintings for San Giovanni Evangelista. But there is a gulf between the two artists' vision of Venice. Carpaccio's work concentrates on the play of colour, in an architectural space which distributes and accentuates the forms, setting things in their own special atmosphere. The freest fantasy replaces Gentile's documentary attitude, and the colour is organized on graded planes of light, obtaining a magical accord between abstract perspective and rational vision of reality. Carpaccio's language is unique in Venetian culture; at times there seems to be a hint of influences connected with Piero della Francesca. The *Portrait of the Man with a Red Beret,* in the Museo Correr, is an indication of the possible origin of Carpaccio's spatial vision in the art of Ferrara, which he might have actually seen on a visit, or known through the presence of De' Roberti in Venice. The combination of crystalline colour in the manner of Antonello and the spatial organization typical of Ferrara, derived from Piero, provided Carpaccio with the essence of his language: the obvious 'narrative' influence exerted by Gentile is in fact the least important element.

One of the numerous *scuole piccole* that arose in Venice in the Middle

Ages, for the purpose of social assistance and pious works, was the one dedicated to St Ursula. When it was suppressed on the fall of the Republic, its most precious possession was luckily preserved, kept in one of the loveliest rooms in the Accademia: the paintings by Carpaccio that decorated its walls. The building itself, mentioned in documents as being in the cemetery of the monks of San Zanipolo, next to the apses of the church, was long believed to have been destroyed. But a lucky observation in 1963 led to the recognition of the roof, which could be traced in the presbytery, subsequently built on top of the little Scuola (Renosto-Zampetti, 'La Cappella di

Campo Santa Maria Formosa. One of the most typical campi of the early Renaissance, with the restrained Palazzo Malipiero-Trevisan (upper left) and the church of Santa Maria Formosa, Codussi's masterpiece.

Sant'Orsola', *Bollettino dei Musei Civici Veneziani,* 1963). Surveys of the masonry structures have led to the discovery of the other outer walls of the Chapel, so that the present reconstruction in the Accademia corresponds perfectly to the original position of the paintings (except for the height above ground, which was slightly greater).

In 1490 Carpaccio began to paint the *Legend of St Ursula* in the small chapel. The legend of the Breton saint was one of the most popular in art, as can be seen from the many previous versions: from the fourteenth-century frescoes by Tommaso da Modena in Treviso, to the marvellous shrine painted by Memling, in the Hospital of St John

in Bruges. Among the various editions of the lives of the saints by Jacopo de Voragine was the magnificent Jenson edition of 1475, translated into vivid, naïve Italian by Nicolò Malerbi, and Carpaccio almost certainly had a copy of it at one time or another. He follows this text on the whole, adding a few variants probably inspired by his own imagination and sensitivity; the legend was a mere pretext, with its crowds, its narrative richness, its departures for distant lands; and the story of Hereus and Ursula proceeds like a great fancy-dress ball in the setting of the rich and gay fifteenth-century city.

The course of the story does not correspond to the dates in which the paintings were actually executed, probably because at first Carpaccio had only a limited amout of space available on the walls; these were cluttered up with the tombs of the Loredan family, which were successively removed from 1492 onwards, according to the school's *Matricula*. The story begins with the *Arrival of the Ambassadors* (*c.* 1500), who ask for Ursula as a bride for the English Prince Hereus. The princess, in her room, lays down her conditions: his baptism and a pilgrimage to Rome with eleven thousand handmaidens. We are at the Breton court, but the lagoon is dotted with sails and gondolas; the costumes of the noblemen, the very buildings (which are clearly based on those of Codussi), leave us in no doubt as to the locality that actually inspired the painter. *The Leave-taking of the Ambassadors,* too, with Kind Dionotus handing over Ursula's reply, takes place in a palace that could be the Doge's, with marble inlay on the walls in the style of the Lombardo family. The crowd upon the bridge and *fondamenta* in the *Return of the Ambassadors* to the English court is once again Venetian, multicoloured and noisy.

The richness of the costumes in the three canvases is extraordinary, and is made more remarkable by the unfailing attention to actual reality: the *Compagno della Calza* (in the centre of the *Arrival*) with the badge of the Compagnia degli Ortolani on his shoulder, and the dandified young men with their vacant gazes but carefully defined physiognomies, as though they were portraits; the interior of the *Leave-taking,* with the scribe writing intently as he is dictated to; or the details of the *Return,* with the Ducal chamberlain and little violinist, and the little monkey on the steps of the dais.

The Departure of the Betrothed Couple (*c.* 1495) is the largest canvas of the whole series, and represents a scene in two parts. On the left we see the English port, while Hereus is saying good-bye to his parents before joining Ursula in Brittany; in the background, a big ship moves off with a favourable wind, but on the sail, in reverse, we see the word *malo:* misfortune for Hereus, a journey without return (and on the base of the flag, in the centre, curls the scorpion, symbol of doom). On the right, we are in Ursula's father's kingdom, and the prince is just disembarking; this is the couple's first meeting, sealed in a long look. Beneath the arc of their joined hands we see the figure of an oarsman, standing still and gloomy, in a silence full of foreboding; slowly Ursula's companion averts her gaze. Further to the right, the engaged couple receive the king's embrace. In the background we see them embarking on the ships which will take them on their voyage to Rome. In the centre Carpaccio has put a standard with the arms of a

◁
Jacopo Sansovino: Apollo. Loggetta dal Campanile, San Marco.

P. 162/163
*Libreria Vecchia (1554), Piazzetta
San Marco. At the time of the
High Renaissance, in the 1530s,
Venice acquired a master: the
architect and sculptor Jacopo
Sansovino. The Libreria Vecchia
was his masterpiece.*

◁
*Scala dei Giganti (1556). Doge's
Palace. Among Sansovino's other
works for the triumphant
enhancement of the San Marco area
were those for the Doge's Palace:
the Scala d'Oro, and the reworking,
with the addition of the statues
of the two Giants, of Antonio
Rizzo's great staircase.*

noble family of Šibenik (Sebenico) in Dalmatia; it is not clear what he meant by this. Equally problematic are the two landscapes. On the left we are in a harbour with two great fortresses; on the right there is a vista of wonderful palazzi. The two fortresses have been identified, through engravings by Reeuwich in the *Peregrinatio* of Bishop Breydenbach, printed in Mainz in 1486, as the towers of Rhodes and Candia. The palazzi have echoes of the Cà d'Oro and a luminous but unidentifiable Renaissance Venetian building.

During the voyage to Rome, Ursula is forewarned of her martyrdom in a *Dream*. Very much cut at the top, the painting has less 'space' than the beautiful drawing in the Uffizi. On the window-sill, the myrtle and carnation symbolize marriage and love. The *Arrival in Rome* shows Ursula, Hereus and their retinue on their knees in front of Pope Cyriac, who receives the pilgrims outside Castel Sant'Angelo. This scene is probably one of the richest in portraits, with the Venetian humanist Ermalao Barbaro standing out in the centre. Castel Sant'Angelo had recently been restored, and perhaps Carpaccio copied it from the rather summary design on a medal struck by Pope Alexander III in 1495.

After the Pope (who was English by birth) and a number of bishops have also embarked, Ursula sets sail for the north, going up the Rhine and anchoring at Cologne, where she is besieged by the Huns. Surprised by the barbarian infidels, the pilgrims are all massacred. At the centre of the *Martyrdom* we see Ursula, who, after having rejected an offer of deliverance in exchange for marriage with the son of the king of the Huns, is transfixed by an arrow. A column divides the scene of the last episode from the *Funeral,* which seems to have been dictated by the wishes of the client, referred to in the coats of arms and portraits.

Deducing what we can from the dates appended to the paintings and from critical examination, it would seem that Carpaccio painted first the *Arrival at Cologne* (1490), then the *Arrival in Rome* (1491), the *Martyrdom* (1493), the *Departure of the Betrothed Couple* (1495), the *Dream* (1495) and last of all the three canvases with the Ambassadors. The legend of St Ursula thus occupied almost ten years in the working life of the artist, and they were the ten crucial years. Before this he had had only a brief period of influence by Antonello and the fortunate contact with Ferrara. Carpaccio travelled an

Cortile della Carità. Accademia. Andrea Palladio, the second great master architect — with Sansovino — of 16th-century Venice, was responsible for San Giorgio, the Redentore, and the restoration of the Doge's Palace after the fire of 1574. In 1561 he had already worked on the Convento della Carità, of which this luminous courtyard façade, in the Accademia, remains.

enormous distance between the *Arrival at Cologne* — that scene in the style of a northern miniature which opens into an endless succession of towers above the greenish water, where the ships float like nut-shells dropped by children — and the *Ambassadors*. In the earliest painting, the painter's narrative vein is revealed in forms which are little more than infantile. Is this a war scene, a dramatic presage of death? And here a reflection in the water under the drawbridge, a bit of green moss clinging to the pink brick, is enough to distract Carpaccio: he is carried away by the passionate detail of his beloved Flemish masters, and all dramatic discourse, all the spatial value of the colours, are confused and lost.

The real Carpaccio appears only in the *Martyrdom,* set against a dramatically diminishing row of great trees in a wood. Here for the first time we have a scene with the Venetian bourgeoisie as its protagonist, painted by its most impassioned and reliable observer: crowds of people, in precise but relaxed poses, filling a landscape that is theatrical but accurate in its detail, beneath a very carefully painted light, which defines the plastic projections in the forms with surprising emphasis. The vitality of Carpaccio's story-telling triumphs in the great scene of the *Departure*. It does not matter whether the characters who accompany Hereus and his father are the Loredan, who commissioned the pictures, or not; the heeling ship, and the other ship unfurling its sails, the crowd on the shores and the onlookers on the bridge and terrace, are all actors in a co-ordinated and extremely lively game, the magical expression of a world transfigured into the symbol of humming, prosperous fifteenth-century Venice.

Perhaps this was another link with Ferrara and the Flemish masters, and with that absolutely original vision which Carpaccio had absorbed from the brilliant court frescoes at the Palazzo Schifanoia. One need only compare the parades and ceremonies by the other painters who were decorating the rooms in the Doge's Palace and the Scuola di San Giovanni Evangelista at this time: Gentile Bellini, Bastiani, Mansueti. Carpaccio's bourgeois have a vitality that sets them quite apart from the puppet-like figures of Gentile (not to mention lesser painters), locked in their stiffly painted outlines against a cardboard background, without any real spatial depth but distorted in an attempt at perspective that is little more than medieval.

For Carpaccio, however, the eye moves in a completely controlled space, with definite distances, where the single details are always entirely vital and precise. The emergence of his chromatic language was determined by a similar process, in forms completely independent of the Venetian tradition but closer to the colour-light synthesis of the Tuscans and northerners. Drawn from Antonello da Messina, already oriented towards crystalline clarity and plasticity, even in the *Departure* Carpaccio's colour takes on local values in each touch, brought out with a precise, almost startling vibration. The people walking along the footbridge of the harbour are faceted prisms offering themselves to the light, so that it may draw brilliant, ringing notes of colour from them: reds, deep blues, greens, intense yellows. In short, this was the birth of a new language of colour, which arose in Venice side by side, and in contrast, with that of Giovanni Bellini. It is by no means a sensual language; it is foreign to any lyrical 'musicality', any veiled quality. On the contrary, it is completely defined, quantitatively measurable.

The essence of Carpaccio's achievement is that he never neglected the

Vittore Carpaccio: The Departure of St Ursula (c. 1495). Accademia. Working in the period of Venice's greatest splendour, Carpaccio often reflects the Republic's seafaring traditions.

rigour of spatial articulation in favour of chromatic effect. Indeed, throughout his career, his concern about the spatial setting of his figures deepened, as he pursued the most surprisingly accurate perspective.

The finest example of his incredible capacity to 'specify', which produces a world that is supremely 'real' but transcends any intention of actually portraying reality, is to be found in the *Arrival of the Ambassadors*. On the left one can see the foreshortened arches of the portico, with the moulding of the marble exposed to the merciless light: one can enumerate every detail, every dimension with absolute certainty. Look at the iron railings, with their brilliant play of shadows: one hundred sun-dials marking the passing of time on the floor of the king's house. Look at the iron gate, open towards us and foreshortened with such precision that we could calculate its

Antonello Da Messina: Pietà. Museo Correr. This is the only work by Antonello now in Venice; he lived here in 1475-76.

exact dimensions: we could even close it to perfection, because below we are shown the bit of carving that will tally with the moulding of the cornice of the pillar. It is a clear-cut design, technical even: it could be handed over to the craftsman for immediate execution.

Carpaccio's interest in architecture, so rare in his time, possibly even unique among his Venetian colleagues, was probably rooted in that early acquaintance with Tuscan cultural circles where architectural themes were part of an ideal geometry fundamental to the spiritual make-up of men of culture. Nor should one forget that Carpaccio's was a very special architecture, because of Venetian ideas of space: architecture that was mirrored by the water, that thrived on reflections, that drew expressive values from the atmosphere of colour which surrounded it. In fact, towards the end of the St Ursula paintings, about 1500, Carpaccio's language could increasingly be defined as a synthesis of perspective drawing and typically Venetian colour.

Gentile Bellini: Miracle of the Cross at San Lorenzo (1496-1500). Bellini has no equal in the depiction of Venetian life, as in the three canvases of the series of the Cross in the Scuola San Giovanni Evangelista.

Golden Age: the Sixteenth Century

The year 1500: Venice was humming, brimming with wealth, intent on celebrating her own glorious triumph. Yet the times, in trade and politics, were not entirely favourable. The Portuguese had discovered the route to the Indies and their ships were circumnavigating Africa, cutting Venice's share of the trade with the Orient; in Venice there was even talk of making a canal through the Suez isthmus, an undertaking that was to be realized only three centuries later. Meanwhile, the great nation states were growing up in Europe, and Venice had to pick her way cautiously through the shifting sands of Italian politics. When Charles VIII of France came down into the peninsula, the Doge managed to profit from the defeat of his own allies and extended his rule over the cities of Apulia, at the other end of the Adriatic. In the division of the kingdom of Aragon, Venice also seized

*Giorgione: La Tempesta
(c. 1508). Accademia Gem of
the great Venetian painting
collection, La Tempesta was
the first painting to achieve a
poetic harmony between
nature and man.*

other cities in the Marches, from Urbino to Rimini, but unleashed the wrath of the Pope, the warlike Julius II. In 1508 the League of Cambrai united half Europe and almost all the Italian States, urged on by the Pope, against Venice. But fortune was on the side of the Republic, which, despite repeated defeats on the mainland, maintained her position at sea and gradually recovered her dominions as far as the borders of Lombardy. She manoeuvred equally skilfully with the Turks and defended her eastern trading-posts.

But the cultural vitality of the city did not falter amid these difficulties: indeed, the beginning of the new century heralded ever greater triumphs. There were numerous printers, from Jenson to Aldus Manutius, who printed the Greek and Roman classics, Aristotle and the Arabian commentators, Dante, Petrarch, the lives of the

Palazzo dei Camerlenghi (1525-28), Rialto. Built by Guglielmo Bergamasco, its white elegance sets off the curve in the Grand Canal near the Ponte Rialto.

Saints, Bembo's *Asolani,* the *Hypnerotomachia Poliphili* with its enchanting woodcuts. Venetian city life also showed a particular tendency to produce 'philosophers', mostly very young, and coming from the main patrician families, who joined the masters of the Studio in Padua, the old university that had now completely entered into the political and spiritual orbit of San Marco. This sophisticated cultural development, though it remained an élite phenomenon, did have noticeable effects on social customs, contributing to the formation of intellectual 'clubs' which often embarked on important artistic under-takings; it encouraged the forming of very considerable collections, particularly of antiquities, for instance that of the Grimani prelates (still partly preserved in the Museo Archeologico), and directly affected the culture of the artists themselves, encouraging them towards genuinely novel themes, and sometimes even towards affectation: we

see this in the young Giorgione and some of his contemporaries, for instance Palma Vecchio and Titian himself.

As far as individual buildings and the shape of the city generally were concerned, the activities of the sixteenth century were extremely important and often decisive. They were probably carried out with some degree of general planning, though no traces of this have been found in documents; however, we can reconstruct it at least approximately, for the benefit of the visitor intending to follow the history of Venice's golden century.

There seems no doubt that the beginning of the sixteenth century witnessed a shift of emphasis to the commercial centre, Rialto. In 1514 — as Vasari records — Frà Giocondo planned a restructuring of Rialto, conceived of as an extensive market area served by canals. From the first decade, the *proto* (this was the name given in Venice to architects with organizational powers in certain sectors) Giorgio Spavento was working on Rialto, and it was probably he who had the idea of erecting big buildings in the 'modern' style by the Ponte di Rialto (a wooden bridge in those days, as it appears in Carpaccio's painting in the Accademia).

The first of these, based on his own designs, was the German trading centre, the Fondaco dei Tedeschi, built on the ruins of an earlier building between 1505 and 1508. This was a grandiose palazzo with a ground-floor gallery and three stories, on a square plan, around a central courtyard. Oddly enough, the traditional Venetian loggias are here on the inside, looking on to the courtyard; they decrease in size towards the top, emphasizing the verticality of the building.

Undoubtedly the main attraction of the Fondaco is the façade on the Grand Canal. Here in 1508, in the broad panels between the windows, Giorgione, the new genius of sixteenth-century Venetian painting, painted a series of allegorical frescoes which were described as one of the wonders of the city even in his own time. Then, in 1509, on the landward façade looking over the *calle,* Titian provided other allegorical representations and a figure of Justice above the main door. Contemporary reports registered the enormous success of this decoration, and there were many other similar ones, on private palazzi in the various *sestieri* of the city. Unfortunately almost all of them have disappeared, corroded by salt and damp. Anyone wishing to gain some idea of so many lost masterpieces can only go by the descriptions and the few eighteenth-century engravings which show the state of the remaining paintings (Zanetti, *Delle Pitture veneziane a Fresco,* 1760). A *Nude* by Giorgione, removed when it was already a mere ghost of its former self, is preserved in the Accademia: there is still a mysterious power in its warm brushstrokes of flaming red and its deep shadows. Long forgotten, Titian's *Justice* also re-emerged several years ago from the smoke-blackened wall of the Fondaco, but the still discernible outlines need to be filled in with the colourful images which are so familiar to us from others of his works, so that we can conjure up the intense, violent chromatic values which the young artist would undoubtedly have used here; only eighteen years old, he was already competing with his master Giorgione, preparing to succeed him after his early death from plague in 1510.

◁

Nicolò de Conti: Detail of Well-head (1556). Doge's Palace. The work of a master gunsmith, it was influenced by the expressive Sansovinian style.

Well-head (16th century).
San Giovanni Crisostomo.

(below) Loggetta del Campanile,
San Marco. Intended to house the
Doge's guard, the Loggetta was
constructed by Sansovino between
1537 and 1549, and decorated by
him with bronze statues of Minerva,
Apollo, Mercury and Peace, and
with numerous reliefs. His
terracotta Madonna is inside.

Meanwhile the rebuilding of Rialto was going ahead, with the build-ing of the nearby church of San Salvador, an impressive work also designed by Spavento (1507) and completed by Sansovino. It is a church of truly monumental proportions, partly because it stands on a tall flight of steps which made possible the building of a crypt. Here the massive scale of the arches of San Marco seems to reappear, evoked in the 'modern' style beneath the three round domes arranged longitudinally in the nave, giving a powerful sense of concentrated space. Next to the church were two cloisters, now only partly visible because of recent alterations.

Naturally, in the designs of the various Venetian *proti,* this general plan for renewal included a project for the rebluilding of the Ponte di Rialto. Indeed, from the first, development proceded as though the new bridge already existed: this produced a line of development westwards, beyond the Grand Canal in the direction of the *sestiere* of San Polo. This was the context for the building of the Fabbriche Vecchie di Rialto (the work of the *proto* Antonio Scarpagnino, from 1520 onwards) which run along the Ruga degli Orefici, which was

Alessandro Vittoria: Doge Antonio da Ponte (c. 1585). Seminario. One of the great sculptors of the second half of the 16th century, Vittoria rivals his contemporary Tintoretto in his play of light.

(below) Palazzo delle Prigioni, San Marco. Prison building, the work of Rusconi, finished by Da Ponte and Contino in 1614.

also to be on the axis of the bridge. Along the left-hand side and part of the right, including the little old church of San Giacomo di Rialto, they constituted a major complex of public buildings. On the Grand Canal, to the left of the Bridge, was the Palazzo dei Dieci Savi, the tax office; on the Campo di Rialto, near the church, was the palazzo housing the officials dealing with trade, navigation and food supplies. The square still has the arcade of the Banco Giro, so-called because of the banking operations which took place there. The Signoria had proclamations read by its heralds from the adjacent column of the Banco; the figure of the dwarf holding up the flight of steps is popularly called *el Gobo de Rialto,* the Hunchback of Rialto: his name, like that of Pasquin in Rome, was used as a pseudonyn by the authors of satires and epigrams attacking well-known figures or public officials. Naturally, as today, the district round the Fabbriche Vecchie was also a market, and the teeming stalls of the Erberia and Naranzeria filled it with colour and movement.

The area towards the Grand Canal, behind the church of San Giacomo, was gradually brought into the sixteenth-century plans for the rebuilding

Sala del Senato. Doge's Palace. Reconstructed after the five of 1574, it was decorated Tintoretto (Pietà above the throne) and by Palma Giovane. The sumptuous golded cornices are by Cristoforo Sorte (1581).

of Rialto. The white Palazzo dei Camerlenghi (1525-28) was built next to the bridge, a building in the style of Codussi, by his follower and successor Guglielmo dei Grigi. More ornate than the others, with its beautifully designed windows and polychrome marble inlay, it follows the curve of the canal; it has several façades, all of which are equally ornate, implying that the architect was already conscious of the function the building was to assume within the city. Further along, also looking on to the canal, Sansovino completed the plan with the Fabbriche Nuove (*c.* 1555), following the scheme of the previous ones, but with greater nobility in the design of the beautiful windows (with tympanums) and solidly constructed façade, squared into panels with pilasters and cornices above the rusticated ground floor. The final touch was the new Ponte di Rialto, a stone bridge by the *proto* Antonio da Ponte (1588-91), whose design was chosen from several plans including one by Palladio, considered too classical.

The rebuilding of Rialto was certainly precipitated by urgent functional needs — the extension of the public offices most closely connected with Venice's growing economic activity and success — and San Marco, the political centre, inevitably had to be brought up to date too, completing the work begun by Codussi with the Torre dell'

Sala del Collegio. Doge's Palace. Reconstructed after the fire of 1574; ceiling by Paolo Veronese. The painting above the throne, The Victory of Lepanto, is by Paolo; the other canvases are by Tintoretto and his assistants.

Orologio and the design for the *Procuratie Vecchie*. These were extended to two storeys high by Guglielmo dei Grigi as far as the end of the Piazza, with curving arcades so that they joined the church of San Gemignano. At the same time the Campanile was restored, and in 1513 the pyramid-shaped belfry was added, in place of the previous flat, octagonal one. On top, a gilded angel showed the direction of the wind to the Venetian galleys.

But the really decisive phase for San Marco began with the arrival of Jacopo Sansovino (1486-1570) whom recent research has identified as the real force behind sixteenth-century Venetian town-planning (Tafuri, *Jacopo Sansovino,* Padua 1969). Driven from Rome when the city was sacked in 1527, the Tuscan architect was received in Venice by Aretino, a man of letters who played an important part in the city's life and culture. In 1529 he was already *proto* of San Marco, with the charge of restoring the dangerous domes. His first success was to secure their structures with chains, a brilliant technical solution. Meanwhile the ruling class had initiated the typically early sixteenth-century policy of trying to accredit the myth of a Venice that was heir to the wisdom and power of the ancients. This brought with it the need to go beyond the traditional schemes, as they had developed

181

Detail of mantel.
Anticollegio, Doge's Palace.

(below) Jacopo Tintoretto:
Crucifixion (1565). Scuola
di San Rocco. Tintoretto's
fame is principally due to
the canvases in the Scuola
di San Rocco, painted
between 1564 and 1588.
The Crucifixion
was one of the first.

since the middle of the fifteenth century, which were orderly and
functional but possibly too discreet. These were to be replaced by a
'learned version' which would embody the demands of a state architecture. The Romano-Tuscan architect Sansovino, with his vast classicizing experience, could hardly have been more suitable.
In the first years Sansovino went through a sort of trial period,

Jacopo Tintoretto: Bacchus and Ariadne (1578). Anticollegio, Doge's Palace. One of the four canvases he painted for this room.

working mainly for clients of the aristocracy and fraternities; this was the period of the Scuola della Misericordia and of the Palazzo Corner at the end of the Grand Canal (1532). This magnificent building, though undeniably a direct continuation, in volume and decoration, of Codussi's later works (Vendramin-Calergi), was in other respects a total contradiction of them. Sansovino, sensing the will of his clients, set out

to create a monumental, rhetorical mechanism suited to symbolizing their boundless ambitions; luckily, his innate tendency to resolve surfaces in painterly nuclei of chiaroscuro enabled him to sink roots easily in the traditional Venetian substratum.

Sansovino's real period as a 'state architect' began with his commission, about 1536, for the Libreria: a building destined to house the gift of ancient manuscripts that Cardinal Bessarion had made to the Republic. At the same time, Sansovino had probably already been commissioned to build the Zecca (Mint) and the Loggetta. At this point, he had decisive powers over the planning of the whole of the new Piazza di San Marco, which was to be his triumph as an artist and was to enshrine the myth of Venice in architecture.

Clearly, Sansovino saw the Piazza as the 'forum of San Marco', to be built as the ancient Romans had built their imperial forums (Lodz, 'La Libreria di San Marco', in *Bollettino del Centro Palladiano,* 1961). Consequently, he tended to organize the architectural prospect as though it were scenery, adjusting the dimensions of his buildings with this aim in mind. It was he who had the brilliant idea of broadening the Piazza, pushing back the old Alberghi Orseolo and thus isolating the Campanile, which thus constituted a positive 'pivot' between Piazzetta and Piazza. Also in the Piazzetta, on a line set well back opposite the Doge's Palace, he then designed the Libreria (built between 1537 and 1554, as far as the sixteenth bay). A second vista was thus created, with the Torre dell'Orologio as its vanishing point, the Mercerie its axis and the two columns on the Molo as its entrance. It is probable that Sansovino had planned to continue the Libreria round so as to have frontage on to the Basin, the Bacino di San Marco (where he was also building the Mint), to balance the mass of the Doge's Palace. But the Libreria was actually completed by Vincenzo Scamozzi, who grafted it in an absurd fashion into the fabric of the Mint, staggering floor and elements as though he wanted to condemn the empiricism of his predecessor.

The Libreria Marciana, or the Libreria Vecchia, as it came to be called, is a building of extraordinary significance for the face of sixteenth-century Venice. Here, too, Sansovino used the emphatically Roman motifs that enabled him to realize those gigantic forms which his clients more or less openly expected of him. With its references to famous Roman buildings (the arches of the Theatre of Marcellus) the Libreria was the masterpiece of the 'state classicism' that the ruling class expected of its very own architect.

But Sansovino's willingness to carry out state policy did not mean that he had to stifle his own particular genius; this lay in an ability to assimilate just enough of the Venetian tradition for his buildings to take their place, without jarring, within the late Roman and Gothic traditions pre-existing in the Piazza, with the golden San Marco and the Doge's Palace. This was an inspired success, made possible

▷

Campanile di San Marco, and Libreria Vecchia.

(below) San Giorgio Maggiore. By Palladio. 16th century Venice was the pivotal time for innovation in the area of San Marco, from the works of Sansovino in the Piazza to the spirited creations of Palladio around the Basin.

P. 186/87
The Ponte di Rialto and the Ponte dei Sospiri, both built in the late 16th century (see p. 188).

by Sansovino's sensitivity in combining scenic values with the highly pictorial ones triumphant in the chiaroscuro of the double loggia of the Libreria and concluded by the luxuriant cornice of foliage and the airy terrace which corresponded to the cresting of the Ducal Palace opposite. This picturesque play of light and shade, distinctly mannerist in tone, does in fact harmonize with the linearity of the surrounding buildings and helps to make the Piazzetta one of the most serenely perfect decorative achievements of Italian town-planning.

Of this vision, as Tafuri rightly points out, the Loggetta was born, standing beneath the Campanile in a position apparently extraneous to the rigorous scenic layout, so as to find justification as a single object, like a piece of furniture, in which the artist could once again demonstrate

Rialto. The centre of the city's commercial life, the Rialto underwent radical transformations in the 16th century. The most extensive was the replacement of the old wooden bridge by Da Ponte's stone one (1588-91).

his faithfulness to the official myth of Venice. The glory of the
Republic is the theme of the reliefs and statues standing in the niches
of the various elements of the graceful construction, with an insistence
that sometimes approaches architectural absurdity. This complex of
allegories is another decisive factor in Sansovino's overall vision, which,
towards the beginning of the sixteenth century, was completely changing the face of the most important part of the city.

Meanwhile, it was Sansovino who suggested other additions to inte-
riors, also around San Marco: in 1555, the staircase and hall of the
Libreria; in 1557 the Scala d'Oro in the Doge's Palace; in 1566 the
Giants on the great staircase named after them, the Scala dei Giganti.
These were always allegorical additions and creations extolling the

Titian: St John the Baptist (mid-16th century). Accademia.
Titian was supreme in mid-16th century Venice. This work reveals
his fullest powers as a colourist.

Republic, further confirming the singular position of this great
architect in the history of the city. The pictorial cycles of the Hall of
the Libreria, by the greatest painters of the later sixteenth century,
celebrate the meeting of Philosophy with Science, and Ethics with Re-
ligion, within the ideal framework offered them by Venice. In the
vestibule, below the staircase, we see Titian's *Wisdom,* and in the hall,
between the ceiling cornices designed by Sansovino with a remarkable
use of perspective, we find *tondi* by Veronese (Song, Music, Honour);
the walls, originally bare, were subsequently decorated with paintings
of the *Philosophers,* mainly by Tintoretto.

The Scala d'Oro is one of the most sumptuous monuments of sixteenth-century Venice; it was intended to give ceremonial access to
the hall of the Collegio and Senate, mainly for illustrious visitors to the
Signoria. Sansovino designed it for theatrical effect, with dramatic

Tintoretto: The Creation of the Animals. Detail. Accademia. The Accademia houses many of Tintoretto's works. Among the most impressive is this lively painting.

perspectives along the steps and landings. The decoration in stucco and gold, by Vittoria, with small fresco panels by G. B. Franco, has a single theme: the exaltation of the power of the Republic on sea and mainland, combining figures from the Old Testament with mythology, ancient history and medieval religious allegory.

The two statues of the Giants, which Sansovino designed in a highly theatrical style for the terrace of the Scala dei Giganti, are part of this same orgy of glorification. With their powerful bulk thrust into Rizzo's slight design, they strain the delicate early Renaissance architecture almost unbearably; but they help to concentrate the optical focus of the vista on to the staircase, visible right from the Piazza through the Arco Foscari, to emphasize the place where the Doge would appear in all his pomp at the main ceremonies.

A calculated theatricality thus guided the planning of sixteenth-century

Paolo Veronese: Mystic Marriage of St Katherine. Accademia.
Compared with Titian and Tintoretto, Veronese is a decorative painter,
with a cool and luminous palette.

Venice, and imposed particular rules on the architects who agreed
to interpret it. In a marginal but no less important sector of activity
we find the Veronese, Michele Sammicheli (1484-1559), who was
commissioned to design the fortifications of the harbour (the Fort of
Sant'Andrea is still in existence) and of many of the islands ruled by
the Republic in eastern seas, including Crete and Corfu. Sammicheli
brought a stock of Roman ideas with him to Venice, clearly visible
in the powerful rustication and tiers of arches of the Fort of Sant'Andrea. But in the few palazzi he was commissioned to design he
accpted the traditional Venetian formula, adapting himself with some

flexibility to the formal patterns of the city. Here we must mention his extremely original Palazzo Corner Mocenigo, which occupies a vast area between the Rio di San Polo and the very beautiful Campo di San Polo: the façade on the Rio marks the appearance of the characteristic rusticated basement which was to feature in most baroque palazzi. In the Palazzo Grimani too, on the Grand Canal, in Rialto, Sammicheli bore in mind his Roman origins, developing archaeological motifs manneristically in the linked and repeated series of triumphal arches, set within a massive frame of pillars.

Unlike Sansovino, Sammicheli never became a town-planner, nor did he make a really important mark on the face of the city. The same fate, almost inexplicably, befell the greatest architect to work in Venice in the sixteenth century, Andrea Palladio (1508-80). This famous Paduan arrived in Venice when he was already launched in his career, after having produced various experimental buildings in Vicenza (Basilica, Palazzo Chiericati) and villas in the Veneto (from Lonedo to the Villa Foscari known as the Malcontenta). His ideas were now clearly moving away from Sansovino's scenic classicism, developing with a mannerist freedom and typically Venetian concern for colour, so much so that he surpassed the Tuscan-Roman mastery of volume and perspective. The forms he created were thus projected into the Venetian countryside or into urban contexts with a sort of abstraction, as though flaunting their flawlessness.

It is clear that such an architectural vision could ill adapt itself to *raisons d'état* as they were put to Venetian builders at the time, nor is it surprising that, as a result, Palladio's activities were somewhat restricted, even marginal. To our modern sensibility, however, they do seem extremely significant, so that it is certainly worth tracking them down where they are still intact. The first Palladian plan in the city was connected with the alteration of the interior of the Convento della Carità (now the Gallerie dell'Accademia). Here Palladio built the wing which looks on to the Rio terrà Marco Foscarini, opening the central section on to the courtyard with a façade in brick, of extraordinary chromatic charm and softness. In the interior, a room with niches *(tablinum)* flanks a stupendous oval spiral staircase with an open well, one of those characteristic pure 'objects' which are the most marvellous things in Palladio's work.

In 1559 Palladio went to the island of San Giorgio Maggiore opposite San Marco, and there rebuilt the first cloister and refectory, with a wonderful and mysterious subtlety in the use of light. But Palladio's genius emerged above all in the church of San Giorgio Maggiore itself, completely rebuilt over the small existing Gothic church. Begun in 1566, it bears the stamp of its creator particularly in the light-filled interior, left completely empty at the crossing under the dome like the spacious hall of some private villa. The chancel is particularly lovely: here Palladio's singular graphic virtuosity created cornices, capitals and windows of great poetic tension, set within a spacious framework full of typically mannerist echoes and gradations of light and colour. Palladio's last masterpieces in Venice are the churches of the Zitelle and the Redentore on the island of the Giudecca. The Redentore, the goal of the Venetians' thanksgiving pilgrimage on the third Sunday in July, in memory of the plague of 1576, seems to personify the poetic lightness of Palladian structures. The façade is reminiscent of so many Palladian villas on the surrounding mainland, with the great staircases leading up to the entrance floor. The geometry of the façade, which gives an almost two-dimensional outline of the structure

Church of Redentore. Designed by Andrea Palladio in 1577, this church is his most elaborate and perfect work in Venice.

(right) Church of San Sebastiano, ceiling (1556). This ceiling is Palladian in style, magnificent paintings by Veronese.

of the interior, is of a limpid solemnity; inside, the single nave, ending with the three-niched presbytery with a late Romanesque air about it, is given a particular softness by the melodious, vibrant light that falls on it, reminiscent of the older architectural traditions of the city.

Though not part of an official state programme of town-planning, the three Palladian churches of San Giorgio, the Zitelle and the Redentore do emerge as elements in an intentional play of volumes vis-à-vis the rest of the Basin of San Marco. Set opposite San Marco, the church of San Giorgio, with its white façade and great dome, is a perfect pendant for the beautifully balanced buildings on the other side of the Basin; while the two landmarks on the Giudecca, to the west, are plainly intended to conclude the whole. As we shall see, Longhena was a later interpreter of this vision of Palladio's and was to complete the charmed circle with his stupendous Baroque church of the Salute.

In 1574 a first fire seriously threatened the centre of the town, attacking the Doge's Palace, where Henry III of France had been entertained that same year. Part of the Doge's apartment was destroyed, and with it the rooms of the Collegio and Senate. Three years later, in 1577, another fire destroyed the part looking on to the Molo and Piazzetta, with the Sala del Maggior Consiglio and Sala dello Scrutinio (where votes were counted), which had the marvellous fifteenth century pictorial cycles of frescoes and canvases.

The Venetians did not quail in the face of disaster. A host of illustrious architects were commissioned to report to the Doge on the state of the Palace and the steps to be taken for its restoration. Palladio's report was very pessimistic and suggested the possibility of a complete reconstruction of the façade; there was talk of blocking up the arches and loggias. Luckily for Venice, the conservative viewpoint

◁

Façade (1549). Scuola Grande di San Rocco. An ornate and unacademic design by Abbondi and others.

Paolo Veronese: Martyrdom of St Sebastian. Church of San Sebastiano.

prevailed and the palace was rebuilt where and as it had been, by the *proto* Antonio Rusconi.

An engraving by Vecellio of 1590 documents the state of the court-yard: on the right the Doge's palace appears entirely rebuilt, with the Sala del Collegio and Sala del Senato above; on the left, we see the massive building which houses the Sala dello Scrutinio. In the background, on the left, the outdoor staircase next to the Arco Foscari was to remain for another few years, then to be replaced by an indoor staircase leading directly to the Scrutinio. In the background, on the right behind the Scala dei Giganti, we see a small courtyard, the Cortile dei Senatori, with the elegant little façade by Rizzo and Pietro Lombardo, ending with a hanging garden by Scarpagnino

▷

Monstrous head (17th century). Campanile of Santa Maria Formosa.

Façade (1683). Santa Maria del Giglio.

dating from about the middle of the century. In the seventeenth century the *proto* Monopola was to attempt to give the whole ground floor gallery some kind of stylistic unity, continuing it under the west building as well the south, under the Maggior Consiglio.

The decoration of the newly restored rooms was entrusted to the major artists of the time, from Palladio himself to Vittoria, Tintoretto and Paolo Veronese. Il was thus, as far as the interiors were concerned, an entirely new palace that emerged toward the end of the century, when after completing the great *Paradise,* Tintoretto gave Venice back her renewed Maggior Consiglio. Luckily, the present-day visitor can still see almost all the works that were in the Palace at that time. One of the most remarkable of these is the Sala del Collegio, whose ceiling was almost entirely painted by Paolo Veronese, between 1574 and 1577: here the symbols of eight *Virtues* surround the three central panels, with a most memorable representation of *Venice Victorious,* placed above the throne where the Doge used to appear with the Signoria. On the other walls are more paintings by Veronese: Doge Sebastiano Venier is portrayed with a view of the Battle of Lepanto, when the Venetian fleet gave decisive assistance in the defeat of the Turks (1572).

Other rooms still have masterpieces dating from the time of the

▷

Palazzo da Lezze (17th century). Rio della Misericordia.

reconstruction after the fire: the Sala del Senato, with the great *Pietà* by Tintoretto between Doges Lando and Trevisan, above the Doge's throne; the Sala del Consiglio dei Dieci, with the ceiling by Veronese (the central painting of *Jove* is in the Louvre and is replaced by a copy); the Sala del Maggior Consiglio with the *Triumph of Venice* by Veronese, Tintoretto's *Paradise* and a very fine series of historical paintings by these same masters and their assistants; the Vicentino, Aliense and Tintoretto *(Battle of Zara)*.

In these same years, from 1563, G. A. Rusconi and Antonio da Ponte began work on the small palazzo of the Nuove Prigioni, the state prisons, next to the Doge's Palace, with a massive rusticated façade, an allusion to its function being seen in the enormous barred windows. Towards the end of the century, Antonio Contino linked the prisons to the Palace with an overhead passage given a melancholy fame by its popular name of Ponte dei Sospiri, Bridge of Sighs, in memory of the unfortunate prisoners who passed across it on their way to judgment.

As we have seen, much of the activity of the Venetian painters of the sixteenth century complemented the extraordinary outburst of architectural production that was changing the face of the city. The Venetian school of painting was reaching unparalleled heights, and, with its own very definite character and the extraordinary personalities who composed it, was pre-eminent in Italy. Even today, the visitor to Venice can see many of the fruits of all this activity on the spot, since many pictorial cycles, as well as many single important works, remain as evidence.

It has been said that Venice, at the beginning of the century, was a 'painted city'; we are told this by the writers on art who went there, starting with the Tuscan Giorgio Vasari, who wrote the most important work on the lives of the artists. The frescoes of Giorgione and Titian, exposed to salt and damp, have unfortunately disappeared, except for the few remains in the Fondaco dei Tedeschi. Recently, the remains of the stupendous frescoes of Pordenone have been removed from the walls of the cloister of Sant'Agnello; a few other badly damaged frescoes can be seen on palazzi along the Grand Canal (for instance near San Stae), but they too are doomed to be destroyed by the corrosive action of atmospheric pollution and other factors. Interior frescoes are less vulnerable, though they too have been exposed to numerous dangers.

One of the greatest pictorial cycles of the sixteenth century that has recently been rescued and restored is the marvellous series of frescoes and canvases by Paolo Veronese (1528-88) in San Sebastiano, a small church which is more or less his own personal museum and includes works from his youthful period (sacristy 1555) to his maturity (ceiling, frescoes of the choir, *c.* 1560) and canvases in the presbytery (1570). A visit to San Sebastiano makes up for many other works destroyed or carried off to the main galleries of the world. Here Veronese's style found its perfect formulation. The aim of his painting was not the idyllic representation of reality, as with Titian or Bassano, nor its visionary transfiguration, it was the exaltation of an abundance of energy and joy. One need only look at the ceiling to feel all the rapture of Veronese's world. The young Esther goes up into a colonnaded portico reminiscent of the Palladian Rotunda, dressed in the most joyous hues ever seen in Venice, in a bright, clear range of colour absolutely characteristic of Veronese. The juxtaposition of shades, the transparency of the shadows, the brilliantly organized composition,

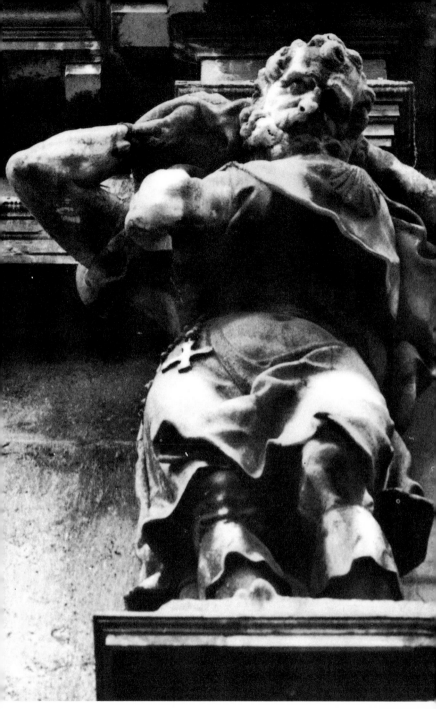

Josse Le Court: Detail of façade, Church of Ospedaletto (c. 1689).
San Zanipolo. Built to a ground plan by Longhena this has one of the most
animated Baroque façades in Venice.

create an unforgettable effect, resonant and luminous. His technique
played an important part in this: it transcends both Titianesque
tonality (the harmonious fusion of colours) and Tintoretto's and
Bassano's luminosity (which can roughly be described as an exaltation
of the values of light contrasting with dark, giving an effect, ultimately,
of white on black). Anticipating modern theories of the decompo-
sition of light, Veronese instinctively discovered the increase in

luminosity deriving from the juxtaposition of two complementary colours. In this way his reds and blues, yellows and violets create on the canvas a myriad faceted planes of light, with an extraordinary effect of unreality and intensity. Local colours take on reflections of the colours that are next to them: black is abolished, and the shadows are coloured, so that luminosity is greater than that of reality itself.

Meanwhile, side by side with Veronese, the parallel but stylistically contrasted personality of Tintoretto (1518-94) was emerging in Venice, at his creative peak in the seventh decade of the century. He painted the three episodes of the *Life of St Mark* (now in the Brera)

for the Scuola di San Marco in a dynamic style using the freest mannerist forms. For the Madonna dell'Orto in Venice he created the complex canvases of the *Last Judgment* and the *Adoration of the Golden Calf,* with a conscious striving for effect which sometimes degenerates into theatricality, but also produces moments of great figurative vitality. In 1564 he decorated the Scuola di San Rocco, a commission he secured by a virtual trick which won him the competition in which Veronese, Schiavone, Salviati and Zuccari also took part (i.e. presenting his work to the Scuola).

The Scuola Grande di San Rocco, with its huge walls entirely covered

◁
Church of Madonna degli Scalzi (1689), Ferrovia. The former church of the barefoot friars, at the steamboat station, was built on Longhena's plan, and has an extremely rich interior, decorated with Baroque sculptures and frescoes by Tiepolo (18th century). The Madonna on the façade (above) is attributed to Falcone.

by paintings of scriptural scenes, was to be the most exciting adventure of his life and was to occupy him until 1587. The paintings include many masterpieces of Tintoretto's symphonic sensitivity and religious feeling, almost always kept at a high level of inner tension. These paintings in San Rocco are in a way secret and intimate; here he worked alone, without help from his now flourishing workshop (in the charge mainly of his children Marietta, Marco and Domenico, and of his son-in-law).

One particularly remarkable painting in San Rocco is the *Crucifixion* in the Sala dell'Albergo, a mighty, organic composition of 1565, in which the complex vision of space moves dizzily into the pyramid-shaped groups occupying the scene. The colour is deep and vibrant

Cà Pesaro. A gem of Baroque Venetian architecture, it was begun by Longhena and completed by Gaspari at the beginning of the 18th century.

under the flickering lights, with a moving, almost expressionist quality. In the paintings of the Salone Superiore (1576-81), Tintoretto stresses the feeling of dynamism, to the point of giving Christ in the garden a simultaneous vision of the various episodes, in their connected and successive unfolding, with a movement that has an extraordinarily vivid narrative effect. While Christ prays in the garden under a reddish light, the apostles are sleeping; at the noise of the soldiers rushing up with Judas, St Peter raises his head, caught in a slash of light; the painter himself seems to be wondering what will happen next. Clearly his mood is now dominated by a concern for narrative. Dynamic necessity causes his technique to become almost summary, offering extremely rapid impressions of reality: a fading crowd along

Chiostri dei Frari. Santa Maria Gloriosa dei Frari. Cloisters, rebuilt in the 17th century with fanciful well-heads and decorative sculptures.

the Jordan, in the Baptism of Christ; Moses and Elijah all silver and light, in the Ascension; a peasant woman shown standing against the light with nervously crossing phosphorescent streaks, in the Nativity. In the paintings of the ground-floor room in San Rocco (1583-87) Tintoretto's language becomes a phantasmagoric flow of light, and in the Santa Maria Egiziaca creates a wonderfully evocative nocturnal effect. This is the artist's most contemplative painting. The saint raises her gaze from her book to the horizon, which is lit up with sulphurous gleams. The leaves and water, the distant hills and outlines of the houses seem to catch fire, to levitate.

Side doorway (18th century). San Nicolò dei Mendicoli. The 18th-century door has an elegant contour, rather like a moulded cornice.

With the Scuola di San Rocco, Tintoretto made his finest contribution to sixteenth-century Venetian painting, a real landmark in the history of the city, which long inspired contemporary artists and also critics (the poetic Marco Boschini, in his *Carta del Navegar Pitoresco,* 1660, has vivid pages on San Rocco). Certainly, comparison between Tintoretto's originals and the work of his successors, though inspired by him, is always unfavourable, indeed it sometimes reflects badly on the reputation of the Master himself. And it was not the square miles of painted canvas by Aliense, Vicentino and Palma Giovane (1544-1628) in the churches, palazzi and Scuole in Venice, that were to save the Venetian painting of the end of the century from a descent into eclecticism and the academic.

Some of the complexes decorated by Palma are more or less intact, for instance the ones in the Scuola di San Fantin (now headquarters of the Ateneo Veneto), a confraternity whose mission was to accompany condemned people to their deaths. The ground-floor room was used for religious ceremonies and had two altars by Vittoria, which are now in San Zanipolo. The ceiling is entirely by Palma and the subject-matter deals with the prayers for intercession of the souls in Purgatory.

Another unusual room decorated by Palma in the style of the late sixteenth century was the Oratorio dei Crociferi, originally built as a hospital opposite the church of the Gesuati and restored by Doge Pasquale Cicogna, between 1585 and 1592. Here are some of Palma's best works, and they give a good idea of how, after the triumph of the brilliant painters of the middle of the century, Venetian paintings was now retreating into the routine drafting of a dignified mannerist prose.

Meanwhile, after the victory of Lepanto, Venice was regaining a position of prestige in the eyes of the members of the European Holy League, but she obtained nothing decisive from the Turks, to whom she had to yield Cyprus in 1573. From that moment onwards, as the Venetians say, the Republic 'drew in her oars' with respect to the expansionist Ottoman policy, and embarked on a prudent policy of compromise that was destined to last two centuries.

Light and Shade: the Baroque

During the first years of the seventeenth century, the Spaniards were gaining supremacy in Italy; the Venetian Republic, with the Papacy, was the only region to preserve any real independence, looking to France in matters of general foreign policy. But the consequences of so many decades of struggle and disagreement were bound to make themselves felt. While Rome had numerous artists, attracted by munificent Cardinals and innovating Popes, Venice languished, further depressed by conflicts with the Papacy on matters of religious jurisdiction, and in the throes of a serious economic crisis brought about by the enormous expenditure and loss of profits caused by the fighting against the Turkish empire in the east.

One cannot really talk of Baroque art in Venice in the way one can in Rome: almost all the social and ideal premises were absent. Another factor that was lacking was that of a reaction against classicism, such as paved the way for the formal revolution elsewhere. For a few decades, at the beginning of the new century, Venetian art stayed on the path of Mannerism, moving on from the neo-Tintorettism of Palma Giovane to the neo-Titianism of Padovanino (to be seen particularly in the beautiful church of the Tolentini, near Piazzale Roma). In Venice, unfortunately, there was no Caravaggio to sweep away the feeble eclecticism of the imitators of the

▷

Church of Santa Maria della Salute (after 1630). Set on the point of Dorsoduro, its great domes give it the look of a ship in full sail.

208

golden age, and none but pale echoes of that glorious realistic revolution reached the city, through the works of passing foreign painters like the Roman Domenico Fetti, the German Liss or the Genoese Strozzi. The painters of the second generation in Venice were not of much importance either; thus, Vecchia re-elaborated a sort of Mannerist version of Giorgione, with portraits of soldiers, helmets and plumed hats, or grotesque and contorted figures of ruffians round tortured and crucified figures of Christ (his main work is in the church of Sant'Antonin in Bragora); or Carpioni, who produced a new Roman classicism with mythological themes, like a little Venetian Poussin.

It was not until mid-century that more genuinely Baroque forms appeared, with the ceilings of Francesco Maffei (c. 1625-60) in Palazzo Nani (now in the museum of Cà Rezzonico), a genuine outburst

Church of Santa Maria della Salute (after 1630). Dogana da Mar.

of whimsical fantasy; or with the stormy Sebastiano Mazzoni (c. 1611-78) who anticipated the style of the imminent eighteenth century with the liquid freedom of his pictorial touch (two altarpieces in the church of San Beneto, 1649).

All in all, the seventeenth century in Venice did not produce one great painter or sculptor; but there was one first-rate personality at work in the field of architecture: Baldassare Longhena (1598-1682), a disciple of Scamozzi. Longhena's particular merit was that be managed to find a language which, though it made concessions to the decorative and fanciful spirit of the Baroque, nevertheless respected the organic tradition of Venetian architecture. His earliest works are the Palazzo Giustinian-Lolin, on the Grand Canal near the Accademia (1623), and the Palazzo Widmann near the Miracoli (*c.* 1630), both of which have fairly traditional forms, taking up

sixteenth-century schemes with slight picturesque variants in the keystones of the windows and in the relationships of the balconies and doorways. Longhena's genius was slow to emerge, but it burst out in all its force in the creation which was to put his name among the greatest of all time: Santa Maria della Salute, on the end of the Dorsoduro peninsula in the centre of the Basin of San Marco.

The Salute was built as a votive church, in memory of the plague of 1630, and its design clearly shows that Longhena had considered the social problem connected with its ceremonial function: it had to be the goal of the state procession which, starting from San Marco, crossed to it each year, on 21 November — as it still does today — over the bridge of boats thrown from the Santa Maria del Giglio

Church of Santa Maria della Salute. Dogana da Mar. This basilica was constructed by Longhena after 1630, to commemorate the miraculous end of an outbreak of plague. It was included in the same urban project as the Seminario and the new Dogana da Mar, the custom house on the extreme point of Dorsoduro. The old Abbey and the church of San Gregorio are in the left foreground.

jetty to the Calle San Gregorio. The Salute had to be clearly visible from San Marco, residence of the Signoria and home of the Doge, and indeed from all parts of the city, to underline the religious meaning of the vow which had brought about its foundation. Longhena thus acted as both architect and planner, introducing a major factor into Venetian topography: by proposing the end of Dorsoduro, the site of the old Ospizio della Trinità, he enabled his church to be set on a sort of wedge which faced boldly over the Basin, thereby securing for it a theatrical aura that is typically Baroque. Today anyone visiting the district round the Salute, or looking at it from the Campanile of San Marco, is bound to notice the totally individual character, the formal autonomy, of Longhena's contribution, which spreads from the church itself to the building of the

Seminario Patriarcale and the rebuilt Dogana da Mar (completed by Benoni about 1680 in absolute harmony with Longhena's work). One need only compare it with the volumes of other adjacent buildings, from those of the small houses along the canal to the abbey of San Gregorio with its church: all structures in brick, with their red medieval roof tiles just a dozen or so feet above the ground. The buildings by Longhena tower above everything round them in size and nobility of material (white Istrian stone), subduing the existing urban environment through the lofty rhetoric of the Baroque. One might be a little dubious about the legitimacy of introducing these architectural forms at all, so dissimilar are they to those hallowed by tradition. The idea of the church with a central plan, determined by the inner space contained within the single huge dome, is in fact most unusual: it may possibly derive from a plan published in 1557 in an engraving by the Roman mannerist Labacco, and has scarcely any Venetian precedents, apart perhaps from an imaginary domed basilica painted by Carpaccio in the *Arrival of the Ambassadors* in the St Ursula cycle (1500). And yet a close look at the minor elements of his composition shows that Longhena uses

a vocabulary that is not too remote from the local one: flights of steps around the octagonal base, cornices, balustrades, lanterns and small campanili, not unlike those designed previously by Sansovino, Palladio and Scamozzi, though with quite different compositional links. Despite these prudent references to Venetian peculiarities, Longhena could still have made a mistake over the volume of the building, which was so completely exceptional that its organic absorption into the Venetian 'scale' was bound to be very difficult. Yet here too he seems to have been guided by an extraordinary figurative sensivity which inspired him to rely mainly on effects of light; thus he was again in the mainstream of Venetian tradition, producing the organic relationship with the surrounding space that we have always found in Venice. Set at the edge of the shifting mirror of the water, approached by flights of steps which fragment the light and thus lighten the weight of the mass, the huge building of the Salute rises from its base, rich with chiaroscuro, up to the intermediate floor with the scrolls and statues, which take all heaviness from it. The result is a characteristic 'optical' effect, which transforms the monument into an inspired piece of Baroque scenery.

Church of San Moise (1668). This has another of Venice's fascinating Baroque façades, by Tremignon with sculptural decorations by Meyring.

Fortune, on the Dogana da Mar. Gilded bronze statue by Falcone.
on the last section of the Dogana, built by Benoni in 1677.

So often compared to a ship with great sails unfurled, moving forward
into the Basin of San Marco, the Salute plays a vital part in the layout
of the very heart of Venice. Opposite San Marco, its bulk picturesquely enlivened by shadowy openings, light-catching cornices, statues
rising like choirs of angels against the sky, the Salute completes a
sequence of perfectly balanced masterpieces, from the Doge's Palace
which rises, transparent as an openwork screen, against the moving
light, to the pale silhouette of San Giorgio, the Zitelle and the
Redentore: from the delightful complexities of the Gothic to the
flawless perfection of Palladio and the picturesque, explosive genius
of Longhena.

Longhena was extremely active in Venice in the middle of the seventeenth century, contributing greatly to that air of sumptuous nobility that was so perfect a reflection of the grandiloquence and generous mood of the times. He worked on the Scuola dei Carmini in Campo Santa Margherita (1668-70), where he designed the lavish façade, and on the Scuola dei Greci in Bragora (1678); on the church of the Scalzi (1660) near the railway station, completed with a façade by Sardi, and on the Spanish Synagogue (Sinagoga Spagnuola) in the Ghetto Vecchio (1654), with its sumptuously modelled interior. But his two masterpieces, which were decisive in the definition of the Baroque face of Venice, are two great palazzi on the Grand Canal, Cà Rezzonico and Cà Pesaro. Here Longhena brings sixteenth-century formulae to their logical conclusion, elaborating and theatric-ally enlarging the ground plans with the addition of a succession of courtyards arranged so that they could be seen, from the water gate, opening off one another like Chinese boxes; creating a most magnificent effect and 'colouring' the façades with deep strokes of chiaroscuro, beneath the beautifully free superstructure of balconies and loggias, supported by the impressive rusticated ground-floor base. The actual size of the palazzo, already increased by Sansovino and Sammicheli, is here taken even further, so that it imposes a crushing presence on the outline of the roofs and façades of the Grand Canal; yet it is contained within a world of forms so characteristically full of light and shade and colour that it is bound by definition to fit easily into the pattern of Venetian art.

Cà Rezzonico (now the Museo del Settecento Veneziano) looks on to the Grand Canal near the Accademia. Begun in 1667 for the Priuli-Bon family, it was abandoned by Longhena after the first floor, and left untouched for over half a century. In the middle of the eight-eenth century it came into the hands of the Rezzonico family, who commissioned Giorgio Massari to complete it. The forms he used were Rococo, but were sensitively matched with those of the existing structure. Massari's only addition was an extremely elegant cere-monial stairway leading to the ballroom at the rear.

Cà Pesaro was begun in 1679, on the site of an earlier Gothic build-ing, parts of which can still just be identified in the courtyard. The front is even more impressive than that of Cà Rezzonico, because of the width of the windows and the way in which the façade 'wraps round', to the depth of two bays, at each side. This last is a most unusual effect in Venice, where façades were conceived as surfaces, as screens of tracery shutting off the reflections of the Grand Canal. It is lavishly ornamented with carvings in typical Baroque style (those on the upper orders are by the Flemish sculptor Le Court, who also carved the altar of the Salute). Remarkably, the east side follows the curve of the little canal that runs alongside it; it was completed, with the second floor, at the beginning of the eight-eenth century, by Antonio Gaspari.

There is little other Baroque architecture in the city comparable to that of Longhena; though it is perhaps worth mentioning the church of San Moisè, in the *sestiere* of San Marco, built between 1632 and 1668; the façade, laden with Baroque decorations, is by Alessandro Tremignon, with the assistance of the sculptor Arrigo Meyring for the numerous statues. In Santa Maria del Giglio the façade (1678-83), by Giuseppe Sardi, is a typical example of Baroque 'triumphal' decoration, with its bas-reliefs and statues celebrating the seafaring Barbaro family, who commissioned the building. This was a very typical phenomenon among Venetian aristocrats in the seventeenth century: even in the funeral monuments in the main churches, they tended to erect themselves theatrical mausoleums which jar with the tradition of Venetian architecture, always elegantly restrained.

Autumn Glory: the Eighteenth Century

The last century in the history of independent Venice is problematical, because it is a century of contradictions. Still close to her golden age, Venice was too full of the memories of past triumphs, and sought an impossible military recovery in the undertakings of Doge Francesco Morosini in the Peloponnese and Morea. Later, caught up in the struggle between the great European powers, she withdrew into her own restricted boundaries, hoping that the upheaval would pass her by unharmed. Hamstrung by a centuries-old system of oligarchic government, Venice nonetheless opened her gates to the most varied cultural influences and was visited by numerous foreign poets, writers, artists and thinkers, who offered telling indictments of her traditional mode of living. Still traditionalist in her own artistic development, Venice cultivated the limited talents of architects who were looking back to Palladio, and of painters who apparently concerned themselves with perpetuating a weary late seventeenth-century academicism; but at the same time she allowed her more inspired painters, such as Sebastiano Ricci and Gianantonio Pellegrini, to move away to sow the seeds of the highly elegant and sophisticated Rococo in England, Germany and France. In mid-century she withdrew her attention from the local re-workings of sixteenth-century classicism (although it was still producing majestic palazzi like the Pisani and Priuli); and promptly discovered French-inspired neoclassicism, through the learned elaborations of Temanza and Selva.

A city of encounters and relationships, Venice saw Casanova mingling with liberal patricians who had read Rousseau and Voltaire; in the theatre she produced the whimsical Carlo Gozzi and the realist Carlo Goldoni; her frivolous ladies pretended to be reading Algarotti's *Il Newtonianismo per le dame;* and Baretti and Gaspare Gozzi laid the foundations of modern journalism. Masquerades, carnivals and gambling houses thrived; and there were more than ten opera houses, where the music of Galuppi, Marcello and Vivaldi could be heard.

These contradictions have often made judgments on eighteenth-century Venice confused; her image is blurred in the myths of historical romance and carnival games. But there is no doubt that, in its amazing richness, the eighteenth century was the most mature, most fertile, most conclusive period in the city's long spiritual and formal progress. With all the perfection of a work of art, now complete, Venice spread over the lagoon with the elegant indolence of a high-class courtesan, though she was never forgetful of her own supreme civilization. In Venice the eighteenth century could be called the century of woman, the century of elegance: but it was also a century during which the face of the city and the genius of its artists concluded a historic

▷

Façade (1709). Church of San Stae. One of the most elegant early 18th-century churches (by Rossi). The façade is adorned with sculptures of high quality.

Façade. Cà Pesaro. Le Court's sculptures (end of 17th century) lend animation to the façade. Now houses two museums, one of modern and one of Oriental art.

cycle which, like all supreme gifts of the spirit, was to become the property of all humanity in the years to come.

In such a situation it was of little importance — at least in so far as it concerns our subject, which is the artistic face of Venice — that the Signoria now had scarcely any money; the coffers had been drained by the long wars with the Turks, and by the inevitable economic decline following the loss of political supremacy in the Italian and Mediterranean arena. All that was needed was the passion for life and love of beauty of one family of Doges, the Pisani, to justify the sumptuous palazzo which rose on the Campo Santo Stefano and whose suites of rooms and porticoed courtyards still retain their original exotic charm even now; all that was needed was a family such as the Rezzonico or Labia to commission Tiepolo to decorate their own great halls, crowded with exquisitely graceful furniture, curiously playful in form and unparalleled anywhere except in the Paris of the Regency.

The city was poor, there were over twenty thousand registered beggars, but there were at least twelve thousand 'family' retainers

Ballroom. Cà Rezzonico. Like the Cà Pesaro, this was not completed until the 18th century. The ballroom, added by Massari around 1750, and frescoed by G. B. Crosato (1753), is the finest room in the palazzo.

or clients who lived in the wake of the patrician families, in the great palazzi, each of which was indeed a positive palace. Popular faith wavered, Jansenism tilted critically at the laxness of the Catholic church, the Preaching Friars had a large following; but the great patrician families guided their own younger sons into a religious career and encouraged the building of churches (San Stae, Gesuati, Pietà, San Marcuola). Their villas, and their country estates, were now a drain on their resources, whereas they had once yielded high incomes, but in the city palazzi were constantly being built, and the old ones were always being modernized and enlarged.

With this in mind, it is not easy for the historian to trace any single coherent line in the enterprises affecting the artistic life and face of the city: everything, in einghteenth-century Venice, seemed to happen by chance, in a sort of burst of unexpected solutions, of brilliant flashes. And there was an obscure feeling, too, that all this was issuing from a source that was now about to dry up, like the last flowering of a great plant that is about to fade.

There was architectural activity all over the city in the eighteenth century, and it is not easy to identify any centres of particularly intense large-scale rebuilding, such as had existed in earlier centuries. Any attempt to understand the main values of this panorama will therefore logically proceed stylistically and historically. At the beginning of the century, architects looked mainly to be traditions of Palladio and Scamozzi: for instance Andrea Tirali, who in 1706 continued work on the church of the Tolentini begun by Scamozzi, adding a showy Roman portico or *pronaos,* with six columns on a high flight of steps: basically, the inspiration is probably related to the Villa Malcontenta by Palladio, one of the most inspiring of all his works, built for the Foscari at the edge of the lagoon, near Fusina. This Palladian portico was an invention which was to enjoy great popularity in the eighteenth century. It reappears in San Simeone Piccolo (opposite the railway station), built by G. A. Scalfurotto between 1718 and 1738. Its huge dome, covered with its marvellous verdigris, is a well-known landmark on the Grand Canal, which reflects its pleasant but somehow grotesque monumentality.

By a strange coincidence, outside the sphere of any conscious town-planning, the builders of the eighteenth century were commissioned several times to work along the Cannaregio, near the church of San Geremia. On this broad, luminous canal, which was part of the direct water route from the centre of Venice to San Giuliano, on the mainland near Mestre, we find the Palazzi Labia, Priuli, Surian and Savorgnan all within a short distance of one another. The last two, by Sardi, were built at the beginning of the century, and the Palazzo Surian in particular has brilliantly designed surfaces which just catch the light with their beautifully animated Serlian windows (a three-light window with the main arch higher than the side ones, topped by two small windows forming a square cornice). In the eighteenth century, Palazzo Surian housed the French embassy, and Jean-Jacques Rousseau stayed there. Palazzo Priuli (*c.* 1753), by Tirali, is very original with its smooth façade, divided horizontally by a clear-cut cornice, which already looks forward to neoclassicism. Palazzo Labia, by Cominelli, stands by the church of San Geremia (also rebuilt in the middle of the century), and has its two façades (with their particularly elegant carved details) looking on to the Cannaregio, at one point clearly visible from the Grand Canal. With one façade on the Campo di San Geremia as well, the palazzo was famous in the eighteenth century for the prodigality of its owners, who commissioned Tiepolo to decorate the ballroom, still one of the most splendid halls of the period.

Alongside and after the 'conservative' group — of whom we have spoken — there were some architects at the beginning of the eighteenth century whose tastes were more advanced, who produced the most lively examples of the Venetian Rococo. The first of these is Antonio Gaspari (1670?-1730?), who began to go beyond the timid imitation of sixteenth-century architecture with motifs drawn from the Roman works of Borromini, following a cultural process which had already borne fruit elsewhere, encouraging the development of seventeenth-century forms into the Rococo. Very few of his numerous projects (preserved in some books of drawings in the Museo Correr) were realized. One of these was the major part of the church of the Fava (1705-35). The façade is still incomplete and bare, but the interior, on a ellipsoidal plan, has a delicate, sophisticated grace, decorated like an ordinary drawing-room with stuccos and reliefs. Naturally the sculptures by Giovanni Marchiori and Gian

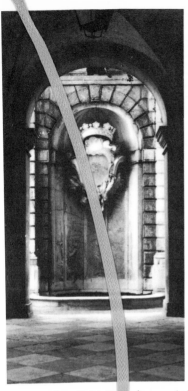

Cà Rezzonico: (left) Coat of arms of the Rezzonico. (right) Green lacquer room furnished with original Venetian lacquer chinoiserie furniture.

(below) The ground floor of the Cà Rezzonico.

Maria Morlaiter, the finest artists of their time, play an integral part in it (some beautiful sketches by Morlaiter are preserved in the Cà Rezzonico).

Giorgio Massari (c. 1686-1766), a very productive architect, also worked with the precious elegance of Gaspari, and some of his buildings are among the most beautiful of eighteenth-century Venice. Firstly, we find him at work in the church of the Gesuati on the Zattere (1725-36), which owes its fascination partly to the frescoed decoration by Tiepolo, the paintings of Piazzetta and Ricci and statues by Morlaiter, constituting the richest and most unified Rococo interior in the city. All the decorative details conspire to give us a typical eighteenth-century interior, luminous with its ivories and greys and slight but surely moulded reliefs. The façade, looking on to the glittering Canale della Giudecca, was inspired by Palladio; it has a lively and pleasing pattern of cornices and columns, assembled with the skill of a cabinet-maker rather than of a real architect.

The second church by Massari, the Pietà (1744-60), was also intended to serve as a concert hall for the young girls cared for in the adjacent institution. There Vivaldi was *maestro di cappella*, and his works for voices and strings must have been played there often. The elliptical plan of the hall and the shallow vaulted ceiling are both intended to obtain better acoustics; while the extreme delicacy of the carving of the cornices of the wall panels, the pulpits and the capitals reveals a very definite interest in these elements on the part of the architect. The ceiling, glowing with frescoed colours, is one of Giambattista Tiepolo's masterpieces (1754), and shows the triumph of the Virgin amid an orchestra of various instruments which extends all around the cornice.

Massari designed many secular buildings, and also worked a lot on the mainland. On the Grand Canal, just opposite Cà Rezzonico, he designed the Palazzo Grassi (1748-72) with extensive façades looking on to the Canal and the Campo di San Samuele, with smooth panels between the windows and a square courtyard, Roman in inspiration; here the gay, delicate touch of Rococo had faded and neoclassical coldness was foreshadowed.

One of the foundations of neoclassicism was the rise of rationalism, the Enlightenment, which found fertile ground during the second half of the eighteenth century, particularly in France. In Venice, neoclassicism was somewhat retarded by the success of the Rococo, particularly in painting, which could boast the names of Pellegrini and Ricci, Rosalba Carriera and G. A. Guardi, not to mention Tiepolo. Neoclassical architecture did not appear until the last quarter of the century. Here too, however, the change was gradual and accompanied by the usual contradictions. As early as the middle of the century, for instance, the British consul Joseph Smith (one of the key figures in the Venetian art world because of his constant patronage of Canaletto, who was launched by him among the English aristocracy as a painter of Venetian views) had Visentini build for him the *palazzetto* on the corner of Rio dei Santi Apostoli near the Grand Canal, in icily neoclassical forms. It was then enlarged and redecorated, after 1784, by the greatest Venetian neoclassical architect, Antonio Selva. In 1760 Tommaso Temanza, a theorist of rationalist architecture rather than an architect proper, designed what is probably the masterpiece of Venetian neoclassicism, the small round church of the Maddalena, on Strada Nuova. Clearly, the inspiration goes back to the Pantheon, even in the interior where chapels were built

Rosalba Carriera: Portrait of Faustina Bordoni. Cà Rezzonico. There are many masterpieces by famous Venetian portraitists in Cà Rezzonico, among which is this portrait of the well-known singer who later moved to Dresden.

within the thickness of the masonry, ringing it all the way round with a delicate touch of elegance; the whole building is very small, almost like a chapel.

Antonio Selva was also responsible for what is perhaps the last important architectural work before the fall of the Republic: the Teatro della Fenice (1792). To gain some idea of the difficulties of fitting a large modern theatre into the urban fabric of Venice, one should wander around the nearby *calli* and *fondamente,* along the canals and little bridges that surround it: it has a perimeter of surprising length and inspiring complexity. In fact, the building is constructed on two main parallel axes, one for the façade, the monumental entrance and grand staircase leading to the foyer, and the other for the auditorium proper, and the adjoining rooms for rehearsals, scenery and so on. The Fenice, inaugurated on 17 May 1792 with the opera *I Giochi d'Agrigento* by Paisiello, still has its

Façade. Cà Rezzonico. Designed by Longhena (1660), this palazzo was built up to the first storey, then carried on by Gaspari and Massari around 1750; its last storey and delicate attic with oval windows are in typical Rococo style.

eighteenth-century grave, even after restorations following a fire, and still maintains a very high level of performance.

Before we conclude our eighteenth-century survey, we should mention at least the most worthwhile activities of certain painters, as painting was a most important feature of Venice at this time. In fact, during this century, the Venetian school can aptly be compared to that of Paris, and its major artists were sought after throughout Europe by the most illustrious clients and collectors.

Little remains in Venice of early Rococo painting, represented by Ricci, Pellegrini, Amigoni — the wandering painters who were active in England and Germany, the Low Countries, Paris and Madrid. Ricci's altarpiece in the Gesuati, Amigoni's in the Fava, and the paintings by Pellegrini in the Gallerie do not give us the full measure of their decorative talents. Their last follower, the mysterious Gian Antonio Guardi (1699-1760), has left perhaps the most significant work of this period, in the organ balcony in the church of Sant'Angelo: the *Legend of Tobias*, painted with the most open-minded and unexpected graphic inspiration, in a fantastic outpouring of iridescent colours, forms dissolving into light, graceful attitudes as in some magical ballet.

Of the other great decorative painters, Giovan Battista Piazzetta

Giambattista Tiepolo: Rezzonico Wedding (1758). Cà Rezzonico. Two salons of the palazzo were frescoed by Tiepolo with two magnificent sequences celebrating the grandeur of the Rezzonico family.

P. 228/229
Glass chandelier Briati.

(1683-1754) is well documented in Venice, both with the *Vision of St Dominic* in San Zanipolo (*c.* 1725-30) and in the luminous altarpieces of the Fava and the Gesuati (1727-1739). Giambattista Tiepolo (1696-1770) was now emerging from his first period, still splendidly Baroque (*St James*, in the church of San Stae, 1717). The pictorial genius of the century, he undoubtedly plays an important part in eighteenth-century Venice and has left his traces in the most various places, sacred and secular. His youthful period, with its strong plastic emphasis and radiant luminescence, is to be seen in the fresco of *St Teresa* at the Scalzi, next to the railway station; also in the Palazzo Sandi at Sant'Angelo (*c.* 1720-25). But the ceiling of the Gesuati (1739) shows him adopting the decorative scheme of Veronese, with its hints of staginess and its lightening of the colour, which became silvery and cold. In Palazzo Labia (*c.* 1745) the *Story of Cleopatra* is primarily costumed melodrama, presented with remarkable theatrical virtuosity and refinement of colour. In the Scuola dei Carmini, at Santa Margherita, there is a whole series of paintings concerned with the *Virgin in Glory* (1739-44) which show the soft but passionate range of colour used by the mature artist and his extraordinary tendency to create forms of supreme beauty, which have all the erotic sensibility and enthusiasm

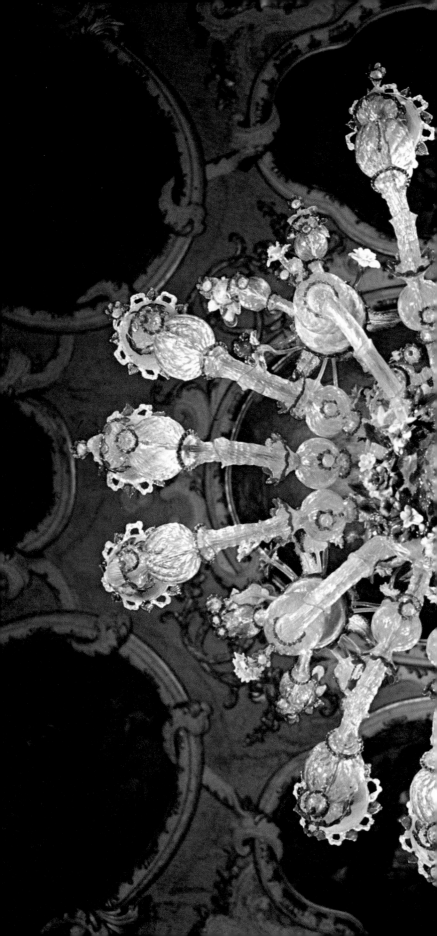

Pietro Longhi: Il Concertino. Accademia. Pietro Longhi was the most faithful chronicler of intimate scenes of luxurious 18th-century Venetian life.

of his time. When he came back from Würzburg, where he had decorated the splendid Residenz for the Archbishop, Tiepolo painted the frescoes for the new church of the Pietà, and then two rooms in Cà Rezzonico, with works of increasing decorative distinction. These were among the last works of the great master, who was in ever greater demand among foreign clients: he worked on the Villa Valmarana in Vicenza in 1757, on the villas of Stra and Verona from 1760-62, in Madrid from 1762 until his death. But Tiepolo did provide eighteenth-century Venice with some of her most magnificent painting.

The absence of original interior decor in the old palazzi is compensated for by the wealth of the Venetian museums, some of which specialize in eighteenth-century material. Rather than to the Accademia, this applies to the Museo del Settecento Veneziano, housed in Cà Rezzonico, which has a wealth of late eighteenth-century collections made by the Venetian nobleman Teodoro Correr, who then gave them

G. B. Piazzetta: The Fortune-Teller. A vibrant use of colour makes Piazzetta one of the most important masters of Venetian popular and religious painting.

to the city. In Cà Rezzonico, in rooms adorned with the delicate furniture of the time, amid carvings, lacquered objects, chinoiseries, precious fabrics, chandeliers in Murano blown glass, we find paintings by all the artists who had helped to create the face of eighteenth-century Venice. There are pastels by Rosalba Carriera (1675-1757), with portraits of the elegant, graceful protagonists of a frivolous, fashion-obsessed but courtly world; here too are the small costume paintings by Pietro Longhi (1702-85), a true master of the 'conversation piece', rivalling the followers of Watteau and of Hogarth in his faithful description of settings and psychologies of his time. There is another remarkable series of paintings by Longhi in the Pinacoteca Querini Stampalia, in Santa Maria Formosa, well worth a visit.

Few of the works of the Venetian *vedutisti* or view-painters — Canaletto, his nephew Bernardo Bellotto and Francesco Guardi — remain in Venice, although there are some in the Accademia and

G. B. Grevembroch. Venetian Courtesan; Pile-drivers. Two watercolours, part of a series illustrating mid-18th century Venetian costumes.

the Galleria Franchetti at the Cà d'Oro; while many of their engravings and drawings are to be found in the Museo Correr. It should however be said that the formation and triumph of the Venetian view-painters, so sought after by foreigners and for this reason irrevocably denied to their native city, go to prove that the 'artistic shape' of the city was now complete, crystallizing around vistas, views of squares and canals, the settings for public ceremonies which themselves are valid as final symbols of a thousand-year-old creative process. As she appears to us in the view of the Basin by Canaletto, or in Guardi's views of state festivals (Louvre), eighteenth-century Venice was at last an entire, perfect, genuine 'work of art'.

And yet, on 12 May 1797, after a thousand years of existence, Venice was to lose her freedom.

Decline

The effects of the fall of the Republic on the level of artistic production and on the face of the city can be seen initially in Piazza San Marco. But first, a brief enumeration of the facts.

The abdication of the last Doge in 1797 had not only deprived Venice of her independence but had brusquely precipitated a political and social crisis that had been brewing for some time. Faced with a rationalist Europe and the ferments of the French Revolution, the Signoria had been adopting ostrich tactics for too long; indeed it had been exerting a discreet but tenacious policy of repression. Having sent reforming patricians off as Podestàs in distant parts and isolated those who, returning from France, attempted to preach the new formulae of freedom and equality, after using censorship to limit the circulation of books of 'philosophy' which might question the conservative regime, and allowing the once flourishing structures in the financial, agricultural and trading field to grow old and tired, Venice was now beginning to find that she had no ruling class. Her last Procurators and Doges were faded shadows of a vanished life, like the crowds of ghostly little figures in some of Guardi's last paintings, insubstantial and fluttering like leaves whirled around by gusts of wind at the beginning of autumn.

It was this ruling class, almost entirely lacking in ideals and authority, which abdicated ingloriously when confronted by the claims of General Bonaparte, conqueror of northern Italy, who had already decided to set up a 'Repubblica Cispadana', subject naturally to France. Venice surrendered without a struggle, and ignominiously became mere currency between the two great contenders, France and Austria. With the treaty of Campoformio, Austria became her ruler. After Napoleon's imperial triumph, Venice experienced another brief period of French domination and then became part of the Napoleonic 'Regno Italico', from 1805-15; this was a moment of apparent revival, on a wave of patriotic enthusiasm which spurred on the more youthful political forces to pursue Napoleonic reforms, particularly evident in the field of art: new buildings were put up, there was the Accademia di Belle Arti, museums and statues by Antonio Canova (a Venetian by adoption, but not very active in the city, where he left only a few early works, in the Museo Correr, such as *Daedalus and Icarus*). But as we shall see, the Napoleonic period also concealed great dangers for the artistic face of the city.

Venice was weary, cut off from all her roots, isolated in the lagoon which seemed to take her back to remote periods of solitude and abandon. Ousted from her position of maritime dominance, Venice was going to have to restructure her own economy; but primarily she was suffering from a serious crisis in morale. Two generations at least would have to pass, from the moment when the standard of St Mark was lowered for the last time at San Marco, before the city could be reborn as a social entity and set off on a new course within the framework of the young Italian state; she had to adjust

Campo San Polo. One of the liveliest of Venetian squares, characteristically 18th-century in style. Massari's monumental Palazzo Tiepoli (1750) in the centre; in the foreground the Gothic church of San Polo.

to the new circumstances, which were hustling her from being the capital of an empire into becoming a modern city, with its own problems of survival and of adaptation to the unexpected system. The nineteenth century therefore also marks the moment of decline for 'Venice the work of art', whose thousand-year progress we have been following. The political turn of events, which annulled all independent decisions, also interrupted that unbroken artistic tradition which had always been at the core of the successive transformations

Palazzo Civran (mid-18th
century), Rialto. In
neoclassical style.
Attributed to Massari.

(below) Palazzo Grassi
(mid-18th century)
Grand Canal. Facing Cà
Rezzonico, it exemplifies
the neoclassical tendency
evident in Massari's work
after mid-century.

▷

Virgin Immaculate (18th
century). Cà Rezzonico.
On garden wall; probably
by Morlaiter.

Church of Maddalena (end of 18th century). Tommaso Temanza's neoclassical masterpiece.

of the face of the city. Completely heterogeneous elements now found acceptance there, extraneous personalities felt entitled to interpolate experiments that were not rooted in local artistic tradition. This was the chief explanation for the aesthetic failure of works which might have found acceptance elsewhere, and this is also the explanation for some ill-advised demolition, typical of the widespread nineteenth-century process of 'redevelopment' of historic centres in many Italian cities.

Luckily for Venice, the Napoleonic phase lasted only a few years; but is is hard to justify the sometimes irreparable damage that it did cause. Unfortunately, the 'modernizing' operation began in Piazza San Marco and was rationalized by the pretended need to adapt the Procuratie Nuove as residence of the Viceroy, Eugène Beauharnais, who usually lived in Milan. In the course of their transformation into the Palazzo Reale, the Procuratie underwent various minor changes which may indeed have proved of positive value, given the charm and grace with which some neoclassical Venetian painters such as Giuseppe Borsato and Carlo Bevilacqua decorated some of the rooms (now part of the Museo Correr). At the top of the main staircase the Sala Napoleonica was created: an oval room for ceremonial occasions, pleasantly decorated in the Empire style and unfortunately partly retouched after 1866.

But the Napoleonic conversion also had more serious consequences. The Viceroy's residence had to be given a completely new orientation, creating an entrance on to the Piazza itself, on the side opposite the Basilica. Here, in the middle, was Sansovino's church of San Gemignano, with its elegant and animated façade complete with tympanum and small towers, linked at both sides to the narrow Procuratie Vecchie and the broader Procuratie Nuove: one of the typical stylistic clusters which contributed so much to the 'colour' of Venetian townplanning. The Napoleonic architects (Carlo Antonini and G. M. Soli, 1807-15) did away with this whole charming corner of the scenery of San Marco and replaced it with a massive screen consisting of a flat succession of arches, which attempted, hopelessly, to square up the most asymmetrical piazza in the world. Another totally negative element of what became known as the Ala Napoleonica (Napoleonic wing) is the attic storey on the top, which brutally emphasizes the point of contact between the architectural structure and the sky, with a dull, uniform outline htat has no parallel in any other part of the city. The bitter irony of history willed it that, in the centre of this attic, where two Victories were carved to support a medallion with the Emperor's profile, the medallion remained blank: the man responsible for the first modern assault on the city had fallen from grace in the interim.

Other no less damaging changes were made around the nucleus of this refurbished palace: if the palazzetto of the Guardia Reale at the Ascensione (by Santi, after 1815) was barely tolerable, far worse was the demolition of the old Fondachi del Grano to make room for the Giardinetti Reali. The picturesque Gothic brick façade which, as we see in paintings by eighteenth-century view-painters, gave a touch of medieval flavour to the old port of the Venetian merchants,

▷

Church of San Simeone e Giuda (1738). G. A. Scalfurotto's neoclassical work is a curious imitation of the Pantheon in Rome.

*The Caffè Florian (19th-century lithograph). The famous café on Piazza
San Marco, established in the 18th century, was at
the height of its splendour in the 19th century.*

was replaced merely by dreary pathways running between the bordered flowerbeds of an uninteresting garden, and a minute building in glaring Istrian stone which originally served as a Kaffeehaus. It is a neoclassical *tempietto,* a little round temple, doomed by its own architectural absurdity to constant changes of function: from being the headquarters of the Bucintoro rowing club (the name it still goes by) to being an air terminal; a permanent incongruity, from the moment it was taken out of that English garden which clearly inspired Santi when he created it.

Another district seriously affected by early nineteenth-century activity was Castello. Here, traditionally, there were a number of convents and churches, which were suppressed by the Napoleonic laws. In their place, Selva planned the present Giardini Pubblici (1810). Unfortunately, this meant the disappearance of a very typically Venetian district inhabited by workers, fishermen, lace-makers and threaders of Murano glass beads. Slum clearance too began at Castello, with the Via Eugenea (now Via Garibaldi): this was to be the arrival

View of the Piazza San Marco (engraving, c. 1742). In this print after a Canaletto drawing one can see the west wing of the Procuratie, which Napoleon demolished at the beginning of the 19th century in order to build the great staircase of Palazzo Reale.

point for a road across the lagoon, over the *barene* of Castello and the islands of Sant'Erasmo and the Vignole.

Many other innovations were connected with the idea of giving Venice new commercial and social structures. After the suppression of the Benedictine convent, a new harbour, the Porto Franco, was installed just off the island of San Giorgio, and was to have given new life to the paralyzed Venetian market. The warehouse along the water's edge and the small dockyard, by Mezzani (1810-15), are an arbitrary but not unpleasing addition to the general prospect of the island. Opposite, during the Austrian period, the Magazzini del Sale (salt warehouses) by Pigazzi (1855) were erected on the Punta della Dogana.

Meanwhile, there was a growing conviction in Venice that the city's life could not be based exclusively on the sea, and people began to think about a link with the mainland. This decision was fundamental for the life and future of the city; possibly its consequences can be fully appreciated only today. The historic destiny of the island

which had grown up in the centre of the lagoon was reversed; the lagoon had once been seen as a crucial ally, now it was a useless obstruction to the expansion of traffic with the *terraferma,* of which Venice was no longer the queen, but a slave. So in 1823 Luigi Casarini put forward the first plan for a causeway from San Marziale in Cannaregio to Campalto, soon to be imitated by Abate Buttacalice and the engineer Picotti, who envisaged a real bridge across the lagoon, ending in the north part of Cannaregio, at the Misericordia (1830). The invention of the railway led to the Bacanello-Biondetti plan, of 1835, which suggested that the railway be carried on a bridge passing behind the Giudecca and ending at San Giorgio. At this point, the Austrian government itself saw the strategic convenience of a railway link between the capital of the Lombard-Venetian kingdom, Milan, and Venice, its military port in the northern Adriatic. So between 1841 and 1846 the engineer Meduna worked on the railway bridge, from Mestre to the nearest point of the city, the district of Santa Lucia where the station now stands. Unfortunately, the convent and Palladian church of Corpus Domini paid the price, and the whole bank of the Grand Canal suffered; this was one of the most delightful parts of it, recorded for posterity several times by Canaletto (London, National Gallery) and Guardi (Castagnola, Thyssen collection).

'Progress' came to Venice on smoke-garlanded steam engines, which linked the historic island to the mainland: the centuries of haughty isolation were over.

Whether the inevitable link with the mainland brought Venice gain or loss, is a problem which town-planners of today have only now begun to discuss, and they have not yet reached any conclusion. Looking at the statistics, it would seem that, rather than increasing population and trade, the bridge had a negative effect, if anything draining the city of its economic and productive resources and encouraging development on the mainland. Admittedly, from the start other elements helped to confuse the issue, for instance Venice's glorious revolt against the foreigner in 1848-49, which ended unsuccessfully and completely exhausted all the city's economic potential. Austria's reprisal was to embark on a policy favouring the port of Trieste, pouring in capital and commercial opportunities; nearly two hundred firms moved out of Venice during those years, a sure sign of positive economic failure (Bassi, in *Urbanistica* 52, 1968). Dozens of palazzi were abandoned, and indeed, to forestall their demolition, the government had expressly to forbid it.

Naturally, amid such difficulties, little large-scale building work was done. But one of the most noticeable additions was the iron bridge that the Austrians built between 1853-60, in front of the railway station, shortly to be followed by the bridge at the Accademia: another of the traditional characteristics of Venetian traffic thus crumbled, with the new road system replacing the ancient means of water travel. Naturally, this innovation made its mark on the face of the city. Space was needed for the new streets that extended from the bridge: one example of this was the demolition of buildings opposite the station, particularly at the Accademia and on the Campo di San Vidal, where Canaletto's painting in the National Gallery in London still shows us the original 'stonemason's yard' that used to be there.

The annexation of Venice by the new kingdom of Italy, after 1866, brought some improvement, reversing the disastrous tendency that

Federico Zandomeneghi: Archangel Gabriel (1822). Campanile, San Marco. Restored after the collapse of the Campanile on 14 July 1902.

had developed under the previous regime. The city now drew her revenue increasingly from tourism, as can be seen, from the very beginning of the century, from the use made of the Lido, which became one of the smartest international seaside resorts. The city was recovering economically, but the integrity of her fabric was now seriously threatened. Unfortunately, another negative element here was the almost complete withering of any worthwhile artistic production: painting was now represented by the mediocre talent of a school which at first (with Giacomo Favretto) seemed intent on perpetuating only the intimist aspects of the realistic painting of the previous century; then, with Ciardi, it turned to landscape once again and produced a rather duller parallel to the Tuscan Macchiaioli (a visit to the Museo d'Arte Moderna in Cà Pesaro can only confirm this judgment).

The burst of economic activity at the end of the nineteenth century, increasing specialization in industry and faster commercial movement generally demanded a number of sacrifices from Venice, which unfortunately produced glaring scars on the face of this 'work of art'. The filling in of canals (in Via Garibaldi, in Piscina San Samuele and in Cannaregio) altered the movement of the tides. Large-scale demolition, which was said to be justified by the needs of a road traffic which in reality did not demand them at all, produced the flat, undistinguished façades of Via Vittorio Emanuele (now Strada Nuova) (1867), of Via 22 Marzo in San Marco (1876) and Via 2 Aprile in Rialto (1885). At the same time architectural eclecticism was at its height, producing both grotesque imitations of the antique like the Mulino Stucky on the Giudecca (c. 1880), and "Gothic" horrors like the Pescheria (fish market) by Laurenti and Rupolo (1907). The same spirit was responsible for the arbitrary and clumsy restorations of the Fondaco dei Turchi (Berchet 1869) and Palazzo Cavalli at the Accademia (Boito 1896), which thus became almost unrecognizable. And of course this did not prevent extreme poverty from being rampant among the less fortunate social classes, many of whose filthy ground-floor dwellings were often flooded at high-tide. In 1891 the first census carried out prior to organizing a programme of slum clearance (by Boito) claimed that 1544 of such dwellings were uninhabitable (in 1935 the Vivante survey found that they had risen to 3441).

So, by the beginning of this century, Venice had started upon her new phase of history, as a mere factor in an Italian economic, social and cultural system, and adapted herself despite everything to the vicissitudes of her national life. It became increasingly difficult for her rulers, artists, planners and men of good will to preserve that absolutely unique outlook that her history and her very special shape had accorded her. The actual idea that, at the end of the eighteenth century, Venice had attained the state of a perfect 'work of art' was not clearly present, or was forgotten; and the various laments raised by Romantic or post-Romantic writers around what was obscurely felt to be her imminent death-bed, were powerless to awaken sleeping consciences.

Despite all this, one can honestly say that, on the whole, the face of Venice has been preserved; indeed, she remains the best preserved of all the historic cities in Italy, and perhaps in the world.

Venice Must Live

Present-day planning problems in Venice are all subordinate to the problems of preserving and revitalizing the city itself.

Industrial policy between the wars tended to reconsider the problem of intensive residential districts for Venice, and produced a rash of working-class districts now relegated to the outskirts of the historic

▷

Campanile (1688). S. Maria Formosa. Its graceful Baroque outline dominates the animated square.

centre: Sant'Anna and San Giuseppe in Castello, San Rocco near the Frari, San Giobbe near the railway, the Madonna dell'Orto in Cannaregio. In 1928 the district of Sant'Elena was built, with an initial population of at least five thousand. After this, and particularly after 1945, the Lido was intensively built up, so that it was no longer a tourist attraction but, in many places, just another dismal suburb. Anyone wanting to verify the absurdity of such superstructures in terms of town-planning, has only to go to Sant'Elena where, between a false 'campiello' and a disproportionately wide 'calle', they will find indescribable façades where concrete Gothic arches are unsuitably juxtaposed with prefabricated entablatures worthy of the Milanese suburbs. Naturally, the dispersal of intensive residential

Francesco Guardi: The Opening of the Teatro della Fenice (1792). Museo Correr. At the end of the 18th century, with this elegant neoclassical theatre by Selva, the glorious tradition of Venetian art came to an end.

zones around the outskirts of the city made the transport situation more difficult than ever, so that the original *vaporetti,* which began to operate at the beginning of the century, were joined by faster *motoscafi diretti, circolari* and *pendolari,* with disastrous consequences for the foundations of the Venetian houses looking on the canals, whose waters were in constant movement.

Apart from the aesthetic horror of the new districts, mass culture is also responsible for impairing a series of useful social functions, not least of all the contradiction of the traditional Venetian rule which had always rejected 'horizontal' development, i.e. the proliferation of suburbs outside the original nucleus. On the contrary, the ancient republic had always tried to contain her proletariat

within the heart of the city, if anything distributing stratification 'vertically', i.e. over the various floors of the same building or groups of buildings, or at least by building the more modest houses near the noblement's residences.

The current decline in building, a consequence of dispersal into the suburbs, has caused and is still causing a constant drift towards the mainland, so that today the flow of commuters from the mainland to the island is actually double that in the reverse direction, inverting a traditional rule of balance. The statistics of recent years are significant: the average age of the population is over thirty-eight; there are only 120,000 residents, and they diminish at an average of three thousand every year. On the other hand, the population of the other islands is relatively stable (about 50,000), and the population of the mainland area has soared (now over 200,000).

A 'greater Venice' has thus grown up around the historic island, making the overall population of the *comune* about 370,000. A consoling fact in its way, but one which has a very specific bearing on the situation of the historic centre, which must be kept at what is now an absolute minimum; and at the same time its own structure and functions must be strengthened and redefined. It must be obvious to anyone that the face of the city is closely linked to its vitality: a city without inhabitants, or indeed a museum-city, would inevitably be condemned to decay, and ultimately death.

In fact, present-day architectural activity in Venice has suffered from all the main planning problems we have mentioned. On the one hand, speculation and banality have contaminated those parts of the city nearest the terminals: the hideous railway station, or the slabs of concrete around Piazzale Roma, with its admittedly indispensable garages, are beneath contempt. The creation of new canals like Rio Nuovo, to speed up travel from the terminals towards the centre, has created vast empty areas promptly lined with dreary buildings, a gloomy example of architectural compromise between innovators and conservatives neither of whom bore in mind the real rules of art in Venice.

Must it therefore be impossible to build any contemporary work in Venice? No, said Le Corbusier emphatically in 1944: 'Centuries have passed, providing endlessly divergent viewpoints, antitheses, reversals of power ... the one thing that matters is that the new architecture should retain the old poetic quality'. Yet the absurd thing is that in Venice building has continued, within the limits laid down by law and by building regulations, in this unbearable 'compromise style' while Frank Lloyd Wright was prevented from building his *Casa Masieri* near Cà Foscari (1953-54), described by its creator as an airy structure, respectful of the most genuinely Venetian traditions, slender stelae of marble solidly set on concrete piles rising from the water like reeds. Undoubtedly, the risk of being presented with too personal a construction was worth taking, in view of its poetic value, and its respect for Venice's architectural tradition of insubstantiality and theatricality.

Contemporary art — when it really is art — present difficulties and meets with incomprehension, and this may be why the most modern plans are still on their champions' drawing boards. However, there is hope that Le Corbusier's 1965 project for a new hospital at San Giobbe will be carried out in the near future; very small in volume, it is a richly transparent structure, conceived as a real Venetian *quartiere* or block, with its courts and alleyways, so that, although it will be made entirely of concrete, it will fit perfectly into the fabric of the city. Louis Kahn's impressive plan for a Palazzo dei Congressi (1969) has a similar justification: it is to be situated in the gardens of the Biennale, and has been designed in such a way that, even in its functional modernity, it retains typical elements of the urban structure of Venice, including a sort of large hall designed as a piazza.

Anyone who loves Venice will be only too delighted that the whole world should have been inspired to design buildings for her; and it is the proof, provided by masters whose art will endure, that Venice must live.

The economic problem of modern Venice is closely bound up with its extensions on the mainland, which occupy the whole of the edge

Palazzo Franchetti, Accademia. Restored in 1896 by Boito,
who distorted its original Gothic elegance by his additions.

Pescheria (early 19th century), Rialto. This fish market, by Rupolo and Laurenti, is an example of early 19th-century architectural eclecticism.

of the lagoon. This is the problem of a young and enterprising population, mostly involved in commerce and industry. From 1917 onwards Porto Marghera, on the edge of the lagoon, rapidly assumed a position of enormous importance, comparable even to the 'industrial triangle' of Milan, Turin and Genoa. A road bridge (1933) linked Marghera to Venice, completely inverting the traditional relationship: now it was Venice that was an appendage to its own mainland suburbs. Mestre, born as a bridge-head for the Republic, has grown enormously (today it has more than 120,000 inhabitants): it is a commercial junction, a meeting point of important road and rail systems for Padua, Bologna, Treviso, San Donà and Trieste. The international Marco Polo airport, a few kilometres away, attracts a great deal of traffic and is the third most important in Italy after Rome and Milan.

Can this mainland 'economic lung' help to give life to the historic centre which gave it birth, or must it be the cause of its gradual decay? This is the main object of study for town-planners; they are exerting their ingenuity to find a solution which will link the two centres in some kind of productive symbiosis, and will also play a decisive part in the future of Venice as a work of art.

Complete control of the relationship between insular Venice and mainland Venice must be pursued by means of an organic plan which will clarify problems of mutual development and responsibility once and for all.

The historic island is still the headquarters of administration, the city centre of greater Venice; improvement of her urban fabric must be guaranteed, with restorations which should discourage no one, of whatever social level, from continuing to live there; rapid means of communication with the mainland are being provided (the possibility

▷

A. Dal Zotto: Monument to Carlo Goldoni (1883). Campo San Bartolomeo.

of an underground railway is now being looked into) to facilitate trade and avoid the harm that could be caused by the intensification of water traffic. Venice will always be primarily a tourist centre, and this in turn implies an extremely busy port. Tourism is closely connected with cultural activity; and Venice is an island of study, both nationally, with her already flourishing University, and internationally, with the growth and founding of cultural centres such as the Biennale, the Giorgio Cini and Querini Stampalia foundations, the international University of Art and her own well-endowed libraries and museums. The production of hand-made goods, particularly of Murano glass, will continue to be another source of the city's income, along with other traditional specialities (furniture-making, carving, leatherwork, embroidery etc).

One essential consideration for the success of such projects is, of course, the physical survival of the city, which has recently caused such grave alarm. Apparently, the natural sinking of a few centimetres per century has seriously increased. Feverishly undertaken studies have shown that in recent years Venice has been sinking at a rate of about five millimetres a year. If this continued, the consequences would be frightful. The high tides of the last few decades are making themselves felt more and more, but the reason is not clear. Those experts who attribute the sinking to some thousands of artesian wells needed by factories, or to the deepening of canals leading into the harbours, or the reduction of the lagoon basin (which was once almost twice the size and is now lessened by the area taken up by industrial zones and banked-in fishing beds) meet with opposition by champions of industrialization, who attribute the phenomena to purely geophysical causes. Here too science is at work, and there is no doubt that modern technology can save Venice, even if it has to resort to the extreme remedy of controlling the impact of the rise and fall of the tides with mobile dykes and partitions.

Other evils which threaten Venice undoubtedly come from the factors of everyday life itself: from the chemical detergents which pollute the waters of the lagoon, progressively destroying its fish; from the 'smog' produced by heating systems, and the industrial smoke that threaten the whole city, blackening it, corroding it, attacking its surface with a leprous growth. It has unfortunately been proved that frescoes and paintings, and particularly sculptures exposed to the effect of the polluted atmosphere, have deteriorated visibly over the last twenty years, quite disastrously in some cases.

But all this, too, is being tackled with energy and modern techniques. Special government bodies have been formed to take care of the suffering works of art, with highly organized and efficient laboratories; a nation-wide law has prevented the use of the most harmful fuels and is agitating for their total elimination. Venice could be given back that clean air which has kept her intact for so many centuries.

In the meantime, the Venetians themselves had begun to fight for their city; new factions, inspired by the desire to ensure her preservation and her very life, were battling on the borders of political and civil struggle, indicating the urgency of the problem. Then the whole

▷

Piazza San Marco at high tide. The sea often makes a lagoon of the Piazza; this creates a spectacle for curious visitors, but is one of the ominous signs that make the future of the city a matter of great concern.

Piazza San Marco, from the Campanile. The Piazza is in the form of a trapezoid (175 x 82 x 57 metres). The 18th-century decorations in Istrian stone stand out on the pavement, a harmony in black and grey which subtly underscores the city's inimitable grace.

world came to their aid — scientists and scholars, scientific foundations, international organizations. UNESCO took action, and the Director General, René Maheu, said in his 1969 appeal: 'Venice needs us. We must, we can save her.' But at the same time — and this is what is particularly moving — thousands of ordinary

Gondola in the boatyard of San Trovaso.

people from all over the world took action too, people for whom Venice was just a brief memory, an idyllic weekend, a postcard, a mirage: one of those golden myths to which we cling obscurely, to avoid going down under the juggernaut of mass culture — every man's inmost dream.

Map of Venice PP. 262/263.

P. 264
The domes of San Marco, reflected in the waters of the flooded Piazza.

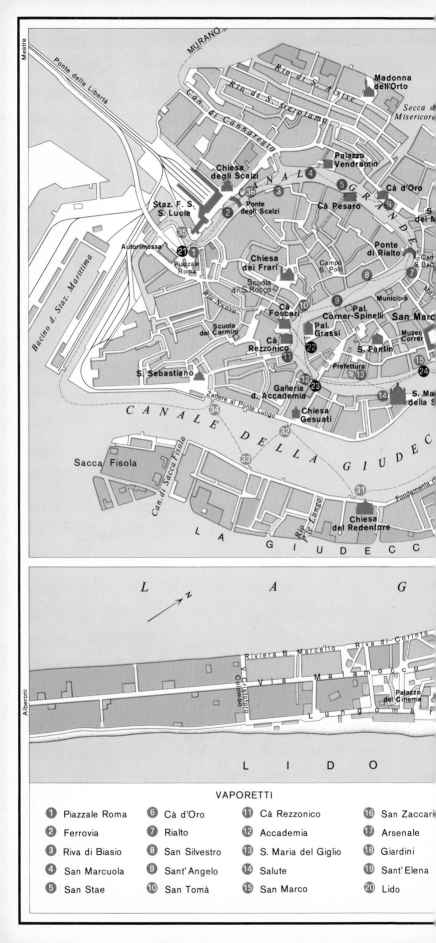

Mestre

MURANO

Ponte della Libertà

Can. di Cannaregio

Rio di S. Anvise

Rio di S. Gerolamo

Madonna dell'Orto

Secca di Misericorde

CANAL GRANDE

Palazzo Vendramin

Chiesa degli Scalzi ③⑥

Cà d'Oro

③

④

⑤

Staz. F. S. S. Lucia ②

Ponte degli Scalzi

Cà Pesaro

⑥

S. dei M

35

Ponte di Rialto

Can. S. Bart

Autorimessa

㉑①

Piazzale Roma

Chiesa dei Frari

Campo S. Pold

⑦

Scuola di S.Rocco

⑧

Rio Nuova

Cà Foscari ⑩

⑨

Municipio

Scuola del Carmini

Cà Rezzonico

Pal. Corner-Spinelli

San Marco

Pal. Grassi

Me

⑪

㉒

S. Fantin

Museo Correr

S. Sebastiano

Galleria d. Accademia

⑫ ㉓

Prefettura

⑬

㉕

㉔

Zattere al Ponte Lungo

Chiesa Gesuati

⑭

S. Ma della S

㉞

C A N A L E   D E L L A   G I U D E C

㉜

Sacca Fisola

Can. di Sacca Fisola

㉝

G I U D E C C

Rio P.te Lungo

㉛

Fondamenta

Chiesa del Redentore

L A   G I U D E C C A

L   A   G

↗ z

Riviera B. Marcello

Riva di Corinto

V. Cristoforo Colombo

V i a   M a l a m o c c o

Palazzo del Cinema

Alberoni

Lungoma r

L I D O

VAPORETTI

① Piazzale Roma	⑥ Cà d'Oro	⑪ Cà Rezzonico	⑯ San Zaccari
② Ferrovia	⑦ Rialto	⑫ Accademia	⑰ Arsenale
③ Riva di Biasio	⑧ San Silvestro	⑬ S. Maria del Giglio	⑱ Giardini
④ San Marcuola	⑨ Sant'Angelo	⑭ Salute	⑲ Sant'Elena
⑤ San Stae	⑩ San Tomà	⑮ San Marco	⑳ Lido

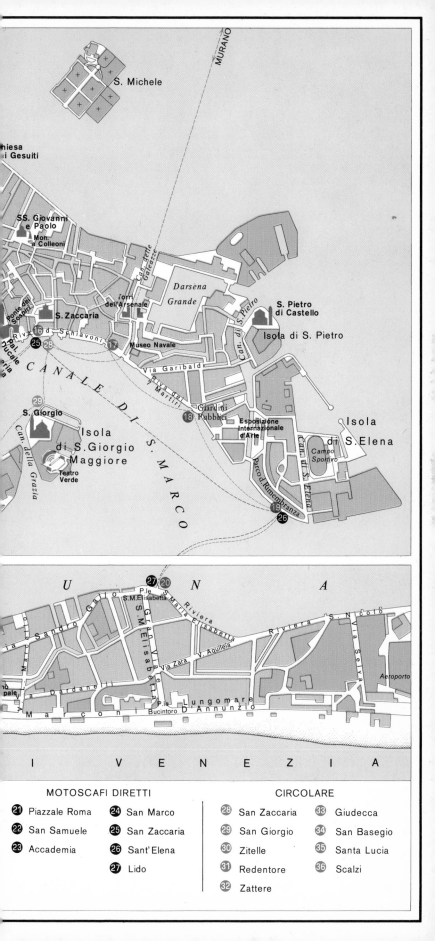

S. Michele

MURANO

Chiesa
dei Gesuiti

SS. Giovanni
e Paolo
Mon.
a Colleoni

S. Zaccaria

Ponte dei
Sospiri

Torre
dell'Arsenale

Darsena
Grande

Can. delle Galeazze

Pal.
Ducale

Riva d. Schiavoni

16

25 28

17

Museo Navale

Via Garibaldi

Riva dei 7 Martiri

S. Pietro
di Castello

Can. di S. Pietro

Isola di S. Pietro

29

S. Giorgio

Isola
di S.Giorgio
Maggiore

Can. della Grazia

Teatro
Verde

CANALE DI S. MARCO

18

Giardini
Pubblici

Esposizione
Internazionale
d'Arte

Campo
Sportivo

Can. di S. Elena

Isola
di
S.Elena

Parco d. Rimembranza

19
26

U

27 20

N

A

P.le
S.M.Elisabetta

Via S. Maria Elisabetta

Riviera

S.Sandro Gallo

Gran Viale S.M.Elisabetta

Via Zara

V. Aquileia

Riviera S.Nicolò

Via Selva

Aeroporto

nicipale

Via Dardanelli

P.le
Bucintoro

Lungomare
D'Annunzio

Marconi

I   V   E   N   E   Z   I   A

MOTOSCAFI DIRETTI

21 Piazzale Roma   **24** San Marco

22 San Samuele   **25** San Zaccaria

23 Accademia   **26** Sant'Elena

                27 Lido

CIRCOLARE

28 San Zaccaria   **33** Giudecca

29 San Giorgio   **34** San Basegio

30 Zitelle   **35** Santa Lucia

31 Redentore   **36** Scalzi

32 Zattere

Museums and Galleries

Page references in italic refer to the captions.

Biblioteca Nazionale Marciana
Libreria Sansoviniana, S. Marco 7. Weekdays, 10.00-12.00.
The Vestibule and great gilded Salone of the Libreria Sansoviniana, rooms adapted in 1597 by Scamozzi to house the collection of antiquities of Domenico and Giovanni Grimani, now house the permanent exhibition of bindings of the Biblioteca Nazionale Marciana. The collection includes the deed of gift in which Cardinal Bessarion donated his precious collection of Latin and Greek manuscripts in 1468, the first nucleus of the library; one of the most famous masterpieces of the art of illumination, the Grimani Breviary; the first two books printed in Venice; some Aldines, including the *Hypnerotomachia Poliphili*, the most famous and beautiful book of the 15th century; and Fra Mauro's *Planisferio*. 18, 64.

Collezioni della Fondazione Giorgio Cini
Island of S. Giorgio. Vaporetto and motoscafo S. Giorgio. Visits on request. Manuscript illuminations, drawings and illustrated books.

Collezione Peggy Guggenheim
Palazzo Venier dei Leoni, S. Gregorio 701. Vaporetto Salute. Summer only, Mondays, Wednesdays and Fridays 15.00-17.00.
Since 1947 the well-known connoisseur Peggy Guggenheim has brought together her collection of abstract and surrealist paintings and sculptures in the only storey ever completed of the ambitious palazzo designed in 1749 by Lorenzo Boschetti for the Venier family. All tendencies within contemporary art are represented.

Gallerie dell'Accademia
Campo della Carità. Vaporetto Accademia. Weekdays (not Mondays) 9.30-16.00; Sundays and public holidays 9.30-13.00.
In 1807 the Accademia dei Pittori e Scultori, founded in 1700, transferred its headquarters from Fonteghetto della Farina to the 15th-century buildings of the Scuola and church of Santa Maria della Carità and to the Convento dei Canonici Lateranensi, designed by Palladio in 1560. The requirements of the new academy involved unfortunate alterations. The church was divided into two floors: the lower one, used for teaching purposes, and the upper, with its collection of statues and paintings for the use of students. Other paintings from churches and suppressed monasteries were subsequently added. In 1814, paintings removed from Venice by Napoleon were brought here from the Louvre. During the 19th century, considerable bequests by Venetian noblemen enriched the collection. In 1882 the Gallerie became independent, the casts were taken to the Accademia, the bronzes and marbles to the Doge's Palace (they are now in the Cà d'Oro). The Gallerie now became the main collection of Venetian paintings. Works by the Bellinis, Giorgione, Carpaccio, Titian, Veronese, Bassano, Tiepolo, Canaletto, Guardi, Carriera, P. Longhi. 74, 80, 82, 97, 99, 111, 118, 120, 128, 153, 155, 156, 158, 159, *167*, 177, 193, 212, 217, 226, 230, 231.

Galleria Giorgio Franchetti
Cà d'Oro, junction of Cannaregio and Grand Canal. Weekdays 9.30-16.00, Sundays and public holidays 9.00-12.30.
Built by Marino Contarini during first decades of 15th century, using Lombard workmen including Raverti, and, during a second phase of activity, Venetian *tagliapietra* (stone-carvers) headed by Bon. This palazzo has been severely maltreated over the centuries. Finally Barone Giorgio Franchetti, who had acquired it in 1896, undertook intelligent restoration; at his death it was bequeathed to the state together with his rich collection of works of art, consisting of paintings and sculp-

tures by Venetian, Tuscan and Flemish artists of the fifteenth to eighteenth centuries, including Mantegna, Vittoria, Guardi and Van Dyck. 83, 88, 99, 100, *113*, *115*, 148, 166, 231.

Galleria Internazionale d'Arte Moderna

Cà Pesaro. Vaporetto San Stae. Weekdays (not Mondays) 9.00-17.00; Sundays and public holidays 9.00-12.30.

Founded in 1897 to bring together the most important works exhibited at the Biennale. It has always been housed in Cà Pesaro, the palazzo designed and completed by Antonio Gaspari in the first half of the 18th century. The palazzo belonged at one stage to the Gradenigo and finally to General Giuseppe La Masa, whose widow left it to the municipality of Venice with the condition that it should encourage young artists, particularly struggling ones. In this way the Opera Bevilacqua La Masa was founded, a foundation administered by the municipality and now in Piazza S. Marco (Procuratie Nuove), while Cà Pesaro has been given over to the Galleria Internazionale d'Arte Moderna and the Museo d'Arte Orientale.

Museo Archeologico

Libreria Sansoviniana, Piazzetta San Marco 17. Weekdays (not Mondays) 9.30-16.00; Sundays and public holidays 9.00-13.00.

Original nucleus consisted of bequest by Cardinal Domenico Grimani (1523). Collection was exhibited in anteroom of Libreria Sansoviniana and enlarged by the antiquities of Giovanni Grimani. Numerous bequests during the seventeenth and eighteenth centuries. After the Second World War it also included the archaeological collections loaned it by the Museo Correr. In the first courtyard is the famous statue of Marcus Vipsanius Agrippa. In the twenty rooms on the first floor, bronzes and marble statues, particularly of the Roman and Hellenistic eras. 175.

Museo d'Arte Orientale

Cà Pesaro. Vaporetto San Stae. Weekdays (not Mondays) 9.30-16.00, Sundays and public holidays 9.00-12.30. Oriental art.

On the death of the Conte di Bardi, his extensive collection of Eastern works of art and objects, which he kept in the Palazzo Vendramin-Calergi, was partly divided up among museums and private foreign collectors. All that remained was claimed by the Italian government after the First World War and displayed on the third floor of Cà Pesaro. Works from the Far East, tenth to eighteenth centuries. *204, 217, 220.*

Museo Correr

Procuratie Nuove, Piazza S. Marco. Weekdays 9.00-17.00; Sundays and public holidays 9.00-12.30. Historical collections and Venetian paintings.

In 1830 the nobleman Teodoro Correr donated his extremely rich art collection to the city of Venice. Open to the public in the founder's home, at San Zan Degolà, it continued to grow and ultimately came to require a new home. This was the nearby Fondaco dei Turchi on the Grand Canal. Then, further enlarged, it was transferred to the Procuratie Nuove in Piazza S. Marco. But even this soon proved inadequate. So the Institute was divided into various collections: the Museo Vetrario (museum of glassware) at Murano, the Museo del Settecento (18th-century collections) at Cà Rezzonico, the Museo Goldoniano and Centro di Studi Teatrali in Carlo Goldoni's house at S. Tomà. The Procuratie Nuove continued to house the Museo del Risorgimento, the Raccolte Storiche and the Quadreria.

Museo del Risorgimento. Relics, emblems, paintings, portraits, uniforms, banners and documents conjure up the Napoleonic period, domination by Austria and the period of the Risorgimento.

Raccolte Storiche. Documents of Venetian public life, official robes of the Republic, portraits of the Doges, banners and coins, naval relics, etc.

Quadreria. Paintings of the Venetian school, fourteenth to sixteenth centuries: Bellini, Carpaccio, Antonello da Messina, Cosmè Tura, Dirc Bouts, Van der Goes, Lotto. 27, 63, 64, 97, 118, 137, 153, 154, 156, 157, 222, 231, 233, 240.

Museo dell'Estuario

Island of Torcello. Vaporetto Torcello. Daily, 10.00-17.00. Historical.

The Museo dell'Estuario has been housed in the Palazzo del Consiglio and Palazzo dell'Archivio in Torcello since 1887.

Today it contains archaeological finds from the islands of the estuary, documents concerning Torcello, etc.

Museo di Icone dell'Istituto Ellenico

Scuola dei Greci, near ponte dei Greci. Vaporetto S. Zaccaria. Weekdays and public holidays 9.00-12.30. Sacred paintings by Greeks and Cretans faithful to the Byzantine tradition and active in Venice, mainly after the fall of Constantinople in 1453.

The community of Orthodox Greeks, which flourished in Venice as early as the 14th century, obtained permission in 1498 to group itself into a *confraternità* or religious and charitable brotherhood, electing as its patron saint St Nicholas of Myra. In the 16th century the Chiesa de' Greci was built; in the 17th century Longhena was commissioned to design two buildings, the college for the education of the young and the refuge for poor or sick Orthodox Greeks, on whose mezzanine floor the Museo di Icone now is. The Greek community, which was repossessed of its goods at the end of the Second World War, made a gift of it to the Greek state in 1949, when Greece, in agreement with the Italian government, founded an institute of Byzantine and post-Byzantine studies in Venice. 217.

Museo del Settecento Veneziano
Cà Rezzonico, S. Barnabà 3136. Vaporetto Cà Rezzonico. Weekdays 9.00-12.30, 14.30-18.30. Sundays and public holidays 9.00-12.30.
The building, which was begun in the second half of the 17th century by Longhena and finished only in 1756 by G. Massari, was acquired by the municipality of Venice in 1931 to house the 18th-century collections of the Museo Civico Correr (paintings, lacquered objects, costumes, furniture, marionettes etc.). Includes works by Tiepolo, Longhi, Guardi, Rosalba Carriera, Morlaiter. 97, 211, 217, 221, 223, 225, 226, 227, 230.

Museo Storico Navale
Granai dell'Arsenale. Riva degli Schiavoni, Campo Angelo Emo 2148. Weekdays (not Tuesday) 9.30-12.30, 14.30-16.30. Sundays and public holidays 9.30-12.00.
This museum occupies the building that was formerly the Republic's Granaries. It contains objects commemorating the seafaring past of various regions of Italy and of the Venetian Republic, and others relating to the Italian Navy up to the last war.

Museo Vetrario
Fondamenta Giustinian 8, Murano. Motoscafo Murano Museo. Weekdays 9.00-12.30, 14.30-18.30. Sundays and public holidays 9.00-12.30.
In 1861 the municipality of Murano set up this glass museum in several rooms in the late 17th-century palazzo of Bishop Marco Giustinian in the centre of the island. Today the collection, to which the glassware of

the Correr collection was added in 1932, occupies the whole of the *piano nobile* and part of the ground floor. It contains about 4000 pieces of glassware, from the 15th century to the present day. 130.

Palazzo Ducale (Doge's Palace)
Piazzetta S. Marco. Daily, 10.00-16.00.
The first definite information we have about the seat of government is the record of the building, between about 1340 and 1365, of the wing looking on to the Basin, including the Sala del Maggior Consiglio. In 1424 the façade looking on to the Piazzetta was completed. Still florid Gothic in form, the Arco Foscari was built inside the courtyard in 1462-71; the wing between the courtyard and the Rio di Palazzo was Renaissance in style. At the beginning of the 17th century the arches of the portico running along the other façades were completed. The exterior did not undergo any very large-scale modifications, but the interiors, after the fires of 1574 and 1577, were radically transformed at the end of the 16th century.
After having been the seat first of government and municipal offices, then of cultural institutions, the Doge's Palace is now a great art gallery, whose treasures bear glowing witness to the political power of the civilization of Renaissance Venice.
Contains many works of the fourteenth to eighteenth centuries: Titian, Carpaccio, Veronese, Tintoretto, Bassano, Tiepolo, Hieronymus Bosch. 9, 16, 26, 29, 51, 52, 54, 55, 56, 78, *80*, 82, *83*, *84*, 86, 88, 93, 94, 99, 100, 113, *114*, 117, *128*, 130, 137, 138, 140, 141, 156, *165*, 168, *180*, *183*, 184, 189, 190, 195, 200, 216.

Pinacoteca della Fondazione Artistica Querini-Stampalia
S. Maria Formosa 4778. Vaporetto Arsenale. Weekdays 9.00-17.00. Sundays and public holidays 10.00-12.00.
On his death in 1868 Conte Giovanni Querini-Stampalia left his library and collection of paintings to the city. The Pinacoteca still has the typical décor of a noble 18th-century residence, and the paintings are hung as they would have been originally. Works by Giovanni Bellini, Pietro Longhi, Giambattista Tiepolo. 231, 256.

Raccolte d'Arte Orientale e di porcellane
Cà del Duca, S. Samuele 3052. Motoscafo S. Samuele, Vaporetto Cà

Rezzonico. Open summer only (not Tuesdays and Thursdays). Oriental art and porcelain.

In 1961 the Hugues Le Gallais collection of Oriental art and the Marino Nani Mocenigo collection of 18th- and early 19th-century porcelain were brought together in several rooms in Cà del Duca. This palazzo was commissioned by Andrea Corner in 1453, begun by Bartolomeo Bon in 1461, and later became the property of Francesco Sforza in exchange for a palazzo at S. Polo. Confiscated by the Republic, it was given to the Grimani in the second half of the 16th century. All that remains of the first great Renaissance building in Venice is two classical columns and the powerful corner rustication.

Raccolte dei Padri Armeni Mechitaristi

Island of S. Lazzaro degli Armeni. Vaporetto S. Lazzaro degli Armeni. Daily, 15.00-17.00. Donations. Manuscripts, printed books, Venetian paintings.

Originally a leper colony, the island of S. Lazzaro was given in 1717 to the Armenian monk Mechitar (the Comforter) who had fled to Venice from the Turks. The island soon became an educational centre for young Armenians and a centre for the spread of learning in Armenia and the east, through the many translations of devotional and scientific works printed at the multilingual press founded in 1789. Today many people still visit the island, which is an active centre of culture and good works and also has a remarkable collection of illuminated books and paintings by Palma Giovane, Giambattista Tiepolo and Alessandro Longhi.

Raccolte del Seminario

Seminario Patriarcale, Campo della Salute. Vaporetto Salute. Weekdays 11.00-12.00.

The collection was started at the beginning of the nineteenth century and consists of memorial stones and sculptures from suppressed religious buildings. One of the most important subsequent bequests to the growing collection was that of Count Manfredini. Includes terracotta busts by Vittoria and Canova. 214.

Scuola di S. Giorgio degli Schiavoni

Calle dei Furlani 3259, Castello. Vaporetto S. Zaccaria. Weekdays 10.00-12.00, 15.00-17.30. Sundays and public holidays 9.00-12.00.

The Dalmatian *confratelli* of the Scuola di S. Giorgio degli Schiavoni, officially recognized in 1451, built

their own premises at the end of the 15th century, commissioning Vittore Carpaccio to decorate them. The famous cycle of commemorative canvases (*teleri*), originally in the upper room, was moved to the ground floor in 1551 when the Scuola was rebuilt.

Scuola di S. Maria del Carmine

Campo S. Margherita, Calle delle Scuole. Vaporetto Cà Rezzonico. Weekdays 9.00-12.00, 14.00-17.00, Sundays and public holidays 9.00-12.00.

Built in the second half of the 17th century, to a design by B. Longhena, who supervised the construction of the two façades. Upper room has a ceiling painted by Giambattista Tiepolo (1739-44). 217, 227.

Scuola Grande di S. Rocco

Campo S. Rocco. Vaporetto S. Tomà. Weekdays 10.00-13.00. Sundays and public holidays 9.00-13.00.

Founded in 1478, within the space of a few years the Scuola di S. Rocco had already become a *scuola grande*, one of the most flourishing in Venice. At the beginning of the 16th century work began on the building of the premises. At the fall of the Venetian Republic (1797) the *scuola* was suppressed and its art treasures and furnishings largely dispersed. But in 1806 it was reopened, still in possession of an impressive number of works of art. It now contains the main work of Tintoretto, in 35 great canvases painted between 1565 and 1580, and works by Titian and Tiepolo. 203-207.

Tesoro e Museo Marciano

Basilica di S. Marco. Treasury: weekdays 10.00-17.30, Sundays and public holidays 14.00-16.30. Museum: daily 9.00-17.00.

The Treasury of S. Marco, which probably dates back to the thirteenth century, became one of the richest and most important in all Europe with its extensive collection of precious plate, church ornaments and relics. Often dispersed by fires and restorations, it underwent its most disastrous and irreparable violation in 1797, when, after the fall of the Venetian Republic, the revolutionary government of the Cisalpine Republic had the precious objects taken to the Zecca to melt them down for their gold and silver. All that escaped destruction was arranged in its present site in 1832. In the church itself is one of the masterpieces of jewellery of all time, the Pala d'Oro. In the Museo Marciano are the four famous Byzantine bronze horses. *45, 64, 80, 156.*

Ala Napoleonica *Vaporetto Arsenale (17).* Piazza S. Marco, opposite S. Marco. In 1807, at Napoleon's behest, the church of S. Gemignano and five arches of the Procuratie Vecchie were demolished so that a grandiose ballroom could be added to the adjacent Palazzo Reale. This 'Napoleonic wing' was begun in 1810 by the neoclassical architect Giuseppe Soli. 240.

Angelo Raffaele, Church *Vaporetto Cà Rezzonico (11).* Extremely old foundation (7th century); the present building is by Francesco Contino (1618); the façade is later (1735). Inside: 18th-century organ case in five panels; Giannantonio Guardi: *Legend of Tobias,* F. Fontebasso: *St Liberalis and Saints.* 18, 56.

Arsenal *Vaporetto Arsenale (17).* Founded, apparently, in 1104, enlarged 14th-16th centuries. This occupied the extreme north-east part of Venice, between the canal of S. Pietro di Castello, S. Martino and S. Francesco della Vigna. 28, 49, *120.*

Biennale di Venezia *Vaporetto Giardini (18).* Permanent exhibition site with national pavilions.

Bridge of Sighs *See* **Ponte dei Sospiri.**

Campanile di S. Marco *Vaporetto San Marco (15).* Begun in 9th century, it took on its definitive form in 1513 under the direction of the *proto* Bon from Bergamo, who probably took up the plan of his predecessor Giorgio Spavento. It collapsed in 1902 and was rebuilt. 181, *184,* 188, 213.

Campo di S. Angelo *Vaporetto S. Angelo (9).* So-called from the extremely ancient church dedicated to the Archangel Michael, demolished in 1837. 18, 226.

Campo S. Margherita *Vaporetto Cà Rezzonico (11).* Enlarged and given its present form in the second half of the 19th century, by filling in various *rii* (canals) that converged in it. Takes its name from the church of S. Margherita, closed down in 1840, and later turned first into a Protestant church, then into a cinema. 217

Campo S. Polo *Vaporetto S. Tomà (10).* Largest *campo* in Venice, was used for popular meetings, festivals and 'bullfighting. Among its most important buildings: Palazzo Tiepolo, formerly Maffetti, 18th century; Palazzo Soranzo, with a 15th-century Gothic façade; Palazzo Donà, 16th century; Palazzo Corner-Mocenigo, 16th century, by Michele Sammicheli. The church of S. Polo itself is 15th-century Gothic. 193, *234.*

Campo S. Samuele *Motoscafo S. Samuele (22).* On Grand Canal opposite Cà Rezzonico. On the right of the Campo, Palazzo Grassi; on the left, Palazzo Barnabò (formerly Cappello, then Malipiero). In middle of *campo,* small campanile of S. Samuele, end of 12th century, with very old church beside it, largely rebuilt in 1685. 224.

Campo S. Zanipolo *Vaporetto or Motoscafo San Zaccaria (16,25).* After Piazza S. Marco, the most important square in Venice. In 1496 Andrea Verrocchio's monument to Colleoni was put up here; the main buildings are the Scuola di S. Marco (now the Ospedale Civile), and the church of S. Zanipolo (SS. Giovanni e Paolo) which was long the resting-place of the Doges. *122,* 128.

Cà Da Mosto *Vaporetto Rialto (7).* Venetian house of the Veneto-Byzantine type, 13th century. Originally home of the Da Mosto family, famous navigators (Alvise Da Mosto). From the 16th century until the end of the 18th, it was the Albergo del Leon Bianco, the most famous inn in the city; princely visitors included Emperor Joseph II. 50, 51, 54.

Cà Foscari *Vaporetto S. Tomà (10).* Built by Doge Foscari from 1452 in the Gothic style. Now headquarters of University. 97, 252.

Cà d'Oro *See* Index of Museums: **Galleria Giorgio Franchetti.**

Cà Rezzonico *See* Index of Museums: **Museo del Settecento.**

Corpus Domini, Church and Convent (demolished). Cannaregio. Demolished prior to building of railway station. 246.

Corte del Milion *Vaporetto or motoscafo Rialto (7).* Near S. Giovanni Crisostomo, and so-called after *Il Milione* by Marco Polo, who is said to have lived there. *31, 37.*

Dogana da Mar *Vaporetto Salute (14).* Near church of Salute; built by Giuseppe Benoni (second half 17th century) on site originally occupied by tower with high crested walls. Two outer wings rebuilt in 1835-38 by G. A. Pigazzi. 214, *216.*

Doge's Palace *See* Index of Museums: **Palazzo Ducale.**

Fabbriche Nuove di Rialto (Arcade of Erberia) *Vaporetto Rialto (7).* Built to plans by J. Sansovino (*c.* 1555), they were extended along Grand Canal for the length of 25 arcades. 180.

Fabbriche Vecchie di Rialto *Vaporetto Rialto (7).* Originally centre for officials of trade, navigation and food supplies; now Law Courts. Built for Signoria 1520-22, to plan by Scarpagnino. 178, 179.

Fondaco dei Tedeschi *Vaporetto Rialto (7).* On Grand Canal at Rialto; now Post Office. Original building burnt in 1505, new one by Spavento and Abbondi. Originally decorated with frescoes by Giorgione and Titian. 177.

Fondaco dei Turchi *Vaporetto S. Stae (5).* On Grand Canal. Almost completely rebuilt during 19th century by Berchet, on old model. Veneto-Byzantine façade, 12th–13th centuries. In 1621 Republic granted it as Fondaco to Turkish merchants, who kept it until 1838. Now Museo di Storia Naturale. 50, 54, 128, 200, 248.

Fort of St. Andrea *Opposite S. Niccolò (Lido).* Built in 16th century by Michele Sammicheli. 192.

Frari, Church *See* **S. Maria Gloriosa dei Frari.**

Gesuati, Church *See* **S. Maria del Rosario.**

Gesuiti, Church *See* **S. Maria dei Gesuiti.**

Giardinetti Reali *Vaporetto or motoscafo S. Marco (15, 24).* Public gardens on Riva del Bacino, laid out on the orders of Napoleon, who had the old Fondaci del Grano demolished. 240.

Giardini Pubblici *Vaporetto Giardini (18).* Laid out by Selva in 1810 on land formerly occupied by typical working-class district. 244.

Libreria Sansoviniana *Vaporetto or motoscafo S. Marco (15, 24).* Piazzetta S. Marco. Built by Sansovino (1537-54) to house library given to Republic by Cardinal Bessarion. Now the Biblioteca Nazionale Marciana. (*See* Index of Museums.) 184, 188, 189, 190.

Loggetta di S. Marco *Vaporetto or motoscafo S. Marco (15, 24).* Built 1537-49 by Sansovino; became guardroom for the guard of Arsenalotti. Rebuilt in 1912 after the Campanile fell. *178, 184, 188.*

Maddalena, Church *Vaporetto S. Marcuola (4).* Built to design by Temanza at end of 18th century. Interior: Giandomenico Tiepolo, *Last Supper.* 224, *238.*

Madonna dell'Orto, Church *Vaporetto Cà d'Oro (6).* Built mid-14th century by Fra Tiberio da Parma as S. Cristoforo; changed its name when old image of Virgin, found in neighbouring garden (*orto*), was brought into church. Rebuilt 15th century, using some pre-existing material. Interior: Jacopo Tintoretto, *Last Judgment, Presentation of the Virgin.* 57, 102, *104,* 106, 107, 110, 137, 203, 248.

Mercerie. From S. Marco to Rialto, this is the liveliest street of the city, with its many shops and bars. 128, 184.

Mulino Stucky *Vaporetto or motoscafo Accademia (16, 23).* Dorsoduro. Mills, built about 1880 in neo-Gothic style. 248.

Oratorio dei Crociferi *Vaporetto S. Zaccaria (16).* Built originally as hospital in 12th century (opposite church of S. Maria dei Gesuiti). Restored 1585-95. Contains some of Palma Giovane's finest works. 208.

Palazzo Albrizzi (now **Rubin de Cervin**) *Vaporetto S. Silvestro (8).* S. Polo 1940. Built at the end of the 17th century, is one of the most splendid of Venetian patrician residences. Salone with stuccoes of early 18th century; furnishings of the period.

Palazzo Ariani (afterwards **Minotto**) *Vaporetto Cà Rezzonico (11).* Dorsoduro 2376. Gothic palazzo with one of the first examples of Venetian Gothic composite windows, Oriental in inspiration. 56.

Palazzo Barozzi (now demolished) S. Moisè. Appears in De' Barbari plan of 1500. Consisted of more or less square block with its east side on the *rio*, crested walls and towers. On its façade it had a broad ground-floor portico topped by a loggia, anticipating Doge's Palace. 54, 56.

Palazzo Barzizza *Vaporetto S. Silvestro (8)*. Here there are important remains (paterae, capitals, columns of the central window complex) of the original Veneto-Byzantine building of the 12th-13th century. 51.

Palazzo Bernardo *Vaporetto S. Silvestro (8)*. Ponte Bernardo. An interesting and well-preserved example of Venetian Gothic architecture of the 'florid' period (15th century). 97.

Palazzo dei Camerlenghi *Vaporetto Rialto (7)*. Built between 1525 and 1528 for the Camerlenghi or city treasurers. 174, 179.

Palazzo del Cammello (or **Mastelli**) *Vaporetto Cà d'Oro (6)*. Near Madonna dell'Orto. So-called from a relief of a man dragging a camel. Belonged to the three brothers Rioba, Sandi and Alfani, merchants who came from Morea in 1112 and took on the name Mastelli. Upper floor still has traces of Gothic forms (15th century) in central row of windows and corner balcony. *35*, 38.

Palazzo Cavalli *Vaporetto or motoscafo Accademia (12, 23)*. On Grand Canal opposite Accademia. Gothic building of 15th century. About 1896 large-scale restorations and erratic additions carried out under the direction of the architect C. Boito, who added a grand inside staircase. Now premises of the Federal Institute of Savings Banks of the Veneto. 248.

Palazzo Contarini del Bovolo *Vaporetto or motoscafo S. Marco (15, 24)*. By S. Luca. Notable for its unusual spiral staircase (Scala del Bovolo, q.v.). 134.

Palazzo Contarini-Fasan *Vaporetto or motoscafo S. Marco (15, 24)*. On Grand Canal (opposite Salute); the name (Fasan, pheasant) apparently derives from the owners' passion for shooting. Highly ornate Gothic building. Traditionally known as 'Desdemona's house'. 97, *117*.

Palazzo Corner-Mocenigo *Vaporetto S. Silvestro (8)*. Now headquarters of Customs Office. Built in 16th century by Michele Sammicheli, on a vast site between Rio and Campo S. Polo. 193.

Palazzo Corner-Spinelli (now **Salom**) *Vaporetto S. Angelo (9)*. On Grand Canal. One of the finest palazzi of Renaissance Venice. Built by M. Codussi. 127, *143*, 183.

Palazzo Dario *Vaporetto Salute (14)*. Grand Canal, opposite S. Maria del Giglio. Remarkable for the lively polychromy of the marble decoration of the façade. Built about 1487, apparently to a design by P. Lombardo. *137*.

Palazzo Donà *Vaporetto S. Tomà (10)*. Grand Canal (Traghetto Accademia). Veneto-Byzantine style of 12th–13th centuries. Known as 'Palazzo della Madonnetta' from the relief of the Virgin and Child, after school of Donatello (15th century). 51.

Palazzo Ducale *See* Index of Museums.

Palazzo Farsetti *Vaporetto Rialto (7)*. Grand Canal near Rialto; apparently built in 12th century for the Dandolo family; acquired by the Tuscan Farsetti family in 1669. Here Filippo Farsetti collected the plaster casts which subsequently went to form the Accademia Farsetti. Municipal offices since 1898. 51, 54.

Palazzo Giustinian *Vaporetto or motoscafo S. Marco (15, 24)*. Grand Canal. Built about the middle of the 15th century. Biennale office and Teatro del Ridotto. 97.

Palazzo Giustinian-Lolin (now **Levi**) *Vaporetto or motoscafo Accademia (12, 23)*. On Grand Canal. Youthful work of B. Longhena (1623). 211.

Palazzo Grassi *Motoscafo S. Samuele (22)*. On Grand Canal; by G. Massari (1748–72). Roman in inspiration, it anticipates neoclassical coldness. Headquarters of Centro Internazionale delle Arti e del Costume. 224, *236*.

Palazzo Grimani *Vaporetto S. Angelo (9)*. On Grand Canal; by M. Sammicheli (16th century), manneristically developing classical motifs in the series of great arches linked within a massive framework of pillars. Seat of Court of Appeal. 193.

Palazzo Labia *Vaporetto Ferrovia (2)*. On Grand Canal (S. Geremia). By Cominelli, first half 18th century. Ballroom decorated by G.B. Tiepolo.

Now offices of Radio Televisione Italiana (RAI). 222, 227.

Palazzo Loredan *Vaporetto Rialto (7).* On Grand Canal, near Rialto. Said to have been founded by Zane family in 12th century; in 14th passed to Piscopia branch of Corner family. In 18th century became property of Loredan family. From 1868, municipal offices, together with neighbouring Palazzo Farsetti. 51, 54.

Palazzo Pesaro *See* Index of Museums: **Galleria Internazionale d'Arte Moderna.**

Palazzo Pisani *Vaporetto or motoscafo Accademia (12, 23).* Campo S. Stefano. Begun in second half of 16th century, completed in 18th. The Pisani spent enormous sums building and decorating it. Now premises of the Conservatorio Benedetto Marcello. 218.

Palazzo Pisani-Gritti *Vaporetto S. Maria del Giglio (13).* On Grand Canal. Gothic building of 15th century, now a hotel.

Palazzo Pisani-Moretta *Vaporetto S. Tomà (10).* On Grand Canal. The name Moretta is a corruption of Almoro, the first member of this branch. An impressive Gothic building (mid-15th century). P. Veronese painted his *Family of Darius* here (in National Gallery, London, since 1857). Tiepolo painted frescoes on ceiling, and Piazzetta the *Death of Darius* now in Cà Rezzonico. 97.

Palazzo delle Prigioni *Vaporetto S. Zaccaria (16).* Second half of 16th century (Rusconi, Da Ponte). Entered across Bridge of Sighs from Doge's Palace. Now houses the Circolo Artistico, which presents concerts of high quality all the year round. *179, 200.*

Palazzo Priuli (formerly **Ruzzini**) *Vaporetto Arsenale (17).* S. Antonin. Gothic building of 15th century, extremely impressive. 218, 222.

Palazzo Reale *See* **Procuratie Nuove.**

Palazzo Rezzonico *See* Index of Museums: **Museo del Settecento.**

Palazzo Sandi-Porto (later **Cipollato**) *Vaporetto S. Angelo (9).* Built in 1725. In salon on *piano nobile,* G.B. Tiepolo's painted ceiling (1724-25) with allegorical figures. Other decorations by Tiepolo in two smaller rooms. 227.

Palazzo Savorgnan *Vaporetto Ferrovia (2).* Cannaregio 349. By Sardi (end 17th century). 222.

Palazzo del Console J. Smith *Vaporetto Rialto (7).* On Grand Canal; by Visentini (18th century). The home of Canaletto's enterprising patron.

Palazzo Soranzo - Van Axel - Barozzi *Vaporetto S. Zaccaria (16).* Near S. Maria dei Miracoli. One of the most interesting Gothic buildings. Built by the Soranzo family 1473-79, on site of Veneto-Byzantine Palazzo Gradenigo. Then passed into possession of the Venier and Sanudo families, and was acquired in 1627 by the Van Axels, rich Flemish merchants who became Venetian noblemen in 1665. On *fondamenta,* Gothic doorway with original wooden panels and old knocker. In courtyard, beautiful open staircase. 98.

Palazzo Surian *Vaporetto Ferrovia (2).* Cannaregio (Ponte delle Guglie). Built first half of 18th century by Sardi. Has beautiful Serlian windows. In 18th century was French embassy. 222.

Palazzo Vendramin-Calergi *Vaporetto S. Marcuola (4).* On Grand Canal; built by Codussi (1504). Residence of Loredan family, then Grimani, then Vendramin-Calergi. Now casino. 128, *144,* 183.

Palazzo Widmann *Vaporetto Rialto (7).* At S. Canciano. 17th-century façade by Longhena. Originally belonged to the Laviotti, then to the Widmanns, merchants from Carinthia who had famous collections of paintings. 212.

Pescheria *Vaporetto Rialto (7).* On Grand Canal; built in 1907 by Laurenti and Rupolo in imitation Gothic style. 248, *254.*

Piazzale Roma *Vaporetto Piazzale Roma (1, 21).* Built 1935; terminus of road linking Venice to mainland. 210, 252.

Piazza S. Marco *Vaporetto or motoscafo S. Marco (15, 24).* Trapezoidal open space with decorated pavement, flanked by S. Marco itself, the Ala Napoleonica, and Procuratie Nuove and Vecchie. *66-67, 74,* 128, 184, 191, *233, 244, 256, 259.*

Piazzetta di S. Marco *Vaporetto or motoscafo S. Marco (15, 24).* Between Libreria Sansoviniana and Doge's Palace. Two columns, in honour of Marco and Todaro, St Mark and St Theodore, patrons of the city, placed there in 1172. 40, *79,* 82, 84, 86, 88, 128, *165,* 184, 188, 195.

Ponte della Paglia *Vaporetto S. Zaccaria (16).* On Riva dei Schiavoni. One of the oldest bridges (1360), rebuilt on old model and broadened in 1847. So called, apparently, from the boats loaded with straw which moored there. At base of end arch: shrine of the Fraglia del Traghetto, the boatmen's guild, with relief of *Madonna dei gondolieri* (1583). 82.

Ponte di Rialto *Vaporetto Rialto (7).* In early times this was the only permanent link between the two banks of the Grand Canal. Originally in wood, was rebuilt in stone by Antonio da Ponte (1588–91). *51, 117, 177, 178, 180, 188.*

Ponte dei Sospiri (Bridge of Sighs) Links Palazzo delle Prigioni with Doge's Palace. Built by Contino towards end of 16th century. 51, 200.

Procuratie Nuove *Vaporetto or motoscafo S. Marco (15, 24).* In Piazza S. Marco; originally residences of Procurators of S. Marco; built later than those opposite (Procuratie Vecchie). Begun by Scamozzi (16th century) on inspiration from the nearby Libreria Sansoviniana, they were completed by Longhena. After the fall of the Republic, Napoleon turned them into a Palazzo Reale. They now house the Museo Correr, Museo del Risorgimento, Museo Archeologico and Biblioteca Correr. 240.

Procuratie Vecchie *Vaporetto or motoscafo S. Marco (15, 24).* Piazza S. Marco; originally residences of Procurators of S. Marco. The present building was put up by M. Codussi, 16th century. *29, 128, 181, 240.*

Redentore, Church *Circolare Redentore (31).* Island of Giudecca. Dedicated to Redeemer (*Redentore*) after plague of 1576. Architect Andrea Palladio, assisted by *proto* Andrea da Ponte. Interior: Francesco Bassano, *Birth of Mary* and *Resurrection.* In sacristy: C. Saraceni, *Ecstasy of St Francis;* A. Vivarini, *Madonna;* L. Bastiani, *Madonna adoring the Child. 93, 195, 216.*

Rio di S. Lorenzo *Vaporetto S. Zaccaria (16).* Flanked by beautiful palazzi, reproduced by Gentile Bellini in one of his paintings in the S. Giovanni Evangelista cycle (Accademia). Completed by the 16th-century façade of Palazzo Cappello. 156.

S. Alvise, Church *Vaporetto Cà d'Oro (6).* Church built, according to tradition, with gift of Antonia Venier after apparition of St Louis of Toulouse. Inside: Tiepolo, *Crowning with Thorns, Way to Calvary, Flagellation.* 102, 106.

S. Angelo, Church *See* **Angelo Raffaele.**

S. Antonin, Church *Vaporetto Arsenale (17).* Founded in 4th century, rebuilt at end of 17th on design apparently by B. Longhena. Inside: Vecchia, *Noah's Ark* (his best work); L. Bastiani, *Deposition with the Three Marys.* 18, 210.

Ss. Apostoli, Church *Vaporetto Rialto (7).* A very ancient foundation, restored and rebuilt on various occasions up to the mid-18th century. Interior with single nave: G.B. Tiepolo, *Communion of St Lucy.* 18.

S. Barnaba, Church *Vaporetto Cà Rezzonico (11).* By Lorenzo Boschetti, 18th century. Interior: C. Cedini, *Apotheosis of St Barnabas,* on ceiling.

S. Bartolomeo, Church *Vaporetto Rialto (7).* Founded in 12th century, restored in 18th. Interior: works by Sebastiano del Piombo; J. Rottenhammer, *Annunciation.*

S. Beneto (S. Benedetto), Church *Vaporetto Rialto (7).* Founded probably in the 11th century; the present building dates from the 17th. Interior: B. Strozzi, *St Sebastian;* G.B. Tiepolo, *St Francis of Paola;* S. Mazzoni, *St Benedict Commends the Parish Priest to the Care of the Virgin Mary, St Benedict and St John the Baptist with the Virtues.* 211.

S. Canciano, Church *Vaporetto Rialto (7).* Ancient foundation, restored by Gaspari in 18th century. Interior: N. Renieri, *St Philip Neri;* A. Zanchi, *The Pool of Bethesda, The Miracle of the Loaves and Fishes.*

S. Cassiano, Church *Vaporetto S. Stae (5).* Built in 10th century, restructured in 17th. Interior: organ with paintings by Schiavone; L. Bassano, *Birth of St John, Visitation of St Zacharias;* G.B. Pittoni, *Madonna and Saints;* J. Tintoretto, *Descent into Hell, Crucifixion.* 138.

S. Chiara, Church (demolished). S. Croce. Now barracks. 18.

S. Croce, Church (demolished). Gives its name to one of the *sestieri* of the city. Very ancient, demolished in 1810; one original granite column with capital (11th century) remains, engaged in wall of Papadopoli Gardens on site of the church and convent. 18, 50.

S. Donato, Church *See* **S. Maria e Donato.**

S. Elena, Church *Vaporetto or motoscafo S. Elena (19, 26).* Founded in 13th century on occasion of the translation of the relics of St Helen; rebuilt 1435 by the Olivetan monks. Deconsecrated in 1807, reopened for worship in 1928. On the porch, a sculpture by Antonio Rizzo (1476). 102, 110, 137, 138, 248.

S. Eufemia, Church *Circolare Giudecca (33)*. Founded in 9th century, rebuilt in 18th. Interior: G.M. Morlaiter, *Madonna, Christ.*

S. Fantin, Church *Vaporetto or motoscafo S. Marco (15, 24)*. Built on plan by A. Abbondi and completed by Sansovino (16th century). Interior: Palma Giovane, *Deposition, Doge Mocenigo.*

S. Felice, Church *Vaporetto Cà d'Oro (6)*. Founded in 10th century, rebuilt in 16th. Interior: J. Tintoretto, *St Demetrius.*

S. Fosca, Church *Vaporetto Cà d'Oro (6)*. Rebuilt late 17th-early 18th century. Interior: P.A. Novelli, *St Joseph*; D. Tintoretto, *Holy Family and Donor.*

S. Francesco del Deserto, Church and Friary *Island of S. Francesco del Deserto, near Burano.* Monastic community on the lonely island where St Francis is said to have been shipwrecked. 14th century cloister. 20.

S. Francesco della Vigna, Church *Vaporetto Arsenale (17)*. So called because of the vine given in 1253 by Doge Ziani to the Friars Minor. Rebuilt in 1534 to designs by Sansovino, with a Palladian façade. Interior: G. Bellini, *Madonna and Saints*; F. Fontebasso, chapel of S. Pietro d'Alcantara; P. Veronese, *Madonna and Saints.* The Giustiniani chapel is decorated with sculptures by the Paduan school (end of 15th century).

S. Gallo, Church *Vaporetto or motoscafo S. Marco (15, 24)*. Restored in 18th century. Interior: J. Tintoretto, *Redeemer between St Gall and St Mark.*

S. Gemignano, Church (demolished). S. Marco. The first church of S. Gemignano opposite S. Marco, beginning of 9th century, was demolished at end of 12th to extend Piazza S. Marco. The second church of S. Gemignano was built soon afterwards, also opposite S. Marco; façade by Sansovino. Demolished at Napoleon's behest in 1807 for the building of the Ala Napoleonica. 18, 29, 181, 240.

S. Geremia, Church *Vaporetto Ferrovia (2)*. Founded in 11th century, rebuilt in 13th and again in 18th. The campanile is one of the oldest in Venice (12th century?). Interior: P.A. Novelli, *Presentation in the Temple*; Giovanni Ferrari, high altar; G. Marchiori, *St Francis de Sales, St John Nepomucene, Immaculate Conception.* 222.

S. Giacomo dell'Orio, Church *Vaporetto Riva di Biasio (3)*. Very ancient foundation (possibly 9th century). The name seems to have been connected with a laurel tree (*alloro*) which was said to have stood near the church itself. Rebuilt in 13th century (*c.* 1225) and further altered in 16th. Interior: L. Lotto, main altarpiece; P. Veronese, sacristy ceiling and altarpiece. The campanile is a Veneto-Byzantine construction (12th-13th centuries). 38.

S. Giacomo di Rialto (S. Giacometto), Church *Vaporetto Rialto (7)*. Traditionally regarded as the oldest church in Venice. The building dates back to the 11th century and was connected with the growth of the market of Rialto (1097). The original form was retained in the restorations of 1601. In front of the façade is a characteristic portico, with wooden architraving supported by five columns. The clock on the façade was built in 1410, rebuilt in 17th century. Small campanile *alla romana* (17th century). Interior: L. Bassano, *Birth of Mary.* 18, 19, 179.

S. Giobbe, Church *Vaporetto Ferrovia (2)*. Built mid-15th century in Gothic style by architect Antonio Gambello. P. Lombardo contributed first Renaissance elements (porch and dome). Martini chapel with terracottas in the style of the Della Robbia. Interior: P. Bordone, *SS. Peter, Andrew and Nicholas*; G. Savoldo, *Nativity*; A. Vivarini, *Annunciation.* 123, 126, 155, 248, 252.

S. Giorgio Maggiore, Church and monastery *Circolare San Giorgio (29)*. On island opposite S. Marco. In 10th century a Benedictine church and monastery were built here; destroyed by the earthquake of 1223. In 1559 Palladio began building the present church, refectory and first cloister. The double ramp staircase is by B. Longhena, as are the abbots' quarters and library. After the fall of Venice the monastery was closed. Since 1951 it has been the headquarters of the Fondazione Giorgio Cini, a centre for studies and research on Venice. Interior of church: Tintoretto, *Last Supper, Gathering of the Manna* (chancel); Jacopo Bassano, *Adoration of the Shepherds*; S.

Ricci, *Madonna and Saints*. In sacristy: Carpaccio, *St George*. Wooden choir stalls of 1598. *184, 193, 195, 216.*

S. Giovanni in Bragora, Church *Vaporetto Arsenale (17).* The name may derive from *bragora* (marketplace) or from *bragolare* (fishing trade). Founded in 8th century, restored in 11th and 12th centuries, rebuilt in 1475 in Gothic style. Interior: Cima da Conegliano, *Baptism of Jesus, Constantine*; L. Corona, *Flagellation, Crowning with Thorns*; Alvise Vivarini, *Resurrection*; B. Vivarini, *Madonna and Saints.* 16.

S. Giovanni Crisostomo, Church *Vaporetto Rialto (7).* Built between 1497 and 1504 by Mauro Codussi. Interior: Giovanni Bellini, *St John Chrysostom*; Sebastiano del Piombo, high altar, *Madonna and Saints*; T. Lombardo, marble altarpiece. 127, 178.

S. Giovanni Elemosinario, Church *Vaporetto Rialto (7).* Rebuilt by Scarpagnino (1757–39). Interior, above high altar: Pordenone, *SS. Katherine, Sebastian and Roch.*

Ss. Giovanni e Paolo, Church *See* **S. Zanipolo.**

S. Giuseppe di Castello, Church *Vaporetto Giardini (18).* Conventual church rebuilt about middle of 16th century; originally belonged to Augustinian nuns, then Salesian. Interior: Pietro Ricci, ceiling with *Triumph of St Joseph.* 248.

S. Giustina, Church (demolished). Castello. Closed down in 1810; the adjoining convent is now the headquarters of a school, the Liceo Scientifico G.B. Benedetti. Lower part of façade still in existence, by B. Longhena. 16.

S. Gregorio, Church *Vaporetto Salute (14).* Founded in 806, granted to Benedictines of S. Ilario, who brought abbey of S. Gregorio here. This monastic centre completely lapsed in 1775. The church, now a regional restoration centre, is a Gothic building begun about the middle of the 15th century. 56, 86, 102, 111, 214.

S. Lio, Church *Vaporetto S. Zaccaria (16).* Dedicated in 12th century to St Leo IX ('Lion' in Venetian dialect). Restored internally in 18th century. Interior: G.D. Tiepolo, ceiling fresco; P.A. Novelli, *Saints*; Titian, *St James*; P. Vecchia, *Crucifixion.*

S. Lucia, Church (demolished). Cannaregio. A Palladian church, it used to house the relics of St Lucy, now in S. Geremia. Demolished for building of railway station, which takes its name from this church.

S. Marco, Church *Vaporetto or motoscafo S. Marco (15, 24).* Built 828-1094. Doges' chapel, now cathedral of Venice. Mosaics 12th-18th centuries. Interior: high altar, Pala d'Oro; G.B. Tiepolo, *Holy Family*; J. and P.P. dalle Masegne, iconostasis. 9, 16, 19, 25, 26, 28, 29, 30, 31, 32, 34, 40, 44, *45, 46-47, 49, 51, 52, 53, 58, 59,* 60, *61, 62,* 64, *68, 73, 75,* 77, *79,* 83, *88,* 102, 113, 153, 178, 180, 181, 189, 195, 212, 216, 234.

S. Marcuola, Church *Vaporetto S. Marcuola (4).* By G. Massari, 18th century. Interior: G.M. Morlaiter, sculptures; J. Tintoretto, *Last Supper.* 221.

S. Maria Assunta, Church *Island of Torcello.* Cathedral founded, apparently, in 639 by order of Exarch of Ravenna, Isaac. Rebuilt in 864 and 1008. General impression is of Veneto-Byzantine building of 11th century. Interior: mosaics of Veneto-Byzantine school, 12th-13th centuries. 14, 20, 21, 25, 32, *39,* 40, 79.

S. Maria della Carità, Church *Vaporetto or motoscafo Accademia (12, 23).* Dorsoduro. Gothic building of mid-15th century, now Accademia delle Belle Arti and Gallerie dell'Accademia. (*See* Index of Museums.) 102, 111, 153, *167,* 193.

S. Maria del Carmelo (Carmini), Church *Vaporetto Cà Rezzonico (11).* Built in 14th century, with 16th-century façade. Interior: A. Schiavone, paintings on organ; G.B. Cima, *Nativity;* L. Lotto, *St Nicholas;* G. Diziani: in chancel, *St Helen discovering the True Cross, Plague of Serpents.*

S. Maria e Donato, Church *Murano.* Veneto-Byzantine architecture of 12th century, with three naves and keel vault (*carena di nave*). Mosaic floor with Christian symbols. Apse with loggetta in Lombard style. 45, 73.

S. Maria della Fava, Church *Vaporetto Rialto (7).* So called because of a shop where *fave dolci* (cakes) were made on All Souls' Day. The church was designed by Antonio Gaspari (1711), the presbytery is by G. Massari (1750–53). Interior: G.B. Tiepolo, *Childhood of Mary;* G.B. Piazzetta, *Madonna and St Philip Neri;* Amigoni, *Madonna, Visitation;* Morlaiter, tabernacle and angels on main altar. 222, 226.

S. Maria Formosa, Church *Vaporetto or motoscafo S. Zaccaria (16, 25)*. According to tradition, one of the eight churches built by St Magnus, bishop of Oderzo. Rebuilt (1492) on a model by M. Codussi. Two façades. Interior: Bartolomeo Vivarini, *Triptych*; Palma Vecchio, *Altar of St Bernard, Pietà*. 18, 126, 127, 196, 231, 248.

S. Maria Gloriosa dei Frari, Church *Vaporetto S. Tomà (10)*. Originally called Cà Grande. The *Frari* were the Franciscan Friars Minor. The present building was begun in the mid-14th century. Interior: Titian, main altarpiece, *Our Lady of the Assumption*, Pesaro altarpiece; A. Bregno, Foscari monument; Donatello, *St John the Baptist*; A. Rizzo, Tron monument; J. della Quercia (attrib.), Savelli equestrian monument. In sacristy: P. Veneziano, *Madonna*; Giovanni Bellini, triptych. 56, 57, 102, *103*, 104, 110, 127, 137, 138, *155*, 156, *206*.

S. Maria dei Gesuiti, Church *Vaporetto or motoscafo S. Zaccaria (16, 25)*. First belonged to the order of the Crociferi. Only in 1657, when the Jesuits acquired the nearby monastery, was the church rebuilt; it dated back to the 12th century. Interior: Titian, *Martyrdom of St Lawrence*.

S. Maria del Giglio, Church *See* **S. Maria Zobenigo.**

S. Maria Materdomini, Church *Vaporetto S. Stae (5)*. Building begun *c.* 1502 and completed before 1540. Interior: Byzantine Madonna; V. Catena, *Martyrdom of St Christina*. 49.

S. Maria dei Miracoli, Church *Vaporetto Cà d'Oro (6)*. Cannaregio. Built between 1481 and 1489, designed by Pietro Lombardo with the help of his sons Antonio and Tullio. Painted ceiling by P. M. Pennacchi, V. Dalle Destre and other Bellinian masters. 124, *127*, 144, 212.

S. Maria di Nazareth (S. Maria degli Scalzi), Church *Vaporetto Ferrovia (2)*. Building begun in 1660 for the Discalced Carmelite Friars (*Scalzi*) on a plan by Longhena; the façade is by Sardi. Interior: G. B. Tiepolo's main ceiling was destroyed by a bomb in 1917; other ceilings by Tiepolo in the chapels, *Glory of St Teresa, Christ in the Garden;* Meyring, altarpiece, *Ecstasy of St Teresa*. *203*, 217, 227.

S. Maria della Pietà, Church *Vaporetto or motoscafo S. Zaccaria (16, 25)*. By Massari (1744-60). Designed to be used by girls cared for in nearby institution. The oval plan and shallow vaulted roof were intended to obtain better acoustics. Interior: G. B. Tiepolo, ceiling with *Triumph of the Virgin;* Piazzetta and G. Angeli, altarpiece, *Visitation;* Morlaiter, *Two Archangels;* G. Marchiori, *St Peter;* A. Gai, *St Mark*. In choir: Moretto da Brescia, *Christ in the house of Simon the Pharisee*. 221, 224, 227.

S. Maria del Rosario (Gesuati), Church *Vaporetto or motoscafo Accademia (12, 23), circolare Zattere (32)*. Present church built by the Dominicans who succeeded the 'poor Gesuati' in 1668. The design with the classical façade is by Giorgio Massari. Interior: Morlaiter, sculptures; G. B. Tiepolo, ceiling fresco with *Glory of St Dominic, Three Dominican Saints;* Piazzetta, *Three Dominican Saints;* Sebastiano Ricci, *Pius V and saints;* J. Tintoretto, *Crucifixion*. 208, 221, 224, 226, 227.

S. Maria della Salute, Church *Vaporetto Salute (14)*. Built (1631-81) in commemoration of deliverance from plague, on the vast site of the Ospizio della Trinita, to a plan by Longhena. Interior: Josse Le Court, main altar, *Venice Delivered from Plague;* Titian, *Pentecost;* Luca Giordano, *Presentation, Assumption, Birth of Mary*. In sacristy: Titian, *Altarpiece of S. Marco,* ceiling executed for monks of S. Spirito in Isola; J. Tintoretto, *Marriage at Cana*. 13, 97, 124, 195, *208*, 210, 212, 213, 215, 216, 217.

S. Maria Zobenigo (S. Maria del Giglio), Church *Vaporetto S. Maria del Giglio (13)*. Known as Zobenigo, from the Jubanico family, who apparently founded it in 9th century. Façade built 1678-83 to a design by Sardi. This is the mausoleum of the Barbaro family. Interior: Tintoretto, *The Four Evangelists, Christ with St Justin and St Francis of Paola;* Morlaiter, sculptures on altars; *Via Crucis* by 18th-century artists; A. Zanchi, *Abraham dividing the World*. 28, *198*, 213, 217.

S. Michele in Isola, Church *Vaporetto from Fondamenta Nuova*. Church of cemetery island of S. Michele, by M. Codussi. First Renaissance religious building in lagoons. Interior: G. B. Tiepolo, *St Margaret of Cortona*. 126, 138.

S. Moisè, Church *Vaporetto or motoscafo S. Marco (15, 24)*. Dedicated in 8th century to St Victor, rebuilt in 10th century and rededicated to St

Moses the Black; took its present shape in 1632. Façade by Alessandro Tremignon (*c.* 1668). Meyring in charge of decoration. 14th-century campanile. Interior: G. A. Pellegrini, *Plague of Serpents*; J. Tintoretto, *Christ washing Peter's Feet.* Charming 18th-century sacristy, with bronze relief by Nicola Roccatagliata. 54, *215*, 217 .

S. Niccolò dei Mendicoli, Church *Circolare S. Basegio (34).* Apparently founded in 7th century, subsequently rebuilt on several occasions. Veneto-Byzantine campanile (end 12th century). In front of façade, small 15th-century pillared portico. Interior: paintings of Venetian school. 18, *206.*

S. Niccolò da Tolentino (I Tolentini), Church *Motoscafo Piazzale Roma (21).* Built for Theatine Fathers by Vincenzo Scamozzi. Later façade by Andrea Tirali. Interior: L. Giordano, *Annunciation;* J. Lys, *St Jerome;* Bonifazio Pitati, *Feast of Herod, Herod, Beheading of John the Baptist;* Padovanino, *St Andrew Avellino;* B. Strozzi, *The Charity of St Lawrence;* M. Bortoloni, ceiling frescoes; B. Longhena, high altar with sculptures by J. Le Court. 208, 222.

S. Pantalon, Church *Vaporetto S. Tomà (10).* Built in 17th century. Interior: G. A. Fumiani, ceiling; P. Veronese, *Miracle of St Pantaleon;* Antonio Vivarini and G. d'Alemagna, *Coronation of the Virgin.* In Cappella di Loreto: P. Longhi, frescoes.

S. Pietro in Castello, Church *Vaporetto Giardini (18).* Venice's cathedral until 1807. Church dedicated to St Sergius and St Bacchus here in the 7th century, rebuilt by Bishop Magnus and rededicated to St Peter. Present building by A. Palladio. Interior: Basaiti, *St Peter;* P. Liberi, *Plague of Serpents;* L. Giordano, *Virgin Mary and Souls from Purgatory;* G. Lazzarini, *St Lawrence;* P. Veronese, *SS. John, Peter and Paul.* 16.

S. Pietro Martire, Church *Island of Murano.* Dedicated first to St John the Evangelist. Destroyed by fire in 1474, rebuilt and rededicated to St Peter Martyr. Closed down and gutted in 1808, reopened in 1813. Interior: G. Bellini, *Madonna of Doge Barbarigo, Our Lady of the Assumption;* P. Veronese, *St Agatha in prison, St Jerome in the wilderness.* 156.

S. Polo, Church *Vaporetto S. Silvestro (8).* Founded 9th century, rebuilt in 15th, restored in 19th to its present state. Interior: G. B. Tiepolo, *St John Nepomucene;* G. D. Tiepolo, *Via Crucis;* J. Tintoretto, *Last Supper;* P. Veronese, *Marriage of the Virgin.* 50, 178.

S. Rocco, Church *Vaporetto S. Tomà (10).* The Scuola di S. Rocco was instituted in 1478 and the church begun in 1489. Largely rebuilt in the 18th century by G. Scalfurotto. Interior: S. Ricci, *St Helen finding the True Cross, St Francis of Paola;* J. Tintoretto, in presbytery, *St Roch visiting the Plague-stricken, St Roch in Prison, Healing of the Man Sick of the Palsy.* 248.

S. Salvador, Church *Vaporetto Rialto (7).* Probably founded in 7th century, rebuilt in 12th by Canons Regular of St Augustine. Present building built 1507–34, to a plan by G. Spavento, completed by Sansovino. Façade rebuilt 1663, to design by Giuseppe Sardi. Interior: F. Fontebasso, *St Lawrence Giustiniani;* J Sansovino, Venier monument; Titian, *Annunciation, Transfiguration.* In chapel on left: *Supper in Emmaus,* old copy of lost work by G. Bellini. 18, 178.

S. Sebastiano, Church *Vaporetto Cà Rezzonico (11) or Circolare S. Basegio (34).* Built for Hieronymite Fathers, 1505–48, by Abbondi, alias Scarpagnino. Interior: remarkable fresco decoration, largely by P. Veronese; canvases by Veronese, *Martyrdom of St Sebastian, Martyrdom of Mark and Marcellinus, Crucifixion.* In sacristy: Veronese, *Evangelists.* *195,* 200.

S. Silvestro, Church *Vaporetto S. Silvestro (8).* Founded 9th century, rebuilt 19th. Interior: J. Tintoretto, *Baptism of Christ.*

S. Simeone e Giuda (S. Simeone Piccolo), Church *Vaporetto Ferrovia (2).* Founded in 9th century, the present building dates from the 18th and is the work of G. Scalfurotto. Interior: M. Bortoloni, *St Simon and St Jude.* 222, 240.

S. Stae (S. Eustachio), Church *Vaporetto S. Stae (5).* Façade, *c.* 1709, and interior by G. Grassi. Interior: in presbytery, works of main painters of Venetian 18th century, including G. B. Piazzetta, *Martyrdom of St James;* G. B. Pittoni, *St Simeon;* G. B. Tiepolo, *Martyrdom of St Bartholomew.* 50, 200, *218,* 221, 227.

S. Stefano, Church *Vaporetto or motoscafo Accademia (12, 23).* Built by Augustinians in 14th century. Interior: G. Diziani, *Flight into Egypt, Adoration of the Magi, Massacre of the Innocents;* J. Tintoretto, *Last Supper, Washing of the Feet, Agony in the Garden;* A. Canova, funeral stele for Senator G. Falier. 57, 102, 106.

S. Teodoro, Church *Vaporetto or motoscafo S. Marco (15, 24).* Adjoining S. Marco. Built by G. Spavento, end 15th century. Dedicated to original patron of city, later used as headquarters of Holy Office or Inquisition; now used as Capitular Antesacristy and Canonical Sacristy. 18.

S. Trovaso (Ss. Gervasio e Protasio), **Church** *Vaporetto or motoscafo Accademia (12, 23).* Already in existence in 11th century, rebuilt several times; present building erected 1584–1657. Interior: Giambono, *St Chrysogonus*; P. Malombra, *Coronation of the Virgin;* Tintoretto, *Washing of the Feet, Last Supper.* 82, 117.

S. Zaccaria, Church *Vaporetto S. Zaccaria (16).* Founded in 9th century, transformed in 10th and 11th. Present church (15th century), begun by Giambellino, completed by M. Codussi: Gothic structure. Renaissance detail and façade. Interior: Giovanni Bellini, *Madonna and Saints*; Andrea del Castagno, frescoes in chapel of S. Tarasio; Stefano da S. Agnese, polyptych; Antonio Vivarini, polyptychs. 82, 113, 114, *124,* 134, 138, 156.

S. Zan Degolà (S. Giovanni Decollato), Church *Vaporetto Riva de Biasio (3).* Original structure very old indeed (foundation dating back to 1007), modified on several occasions. Recent restorations have uncovered frescoes probably dating from 12th century. 59.

S. Zanipolo (Ss. Giovanni e Paolo), Church *Vaporetto S. Zaccaria (16).* Built by Dominican friars, 14th-15th centuries. The numerous monuments of Doges make it the Pantheon of Venice. Interior: P. Lombardo, monument to Doge Vendramin (with Tullio Lombardo); G. Bellini, polyptych; L. Lotto, *Alms of St Antonino*; G. B. Piazzetta, in chapel of S. Domenico, *Glory of St Dominic.* Stained glass of main transept after cartoons by B. Vivarini. Cappella del Rosario built by Vittoria (16th century) but damaged by fire in 1867; ceiling now has three paintings by Veronese; on walls, sculptures by Morlaiter. 56, 57, 98, 102, 103, 104,

120, *122,* 127, 141, 142, 143, 144, 153, 155, 158, *201,* 208, 226.

S. Zulian, Church *Vaporetto or motoscafo S. Marco (15, 24).* Rebuilt mid-16th century to design by Sansovino. Interior: Palma Giovane, *Our Lady of the Assumption, Agony in the Garden;* G. da Santacroce, *Coronation of the Virgin;* P. Veronese, *Pietà.*

Salute, Church *See* **S. Maria della Salute.**

Scala del Bovolo *Vaporetto or motoscafo S. Marco (15, 24).* Next to Palazzo Contarini, near Campo S. Luca. Spiral staircase (end 15th century) in cylindrical tower inspired by early campanili on Venetian lagoon. Design of architectural details apparently work of G. Candi, a follower of Codussi. 134, 135, *153.*

Scalzi, Church *See* **S. Maria di Nazareth.**

Scuola dei Carmini *See* Index of Museums: **Scuola di S. Maria dei Carmini.**

Scuola dei Greci *See* Index of Museums: **Museo di Icone dell'Istituto Ellenico.**

Scuola della Misericordia *Vaporetto Cà d'Oro (6).* Scuola S. Maria Valverde, known as Scuola Nuova della Misericordia, one of the six *scuole grandi.* The building was designed by J. Sansovino in 1532 when the brotherhood decided to replace their original premises with larger ones nearby. But it was never completed, and the *Scuola* was suppressed at the beginning of the 19th century. The building now houses a gymnastics society. 99, 183.

Scuola di S. Fantin *Vaporetto or motoscafo S. Marco (15, 24).* Built in 16th century by A. Contino after the fire of 1562. The *Confratelli* or brethren of S. Fantin, S. Girolamo and S. Maria della Giustizia, together, performed the task of acompanying condemned men to their deaths. Hence the name 'Scuola de' Picai' (hanged men) or 'della Buona Morte' (good death). Interior: Palma Giovane, ceiling paintings; Vittoria, busts; A. Zanchi, upper room ceiling, *Last Judgment.* Now Ateneo Veneto (literary academy). 208.

Scuola di S. Giovanni Evangelista *Vaporetto S. Tomà (10).* One of the six *scuole grandi.* Built at end of 15th century and beginning of 16th. Originally decorated by Gentile Bellini and Carpaccio with *Story of the True Cross,* now in Accademia. Now headquarters of Società delle Arti Edificatorie. 127, 156, 157, 168.

Scuola di S. Giorgio degli Schiavoni *See* Index of Museums.

Scuola di S. Girolamo *See* **Scuola di S. Fantin.**

Scuola di S. Marco *Vaporetto S. Zaccaria (16).* One of the six *scuole grandi.* Founded in 1260 with religious and humanitarian aims. Rebuilt after 1485 under direction first of Pietro Lombardo, then of Codussi, lastly of Sansovino. Now hospital (Ospedale Civile). *122,* 127, 128, 130, 131, *133, 156,* 203.

Scuola di S. Orsola (demolished). Castello. Renowned for the famous paintings of V. Carpaccio, now in Accademia. Was situated behind the apse of S. Zanipolo in cemetery of monastery now occupied by other buildings. 158, 159, 161, 170.

Scuola di S. Rocco *See* Index of Museums: **Scuola Grande di S. Rocco.**

Sinagoga Spagnuola *Vaporetto Ferrovia (2).* In Old Ghetto; Spanish synagogue by B. Longhena, 1654. 217.

Stazione Ferroviaria *Vaporetto Ferrovia (2).* Railway terminus built 1841–46 by engineer Meduna in area originally occupied by Palladian churches of S. Lucia and Corpus Domini which were demolished. Rebuilt in 1950.

Strada Nuova Also called Via 28 Aprile. Built 1871–72, with demolition of houses and broadening of narrow streets. Runs along beside Grand Canal, behind Cà d'Oro. 224, 248.

Teatro della Fenice *Vaporetto or motoscafo S. Marco (15, 24).* Built by

Antonio Selva (1792). Restored after fire (1836), still retains its 18th-century grace. 224.

Torre dell'Orologio *Vaporetto or motoscafo S. Marco (15, 24).* Clock tower in Piazza S. Marco. Built by Codussi between 1494 and 1500. 128, *138,* 180, 184.

Via 2 Aprile Near S. Bartolomeo, Rialto. Was broadened in 1885; so called to commemorate 2 April 1849 (Venice's revolt against Austria). 248.

Via Garibaldi *Vaporetto Giardini.* Formerly Via Eugenia. Opened in 1807 after filling in a canal and originally named after Viceroy Eugene Beauharnais. 244, 248.

Via 22 Marzo *Vaporetto or motoscafo S. Marco (15, 24).* Opened in 1876, commemorates Venice's revolt against Austria in 1848. 248.

Zattere *Circolare Zattere (32).* Quay facing south across canal of Giudecca; built 1519. Gets its name from the *zatteroni,* log-rafts, which used to moor here. Today, berthing-place for ships passing through. At end, Stazione Marittima (marine terminal). 224.

Zecca *Vaporetto or motoscafo S. Marco (15, 24).* Built by J. Sansovino (1537–45) as mint, adjoining Piazza S. Marco; in use as such until 1870. In 1905 Biblioteca Marciana moved here. 184.

Zitelle, Church *Circolare Zitelle (30).* On island of Giudecca; church of S. Maria della Presentazione, known as Zitelle (Spinsters) after the foundation of a pious institution for poor girls in 18th century. Façade begun in 1582 and completed in 1586 to a design by Palladio. 193, 195, 216.

Painters, Sculptors and Architects

Abbondi, Antonio (known as Scarpagnino) (Milan, active 1505–Venice 1549). Architect. Church of San Fantin; church of San Sebastian; Fabbriche Vecchie at Rialto; completed Fondaco dei Tedeschi; Palazzo Loredan at S. Stefano; worked on Scuola di S. Rocco.

Amigoni, Jacopo (Naples, 1682–Madrid, 1752). Painter. Works in Galleria dell'Accademia; Cà Rezzonico; church of S. Maria della Fava. 226.

Angeli, Giuseppe (Venice, c. 1709–98). Painter. Follower of Piazzetta. Works in church of S. Maria della Pietà.

Antonello da Messina (Messina, c. 1430–79). Painter. Works in Museo Correr. 138, 140, 157, 167, 168, *170*.

Antonini, Carlo. Roman architect of the Napoleonic era, together with Soli built the so-called Ala Napoleonica on Piazza San Marco on site of demolished church of S. Gemignano. 240.

Appiani, Andrea (1754–1817). Painter. Works in Museo del Risorgimento, Museo Correr.

Bambini, Niccolò (Venice, 1651–1736). Painter. Works in Cà Pesaro; Doge's Palace; Raccolte del Seminario.

Basaiti, Marco (Venice (?), active 1496–1521). Painter. Works in Gallerie dell'Accademia; Museo Correr; church of S. Pietro.

Baseggio, Pietro (Venice, fourteenth century). Architect. Proto (master builder) of Doge's Palace 1340–54/55. 56.

Bassano, Francesco da Ponte (Venice, 1549–92). Painter. Works in Gallerie dell'Accademia; Doge's Palace; church of the Redentore.

Bassano, Jacopo da Ponte (Bassano, 1510/19–1592). Painter. Works at Galleria dell'Accademia; church of S. Giorgio Maggiore; S. Lazzaro degli Armeni. 200, 201.

Bassano, Leandro da Ponte (Bassano 1557–Venice, 1622). Painter. Works in church of S. Cassiano; S. Giacomo di Rialto.

Bastiani, Lazzaro (Venice (?), c. 1452–c. 1512). Painter. Works at Gallerie dell'Accademia; Museo Correr; church of S. Antonin; church of the Redentore. 156, 168.

Bellini, Gentile (Venice, 1429 (?)–1507). Painter. Works at Galleria dell'Accademia; Museo Correr; Museo di S. Marco. 99, 115, 128, 142, *150*, 156, 157, 168, *171*.

Bellini, Giovanni (known as Giambellino) (Venice, c. 1426–1516). Painter. Son of Jacopo. Works at Gallerie dell'Accademia; Museo Correr; Pinacoteca Querini-Stampalia; church of S. Francesco della Vigna; church of the Frari; church of S. Giovanni Crisostomo; church of S. Pietro Martire in Murano; church of S. Zaccaria; church of S. Zanipolo. 113, 115, 120, 126, 127, 140, 142, 149, *150*, 153, 154, 155, 156, 168.

Bellini, Jacopo (Venice, 1396(?)–1470(?)). Painter. Works at Gallerie dell'Accademia; Museo Correr. 114, 115, *117*, 156.

Bellotto, Bernardo (Venice, 1720–Warsaw, 1780). Painter. Works at Galleria dell'Accademia; Doge's Palace. 231.

Benoni, Giuseppe (Trieste, 1618–Venice, 1684). Architect, hydraulic engineer. Completed building of the Dogana da Mar. 214.

Berchet. Architect. In 1879 carried out arbitrary restoration on Fondaco dei Turchi. 248.

Bevilacqua, Carlo. Venetian neoclassical painter. Works in church of Ss. Maria e Donato (Murano); Museo Correr. 240.

Boccaccino, Boccaccio (Ferrara (?), *c.* 1467–Cremona, *c.* 1524). Works at Gallerie dell'Accademia; Museo Correr.

Boito, Camillo (Rome, 1836–Milan, 1918). Architect. Palazzo Franchetti (formerly Gussoni-Cavalli). 248.

Bon, Bartolomeo (active 1422–*c.* 1464). Venetian sculptor. Works in Cà d'Oro; Doge's Palace. 88, 103, 135.

Bon, Giovanni (fifteenth-sixteenth centuries). Venetian sculptor. Collaborated with B. Bon on Cà d'Oro and Doge's Palace. 88, 103, 135.

Bordone, Paris (Treviso, 1500–Venice, 1571). Painter. Works at Galleria dell'Accademia; Cà d'Oro; church of S. Giobbe.

Borsato, Giuseppe (Venice, 1771–1849). Painter. Works at Museo Correr; Palazzo Pisani-Gritti. 240.

Bortoloni, Mattia (Belluno, 1696–1750). Painter. Works in church of S. Niccolò da Tolentino; church of S. Simeone e Giuda.

Bregno, Antonio (da Rigesio) (Como, 1426–1485). Sculptor. Works in church of S. Eufemia, church of the Frari, Doge's Palace. 93, 94, *107*, 135, 137, 142.

Brustolon, Andrea (Belluno, 1662–Mezzaterra, Belluno, 1732). Sculptor, wood-carver. Works at Cà Rezzonico.

Caffi, Ippolito (Belluno, 1809–Vis, 1866). View-painter. Works at Galleria d'Arte Moderna; Museo Correr.

Calendario, Filippo (Venice, first half of fourteenth century). Architect. Creator of Doge's Palace. 56.

Caliari, see Veronese.

Canaletto (Antonio Canal) (Venice, 1697–1768). Painter. Works in Gallerie dell'Accademia. 111, 224, 231, 233, 246.

Candi, Giovanni (fifteenth century). Architect. Attributed work: Scala del Bovolo (Spiral staircase). 135.

Canova, Antonio (Possagno, 1757–Venice, 1822). Sculptor. Works at Museo Correr; church of S. Lazzaro degli Armeni; church of S. Stefano; Palazzo Albrizzi; Raccolte del Seminario. 97, 233.

Carlevaris, Luca (Udine, 1665–Venice, 1729). View-painter. Works at Cà Rezzonico.

Carpaccio, Vittore (Venice, *c.* 1465–1526(?)). Painter. Works at Galle-

rie dell'Accademia; Cà d'Oro; Museo Correr; Doge's Palace; Scuola di S. Giorgio degli Schiavoni; church of S. Giorgio Maggiore. 99, 113, 126, 144, *148*, 156, 157, 158, 159, 161, 166, 167, 168, *169*, 170, 177, 214.

Carriera, Rosalba (Venice, 1675–1758). Painter. Works at Gallerie dell'Accademia; Cà Rezzonico. 224, *225*, 231.

Castagno, Andrea del (Castagno, Mugello, 1420–Florence, 1457). Painter. Works in church of S. Zaccaria. 114.

Catena, Vincenzo (Venice, *c.* 1470–1531). Painter. Works in Pinacoteca Querini-Stampalia; church of S. Maria Materdomini.

Cedini, Costantino (Padua, 1741–Venice, 1811). Painter. Works in church of S. Barnaba.

Ciardi, Guglielmo (Treviso, 1842–Venice, 1917). Painter. Works at Galleria d'Arte Moderna; Pinacoteca Querini-Stampalia. 247.

Cima da Conegliano, Giambattista (Conegliano, Veneto, 1459–1517/18). Painter. Works in Gallerie dell'Accademia; Museo Correr; Cà d'Oro; church of S. Maria del Carmelo; church of S. Giovanni in Bragora. 143.

Codussi, Mauro (Lenna (Valle Brembana, Bergamo) *c.* 1440–Venice, 1504). Architect. Church of S. Giovanni Crisostomo; church of S. Maria Formosa; church of S. Michele in Isola; church of S. Zaccaria (whose façade he completed); Palazzo Corner-Spinelli; Palazzo Vendramin-Calergi; Procuratie Vecchie; Scuola di S. Marco (completed façade); Torre dell'Orologio in Piazza S. Marco. 122, *124*, *126*, 127, 128, 131, 134, 135, *138*, *140*, *141*, 142, *153*, 155, *158*, 161, 179, 180, 183.

Cominelli, Andrea (worked in Venice in first half of eighteenth century. Architect. Palazzo Labia. 222.

Contino, Antonio (Lugano (?), 1566–Venice, 1600). Architect. Bridge of Sighs; Scuola di S. Fantin. 200.

Corona, Leonardo (Murano, 1561–Venice, 1605). Painter. Works in church of S. Giovanni in Bragora.

Crivelli, Carlo (Venice, *c.* 1430/35–last documented in 1493). Painter. Works in Gallerie dell'Accademia.

Dalle Destre, Vincenzo (Treviso, *c.* 1488–1543 (?)). Painter. Works in Museo Correr; church of S. Maria dei Miracoli.

Diziani, Gaspare (Belluno, 1689–Venice, 1767). Painter. Works in Galleria dell'Accademia; Cà Rezzonico; church of S. Maria del Carmelo; church of S. Stefano.

Donatello (Donato di Niccolò di Betto Bardi) (Florence, *c.* 1382/83 (1386?)–1466). Sculptor. Works in church of Frari. 88, 104, 113, 118, 122, 138, 141, 154.

Favretto, Giacomo (Venice, 1849–1887). Painter. Works at Galleria d'Arte Moderna; Pinacoteca Querini-Stampalia. 247.

Ferrari, Giovanni (known as Torretti) (Crespano, 1744–Venice, 1826). Sculptor. Canova's master. Works in church of Gesuiti; church of S. Geremia.

Fetti, Domenico (Rome, *c.* 1589–Venice, 1623). Painter. Works at Gallerie dell'Accademia. 210.

Fontebasso, Francesco (Venice, 1709–1768/69). Painter. Works in Cà Rezzonico; Raccolte del Seminario; church of Angelo Raffaele; church of S. Francesco della Vigna; church of S. Salvador.

Fumiani, G. Antonio (Venice, 1643–1710). Painter. Works in church of S. Pantalon.

Gai, Antonio (Venice, 1686–1769). Sculptor. Gate of Sansovino's loggetta; church of the Pietà.

Gambello, Antonio (worked in Venice in fifteenth century). Architect. Porta dell'Arsenale; began building church of S. Giobbe; began façade of church of S. Zaccaria. *120*, 134.

Gaspari, Antonio (Venetian, 1670 (?)–1750(?)). Architect. Church of S. Canciano (most recent restoration); church of S. Maria della Fava (front part); Palazzo Pesaro, east side. 217, 222, 224.

Ghislandi, Vittore (known as Frà Galgario) (Bergamo 1655–1743). Painter. Works in Gallerie dell'Accademia.

Giambono, Michele (Veneto, active 1420–62). Painter. Works in Gallerie dell'Accademia; Museo Correr; Cà d'Oro; church of S. Trovaso. 82.

Giordano, Luca (Naples, 1632–1705). Painter. Works in Gallerie dell'Accademia; church of S. Maria della Salute; church of the Tolentini; church of S. Pietro.

Giorgione (Giorgio da Castelfranco) (Castelfranco, Veneto, *c.* 1478–Venice, 1510). Painter. Works in Galleria dell'Accademia. 113, 153, 156, *173*, 177, 200, 210.

Giovanni d'Alemagna (Active 1441–Venice 1450). Painter. Works in church of S. Pantalon.

Giovanni di Martino da Fiesole (Tuscan, worked in Venice during first decades of fifteenth century). Sculptor. Works in S. Zanipolo (in collaboration with P. Lamberti); Doge's Palace. 88.

Grassi, Giovanni (active end of seventeenth century). Architect. Church of San Stae.

Grigi, Guglielmo de (Alzano (Bergamo), active *c.* 1515). Architect. Palazzo dei Camerlenghi; completed Procuratie Vecchie. 180, 181.

Guarana, Giacomo (Venice, 1720–1808). Painter. Works in Cà Rezzonico; Doge's Palace.

Guardi, Francesco (Venice, 1712–1793). Painter. Works in Gallerie dell'Accademia; Cà d'Oro; Cà Rezzonico. 231, 233, 246, *250*.

Guardi, Giannantonio (Vienna, 1699–Venice, 1760). Painter. Works in Cà Rezzonico; church of Angelo Raffaele. 51, 224, 226.

Guariento (Padua, 1338–1368/70). Painter. Works in Doge's Palace. 86.

Hayez, Francesco (Venice, 1791–Milan, 1882). Painter. Works in Galleria d'Arte Moderna.

Jacobello del Fiore (Venice, *c.* 1370–1439). Painter. Works in Gallerie dell'Accademia; Doge's Palace. 82.

Jacopo della Quercia (Tuscany, 1367–1438). Sculptor. Works in church of Frari. 88, 104.

Kahn, Louis (lives in Philadelphia). Architect. Plan for a Palazzo dei Congressi in the gardens of the Biennale. 253.

Lamberti, Niccolò di Pietro (Arezzo, active 1403–Florence, 1456). Sculptor. Works in church of San Marco; Doge's Palace. 88, 113.

Lamberti, Pietro di Niccolò (active 1423-1434). Tuscan sculptor. Worked with his father. Works in church of San Marco; Doge's Palace. 88, 113.

Laurenti, Cesare (Mesola (Ferrara), 1854). Painter. In 1907 (with Rupolo) designed Pescheria in mock Gothic style. 248.

Lazzarini, Gregorio (Venice, 1665–Villa Bona, Verona, 1730). Painter. Works at Cà Rezzonico; Pinacoteca

Querini-Stampalia; church of S. Pietro.

Le Corbusier (Charles-Edouard Jeanneret) (La Chaux-de-Fonds, 1887–Cap Martin 1965). Architect. Design for new hospital of S. Giobbe. 252.

Le Court, Josse (Ypres 1627–Venice, 1679). Sculptor. Works in Cà Pesaro; church of S. Maria della Salute; church of San Niccolò dei Tolentini. 217.

Liberi, Pietro (Padua, 1605–Venice, 1687). Painter. Works in church of S. Pietro.

Licinio, Bernardino (Poscante (Bergamo), c. 1489–1549/61). Painter. Works in Gallerie dell'Accademia; Cà d'Oro; church of Frari.

Lippi, Filippino (Prato, 1457–Florence, 1504). Painter. Works at Cà d'Oro; Raccolte del Seminario.

Liss see Lys.

Lombardo, Antonio (1485–1516, active in Venice and Ferrara). Sculptor. Worked with father Pietro and brother Tullio on church of Miracoli; church of San Marco. 142, 143, 144, 149, 153.

Lombardo, Pietro (1435–1515, active in Veneto). Lombard sculptor and architect. Works in church of Miracoli; church of S. Giobbe; church of S. Zanipolo; Palazzo Dario; Scuola di San Marco. 122, 123, 124, *126*, 128, 130, 131, *135*, 138, 141, 142, 143, 144, *155*, 198.

Lombardo, Tullio (c. 1455–1532, active in Venice). Lombard sculptor and architect. Works in church of S. Giovanni Crisostomo. Collaborated with his father Pietro and brother Antonio on building church of Miracoli; works in church of Miracoli; church of San Zanipolo. 127, *133*, 142, 143, 144, 148, 149, 153.

Longhena, Baldassarre (Venice, 1598–1682). Architect. Cà Pesaro; Cà Rezzonico; church of Salute; church of S. Giustina; church of S. Niccolò da Tolentino; church of Scalzi, interior; monastery of S. Giorgio Maggiore; Palazzo Giustinian-Lolin; Palazzo Widmann; Procuratie Nuove; Scuola dei Greci; Sinagoga Spagnuola. 195, 211, 212, 213, 214, 215, 216, 217.

Longhi, Pietro (Venice, 1702–1785). Painter. Works in Gallerie dell'Accademia; Cà Rezzonico; Pinacoteca Querini-Stampalia; church of S. Pantalon. *230, 231.*

Lorenzo Veneziano (Venice, active 1356–72). Painter. Works in Gallerie dell'Accademia; Museo Correr. 76, 78, 80, *90.*

Lotto, Lorenzo (Venice, c. 1480–Loreto, 1552). Painter. Works in Gallerie dell'Accademia; church of S. Maria del Carmelo; church of S. Giacomo dell'Orio; church of S. Zanipolo. *157.*

Luciani, Sebastiano (known as del Piombo) (Venice (?) c. 1485–Rome, 1547). Painter. Works in church of S. Bartolomeo; church of S. Giovanni Crisostomo.

Lys, Johann (Oldenburg (Holstein), c. 1595–Venice, 1629). Painter. Works in Galleria dell'Accademia; Cà Rezzonico; church of S. Niccolò da Tolentino.

Maffei, Francesco (Vicenza, c. 1606–Padua, 1660). Painter. Works in Cà Rezzonico. 211.

Malombra, Pietro (Venice, 1556–1618). Painter. Works in church of S. Trovaso.

Mansueti, Giovanni (Venice, active 1485–1526). Painter. Works in Gallerie dell'Accademia. 156, 168.

Mantegna, Andrea (Island of Carturo (Padua), 1431–Mantua, 1506). Painter. Works in Gallerie dell'Accademia; Cà d'Oro. 113, 142, 143, *153*, 154, 156.

Marchiori, Giovanni (Caviola d'Agordo (Belluno), 1696–Treviso, 1778). Sculptor. Works in church of S. Geremia; church of the Pietà. 222.

Marieschi, Michele (Venice, end of seventeenth century–1743). Viewpainter. Works in Gallerie dell'Accademia.

Masegne, Jacobello and Pierpaolo Dalle (active (1383–1409). Venetian sculptors. Works in church of Madonna dell'Orto; church of San Marco; Doge's Palace. 82, 83, *90*, 107.

Massari, Giorgio (Venice, c. 1687–1766). Architect. Cà Rezzonico, second storey; church of S. Maria del Rosario; church of S. Marcuola; church of S. Maria della Pietà; Palazzo Grassi. 217, 224.

Mazzoni, Sebastiano (Florence, c. 1615 (?)–1685 (?)). Painter. Works in church of S. Beneto. 211.

Meldolla, Andrea (known as Schiavone) (Zara, 1522–Venice, 1563). Painter. Works in Pinacoteca Querini-Stampalia; church of S. Cassiano; church of S. Maria del Carmelo. 203.

Meyring, Arrigo (active in Venice in second half of seventeenth century). Sculptor. Works in church of S. Maria Zobenigo (del Giglio); church of S. Moisè; church of S. Maria di Nazareth. 217.

Michelino da Besozzo (worked in Venice in 1410). Lombard painter and draughtsman. Works in Doge's Palace. 83, 84.

Michieli, Andrea (known as Vicentino) (Vicenza (?), c. 1539–Venice, 1614/17). Painter. Works in Museo Correr; Doge's Palace.

Monopola, Bartolomeo (active in Venice, second half of sixteenth century). Architect. Doge's Palace, unified ground floor gallery; Palazzo Priuli, formerly Ruzzini. 98.

Montagna, Bartolomeo (Orzinovi (Brescia), c. 1450–Vicenza, 1523). Painter. Works in Gallerie dell'Accademia.

Moretto, Alessandro (Brescia, 1498–1554). Painter. Works in church of S. Maria della Pietà.

Morlaiter, GianMaria (Venetian, 1699–1782). Sculptor. Works in Cà Rezzonico; church of S. Eufemia; church of S. Maria del Rosario; church of the Pietà; church of S. Maria della Fava; church of S. Maria Zobenigo (del Giglio); church of S. Marcuola; church of S. Zanipolo. 222, 224.

Nicolò di Pietro (Venice (?), active 1394–1430). Painter. Works in Gallerie dell'Accademia. 80.

Novelli, Pietrantonio (Venice, 1729–1804). Painter. Works on island of S. Lazzaro degli Armeni; church of S. Geremia; church of S. Fosca; church of S. Lio.

Padovanino see Varotari.

Palladio, Andrea (Padua, 1508–1580). Architect. Church of S. Giorgio Maggiore; church of the Redentore; church of the Zitelle; transformation of Convento della Carità; Convento di S. Giorgio Maggiore, cloister and refectory. 180, 193, 195, 198, 215, 216, 218, 222, 224.

Palma Giovane (Jacopo Palma the Younger) (Venice, 1544–1628). Painter. Works in Oratorio dei Crociferi; Doge's Palace; church of S. Fantin; church of S. Pietro;

church of S. Zulian; Scuola di S. Girolamo. 208.

Palma Vecchio (Jacopo Palma the Elder) (Serinalta (Bergamo), c. 1480–Venice, 1528). Painter. Works in Gallerie dell'Accademia; Pinacoteca Querini-Stampalia; church of S. Maria Formosa. 117.

Paolo Veneziano (Venice, c. 1290–c. 1362). Painter. Works in Gallerie dell'Accademia; Museo Correr; Museo Marciano. 73, 74, 75, 76, 78, 90, 94.

Pellegrini, Giovanni Antonio (Venice, 1675–1741). Painter. Works in Gallerie dell'Accademia; Cà Rezzonico; church of S. Moisè. 218, 224, 226.

Pennacchi, Pier Maria (1464–1514?). Painter. Works in church of S. Maria dei Miracoli.

Peranda, Sante (Venice, 1566–1638). Painter. Works in Doge's Palace.

Piazzetta, Giovan Battista (Venice, 1682–1754). Painter. Works in Gallerie dell'Accademia; Cà Rezzonico; church of S. Maria del Rosario; church of S. Maria della Fava; church of the Pietà; church of S. Stae; church of S. Zanipolo. 97, 224, 226, 231.

Piero della Francesca (Borgo San Sepolcro, 1410/20–1492). Painter. Works in Gallerie dell'Accademia. 157.

Pignazzi, Giovanni Alvise (active in Venice in nineteenth century). Engineer and architect. In 1855 completed Magazzini del Sale (salt storehouses) on Punta della Dogana.

Pitati, Bonifacio (Verona, c. 1487–Venice, 1553). Painter. Works in Gallerie dell'Accademia; Cà d'Oro; church of S. Niccolò da Tolentino.

Pittoni, Giambattista (Venice, 1687–1767). Painter. Works in Gallerie dell'Accademia; church of S. Cassiano; church of S. Stae.

Ponte, Antonio da (Venice (?), c. 1512–1597). Architect. Palazzo delle Prigioni (with Rusconi); Rialto bridge; church of the Redentore. 180, 200.

Pordenone (Giovanni Antonio Regillo) (Pordenone, 1484–Ferrara, 1539). Painter. Works in Gallerie dell'Accademia; church of S. Giovanni Elemosinario. 200.

Porta, Giuseppe (known as Salviati) (Castelnuovo di Garfagnana, c. 1520–Venice, c. 1575). Painter. Works in Doge's Palace.

Raverti, Matteo (Milan, active 1385–1436). Sculptor and architect. Cà d'Oro; Doge's Palace, south-east and south-west corners: Drunkenness of Noah, Adam and Eve; Doge's Palace, capitals: Crusaders, Women, Human Races, Nations. 83, 84, 86, 88, 92.

Renieri, Niccolò (Maubeuge, active 1626–Venice, 1667). Painter. Works in church of S. Canciano.

Ricchi, Pietro (Lucca, 1606–Udine, 1675). Painter. Works in church of S. Giuseppe.

Ricci, Marco (Belluno, 1676–Venice, 1729). Landscape painter. Nephew of Sebastiano. Works in Gallerie dell'Accademia.

Ricci, Sebastiano (Belluno, 1659/60–Venice, 1734). Painter. Works in Gallerie dell'Accademia; church of San Giorgio Maggiore; church of S. Maria del Rosario; church of S. Rocco. 218, 224, 226.

Rizzo, Antonio (Verona, c. 1430–c. 1498). Sculptor and architect. Works in church of Madonna dell'Orto; church of S. Elena; church of the Frari; Doge's Palace. 94, 97, *104*, *128*, 137, 138, 140, 142, 191, 198.

Robusti see Tintoretto.

Roccataglia, Nicola (Genoa, active 1593–1636). Sculptor. Works in church of S. Moisè.

Romani, Girolamo (known as Romanino) (Brescia, 1480–1566). Painter. Works in Gallerie dell'Accademia.

Rottenhammer, Johann (Munich, 1564–Augsburg, 1625). Painter. Works in church of S. Bartolomeo.

Rupolo, Domenico (Venice, 1861). Architect and sculptor. In 1907, with Laurenti, built Pescheria in mock Gothic style. 248.

Rusconi, Antonio (Venetian, active 1538–1577). Architect. Rebuilt Doge's Palace after fire; Palazzo delle Prigioni (with Da Ponte). 196, 200.

Sammicheli, Michele (Verona, 1484–1559). Architect, military engineer. Fort of S. Andrea; Palazzo Corner-Mocenigo; Palazzo Grimani. 192, 193, 217.

Sansovino, Jacopo (Jacopo Tatti) (Florence, 1486–Venice, 1570). Architect and sculptor. Completed church of S. Salvador (Monument to Doge Venier), and those of S. Fantin and S. Zulian; church of S.

Gemignano; Fabbriche Nuove at Rialto; Libreria Marciana (as far as sixteenth arch); loggetta; Palazzo Corner; Doge's Palace, Giants; Scala d'Oro; Scuola di S. Marco; Scuola della Misericordia; Zecca. *161*, 178, 180, 181, *182*, 183, 184, 189, 190, 191, 193, 215, 217, 240.

Santacroce, Girolamo da (from Bergamo district, active 1508–1545). Painter. Works in Museo Correr; church of S. Zulian.

Santi, Lorenzo (Siena, 1783–Venice, 1829). Architect. Palazzetto della Guardia Reale, at the Ascensione. 240, 244.

Santi, Sebastiano (Murano, 1789–1866). Painter. Works in church of S. Luca.

Saraceni, Carlo (Venice, 1580–1620). Painter. Works in church of Redentore.

Sardi, Giuseppe (Venetian, 1630–1699). Architect. Church of S. Maria di Nazareth; church of S. Maria Zobenigo: façade; church of S. Salvador: façade; Palazzo Savorgnan; Palazzo Surian. 217, 222.

Savoldo, Gerolamo (Brescia, c. 1480–Venice, c. 1550). Painter. Works in Gallerie dell'Accademia; church of S. Giobbe.

Scalfurotto, Giovanni (Venice, c. 1700–1764). Architect. Church of S. Rocco; church of S. Simeone e Giuda. 222.

Scamozzi, Vicenzo (Vicenza, 1522–1616). Architect. Began work on church of S. Niccolò da Tolentino; completed Libreria Marciana; Procuratie Nuove. 184, 211, 215, 222.

Scarpa, Carlo (living in Venice). Designer. Gallerie dell'Accademia and Museo Correr: decor of various rooms; Pinacoteca Querini-Stampalia: ground-floor courtyard. 155.

Schiavone see Meldolla.

Sebastiano del Piombo see Luciani, Sebastiano.

Selva, Antonio (Venice, 1757–1819). Architect. Enlarged and decorated Palazzo del Console J. Smith; Teatro della Fenice; Giardini Pubblici. 218, 224, 225, 244.

Soli, Giuseppe Maria (Vignola (Modena), 1745–Modena 1823). Architect and painter. With Antonini, built Ala Napoleonica on site of church of S. Gemignano in Piazza S. Marco. 240.

Spavento, Giorgio (Venetian, d. 1509). Architect. Began church of S. Salvador; church of S. Teodoro; designed Fondaco dei Tedeschi. 177, 178.

Stefano da S. Agnese (Active 1369–1434). Painter. Works in church of S. Zaccaria. 82.

Strozzi, Bernardo (Genoa, 1581–Venice, 1644). Painter. Works in Gallerie dell'Accademia; Cà Rezzonico; church of S. Beneto; church of S. Niccolò da Tolentino. 210.

Temanza, Tommaso (Venice, 1705–1789). Architect, hydraulic engineer. Church of Maddalena. 218, 224.

Tiberio, Frà, da Parma (worked in Venice in fourteenth century). Architect. Began building church of Madonna dell'Orto. 107.

Tiepolo, Giambattista (Venice, 1696–Madrid, 1770). Painter. Works in Gallerie dell'Accademia; Cà Rezzonico; church of Pietà; church of S. Maria di Nazareth; church of S. Alvise; church of SS. Apostoli; church of S. Beneto; church of S. Marco; church of S. Maria della Fava; church of S. Maria del Rosario; church of S. Polo; church of S. Stae; Palazzo Labia; Palazzo Sandi; Scuola dei Carmini. 220, 222, 224, 226, 227, 230.

Tiepolo, Giandomenico (Venice, 1727–1804). Painter. Works in Gallerie dell'Accademia; Cà Rezzonico; church of S. Lio; church of the Maddalena; church of S. Michele in Isola; church of S. Polo.

Tintoretto, Domenico (Venice, c. 1560–1635). Painter, son of Jacopo. Works in S. Fosca. 204.

Tintoretto, Jacopo (Jacopo Robusti) (Venice, 1518–1594). Painter. Works in Gallerie dell'Accademia; church of Madonna dell'Orto; church of S. Cassiano; church of S. Felice; church of S. Gallo; church of S. Giorgio Maggiore; church of S. Marcuola; church of S. Maria Zobenigo; church of S. Maria del Rosario; church of S. Maria della Salute; church of S. Moisè; church of S. Polo; church of S. Rocco; church of S. Silvestro; church of S. Stefano; church of S. Trovaso; Libreria Marciana; Doge's Palace; Scuola di S. Rocco. 86, *183*, 190, *191*, 198, 200, 201, 202, 204, 205, 206, 207.

Tirali, Andrea (c. 1660–Monselice 1737). Architect. Church of S. Niccolò da Tolentino, pronaos; Palazzo Priuli. 222.

Titian (Tiziano Vecellio) (Pieve di Cadore, 1488/90–Venice, 1576). Painter. Works in Gallerie dell'Accademia; church of Frari; church of Gesuiti; church of S. Lio; church of Salute; church of S. Salvador; Libreria Marciana. 10, 104, 177, *190*, 200.

Tremignon, Alessandro (Paduan, worked in Venice in second half of seventeenth century). Architect. Church of S. Moisè: decoration of façade. 217.

Tura, Cosmè (Ferrara, c. 1430–1495). Painter. Works in Gallerie dell'Accademia; Museo Correr.

Varotari, Alessandro (known as Padovanino) (Padua, 1588–1648). Painter. Works in Libreria Marciana; Scuola di S. Maria del Carmine; church of S. Niccolò da Tolentino. 208.

Vassilacchi, Antonio (known as Aliense) (Milos (Greece), c. 1556–Venice, 1629). Painter. Works on island of S. Lazzaro degli Armeni; church of S. Antonin; church of S. Lio.

Vecchia, Pietro della (Pietro Muttoni) (Venice, 1605–78). Painter. Works on island of S. Lazzaro degli Armeni; church of S. Antonin; church of S. Lio. 210.

Vecellio see Titian.

Veronese, Paolo (Paolo Caliari) (Verona, 1528–Venice, 1588). Painter. Works in Gallerie dell'Accademia; church of S. Francesco della Vigna; church of S. Giacomo dell'Orio; church of S. Luca; church of S. Pantalon; church of S. Pietro; church of S. Pietro Martire; church of S. Polo; church of S. Zanipolo; church of S. Sebastiano; church of S. Zulian; Libreria Marciana; Doge's Palace. 97, 190, *192*, *196*, 198, 200, 201, 202, 203, 227.

Verrocchio, Andrea (Andrea di Cione) (Florence, 1436–Venice, 1488). Sculptor and painter. Campo S. Zanipolo: equestrian monument to Bartolomeo Colleoni. *124*, 128.

Visentini, Antonio (Venice, 1688–1782). Architect. Palazzo built for Consul Joseph Smith, on Rio dei SS. Apostoli and Grand Canal. 224.

Vittoria, Alessandro (Trento, 1524–Venice, c. 1608). Sculptor and architect. Works in Museo Correr; church of S. Zanipolo; Doge's Palace; Scuola di S. Fantin. *179*, 191, 198, 208.

Vivarini, Alvise (Murano, 1446–1503). Painter. Works in Gallerie dell'Accademia; Cà d'Oro; Museo Correr; church of S. Giovanni in Bragora; church of Redentore. *157.*

Vivarini, Antonio (Murano, *c.* 1415–1484). Painter. Works in Cà d'Oro; church of S. Pantalon; church of S. Zaccaria; church of S. Giobbe. 82, 104 113.

Vivarini, Bartolomeo (Murano, *c.* 1430–1499). Painter. Works in Gallerie dell'Accademia; Museo Vetrario di Murano; church of S. Giovanni in Bragora; church of S. Maria Formosa; church of S. Zanipolo. *117, 153.*

Zanchi, Antonio (Este, 1631–Venice, 1722). Painter. Works in church of S. Canciano; church of S. Maria Zo-benigo (del Giglio); Scuola di S. Fantin.

Zandomeneghi, Federico (Venice, 1841–Padua, 1917). Painter. Works in Galleria d'Arte Moderna. *247.*

Zais, Giuseppe (Canale d'Agordo (Belluno), 1709–Treviso, 1784). Painter. Works in Gallerie dell'Accademia; Cà Rezzonico.

Zuccarelli, Francesco (Pitigliano (Tuscany), 1702–Florence, 1778). Painter. Works in Gallerie dell'Accademia; Cà Rezzonico.

Zuccari, Federico (Sant'Agnolo in Vado, Urbino, 1540–Ancona, 1609). Painter. Works in Doge's Palace. *203.*